Wiley
CMAexcel Learning System
Exam Review 2017

About IMA® (Institute of Management Accountants)

IMA®, the association of accountants and financial professionals in business, is one of the largest and most respected associations focused exclusively on advancing the management accounting profession. Globally, IMA supports the profession through research, the CMA® (Certified Management Accountant) program, continuing education, networking, and advocacy of the highest ethical business practices. IMA has a global network of over 75,000 members in 120 countries and 300 local chapter communities. IMA provides localized services through its offices in Montvale, NJ, USA; Zurich, Switzerland; Dubai, UAE; and Beijing, China. For more information about IMA, please visit www.imanet.org.

Wiley
CMAexcel Learning System
Exam Review 2017

Participant Guide

Part 1: Financial Reporting, Planning, Performance, and Control

The Association of
Accountants and
Financial Professionals
in Business®

Contents

Acknowledgments of Subject Matter Experts

The Wiley CMAexcel Learning System (WCMALS) content is written to help explain the concepts and calculations from the Certified Management Accountant (CMA) exam Learning Outcome Statements (LOS) published by the Institute of Certified Management Accountants (ICMA).

Wiley would like to acknowledge the team of subject matter experts who worked with us to produce this version of the WCMALS. IMA would like to acknowledge the team of subject matter experts who worked together in conjunction with IMA staff to produce this version of the WCMALS.

Meghann Cefaratti, Ph.D., is an associate professor in the Department of Accountancy at Northern Illinois University. She completed her Ph.D. in Accounting at Virginia Tech. Professor Cefaratti teaches financial accounting and assurance services. Her primary research interest involves auditors' fraud risk assessment judgments. Her dissertation was recognized by the AAA Forensic and Investigative Accounting Section in 2011. Additionally, her research has received awards from the Accounting and Information Systems Educators Association and has been published in the Journal of Information Systems, Journal of the Association for Information Systems, Journal of Forensic and Investigative Accounting, and Internal Auditor. She is a former auditor for the Air Force Audit Agency (AFAA) where her audit coverage included Andrews Air Force Base, MD, the Pentagon and various Air National Guard installations. Prior to working with the AFAA, she worked as a tax associate for PricewaterhouseCoopers in Baltimore, MD.

Gary Cokins, CPIM, is an internationally recognized expert, speaker, and author in enterprise and corporate performance management (EPM/CPM) systems. He is the founder of Analytics-Based Performance Management LLC (www.garycokins. com). He began his career in industry with a Fortune 100 company in CFO and operations roles. Then for 15 years he was a consultant with Deloitte, KPMG, and EDS (now part of HP). From 1997 until 2013 Gary was a Principal Consultant with SAS, a business analytics software vendor. His most recent books are *Performance Management: Integrating Strategy Execution, Methodologies, Risk, and Analytics* and *Predictive Business Analytics*. He graduated from Cornell University with a

Bachelor of Science degree in industrial engineering/operations research in 1971 and went on to earn his MBA from Northwestern University Kellogg in 1974.

Daniel J. Gibbons, CPA, Associate Professor of Accounting, has been employed by Waubonsee Community College since 2001. Prior to starting his career in education, he worked in Accounting and Finance for approximately 21 years. He has a Bachelor of Science degree in Accounting from Northeastern Illinois University and a Master of Science degree in Finance from Northern Illinois University. He is a resident of Naperville, IL.

Joseph Kastantin, CPA, CMA, MBA, ACCA, is a Professor of Accountancy at the University of Wisconsin-La Crosse and an alum of KPMG Central and Eastern Europe having worked from 1997–2008 in both full time and part time capacities with KPMG Central Europe in the department of professional practice and training. Kastantin served on the board of directors and audit committee of the North Central Trust Company (now Trust Point) for three years and as chairman of the board of La Crosse Funds, Inc. for four years. Additionally, he served as president and board member for several not-for-profit entities, as CEO of a small manufacturing company, business manager for an auto dealership, controller for a textile wholesaler, and as sole practitioner in public accounting. He has more than 30 published journal articles and books. His most recent publications are on fraud and a practical guide to impairments under IFRS and US GAAP. He served nearly ten years on active duty with the US Army (SFC E-7) with tours in Korea and Vietnam and was an instructor and MOS test writer at the US Army AG School.

Marjorie E. Yuschak, CMA, is fortunate to have enjoyed multiple careers. She had a 21-year career at Johnson & Johnson developing expertise in cost/managerial accounting, financial reporting, and employee stock option programs while working in the consumer, pharmaceutical, and corporate segments of the business. Following that she was an adjunct professor of accounting and faculty advisor to Beta Alpha Psi at the Rutgers Business School, New Brunswick. Marj continues to facilitate the CMA Review courses at Villanova University, which she has done for over five years. She is currently an adjunct professor of accounting at The College of New Jersey. She has a consulting business providing coaching for accounting, communication skills, and small business management. Marj is a member of the Raritan Valley Chapter of the IMA in New Jersey. In addition, she is a Certified Trainer in both AchieveGlobal and DDI (Development Dimensions International) and a member of ATD (the Association for Talent Development).

For the Student

This course is part of the comprehensive Wiley CMAexcel Learning System (WCMALS) exam preparation program. Your classroom materials consist of a *Participant Guide* that includes all the instructor slides. In addition to the classroom materials, the WCMALS Part 2 includes a self-study book and the Online Test Bank. The course makes frequent reference to these tools and uses material from the self-study book as part of the class.

Many of the slides you will see in this course pose a question with an answer appearing on the slide after another mouse *click*. The complete slide with answer appears in your *Participant Guide*. This was done to facilitate study and allow you to focus on the discussion of the question, rather than copying the answer. You are encouraged to answer the questions first without referring to your *Participant Guide*.

Also included in your *Participant Guide* is a number of case study exercises. These exercises are inserted throughout the course at appropriate places to help reinforce learning on particular topics. An answer sheet is provided; however, it is recommended you work on the exercises right in your guide allowing for easy reference when reviewing. As you complete the exercises in class, write your own answers first and then check the answer sheet. Be sure to discuss any questions you may have and come up with methods to develop the answers with your instructor.

Another feature of the course is the in-class review of practice questions for each of the five sections. These questions appear at the end of the respective section in the self-study book. It is important that you have sufficient practice and in-class review of exam-style questions. Therefore, ensure that you participate in the in-class review of these questions and that you fully use the online question tool.

The final session of the course focuses on essay questions, which are part of the Part 2 exam. The session features a discussion of question scoring, example scorecards from ICMA, and strategies for writing answers to essay questions. The final session includes time to complete the practice essay questions in the self-study book.

Updates and Errata Notification

Please be advised that our materials are designed to provide thorough and accurate content with a high level of attention to quality. From time to time there may be clarifications, corrections, or updates that are captured in an Updates and Errata Notification.

To ensure you are kept abreast of changes, this notification will be available on Wiley's CMA update and errata page. You may review these documents by going to Wiley.com/go/cmaerrata.

Session 1

Course Introduction

The Association of
Accountants and
Financial Professionals
in Business

Wiley
CMAexcel Learning System
Exam Review 2017

Part 1: Financial Reporting, Planning, Performance, and Control

Session 1

Learning Outcome Statements (LOS) identifiers appear on the
slides as applicable to highlight where we address each LOS
within the material.

The Association of
Accountants and
Financial Professionals
in Business

Part 1: Financial Reporting, Planning, Performance, and Control

- Section A: External Financial Reporting Decisions
- Section B: Planning, Budgeting, and Forecasting
- Section C: Performance Management
- Section D: Cost Management
- Section E: Internal Controls

The Association of
Accountants and
Financial Professionals
in Business

Course Sessions

Session 1
- Introduction to CMA Credential and Wiley CMAexcel Learning System
- Section A, Topics 1 and 2

Session 2
- Study Tips
- Section A, Topic 2 (continued)

Session 3
- Section B, Topics 1 and 2

Session 4
- Section B, Topic 5

Session 5
- Section B, Topics 3 and 4

Session 6
- Section B, Topic 6

Session 7
- Section C, Topic 1

Session 8
- Section C, Topics 2 and 3

Session 9
- Section D, Topics 1 and 2

Session 10
- Section D, Topics 3, 4, and 5

Session 11
- Section E, Topic 1

Session 12
- Section E, Topics 2 and 3

Session 1 Overview

Session 1 Overview

- Introduction to CMA Credential and Wiley CMAexcel Learning System
- Section A, Topic 1: Financial Statements
- Section A, Topic 2: Recognition, Measurement, Valuation, and Disclosure:
  - Accounts and Notes Receivable
  - Inventory
    - Exercise: Inventory Valuation, LIFO to FIFO

IMA and CMA Program Overview

- Benefits of IMA membership
- Content specifications for CMA exam
- Becoming a CMA candidate
- Taking an exam: registration, testing locations, testing windows
- Wiley CMAexcel Learning System features and overview
- How to access the online practice tests

Benefits of IMA Membership

- Face-to-face networking and professional development opportunities—over 200 chapters around the world
- Subscription to IMA's award-winning publication: *Strategic Finance*
- Online learning courses—learn at your own pace
- Online library—let IMA's cybrarian brainstorm your research requirements
- Opportunity to pursue CMA designation
- Access to IMA's Ethics Center: tools, resources, and advice on ethically sound practices in global business

Part 1 Exam Content Specifications

- Exam: 4 hours total
  - 100 multiple-choice questions (3 hours to complete)
  - 2 essay questions (1 hour to complete)
- Five sections:
  - Section A: External Financial Reporting Decisions (15%)
  - Section B: Planning, Budgeting, and Forecasting (30%)
  - Section C: Performance Management (20%)
  - Section D: Cost Management (20%)
  - Section E: Internal Controls (15%)

The Association of
Accountants and
Financial Professionals
in Business

Steps to Become a CMA Candidate

- Become a member of the Institute of Management Accountants (IMA)

    ‣ Visit the IMA Web site at www.imanet.org
- Pay the CMA Program Entrance Fee

Wiley CMAexcel Learning System, Part 1: Financial Reporting, Planning, Performance, and Control.
Copyright © 2017, Institute of Management Accountants. Published by John Wiley & Sons, Inc.

The Association of
Accountants and
Financial Professionals
in Business

Become a CMA Candidate Early!

By enrolling early you can:
- Receive the monthly CMA *Connect* online newsletter filled with articles and tips.
- Gain access to the ICMA online candidate community.
- Have time to review and prepare all certification requirements and ensure you receive key updates and communications from ICMA.
- Ensure you are eligible to sit for an exam part (only registered candidates can sit for an exam).

Wiley CMAexcel Learning System, Part 1: Financial Reporting, Planning, Performance, and Control.
Copyright © 2017, Institute of Management Accountants. Published by John Wiley & Sons, Inc.

The Association of
Accountants and
Financial Professionals
in Business

How to Register for an Exam Part

After becoming an IMA member and entering the CMA program:

- Complete the online Exam Registration Form; select the exam(s) you plan to take and pay the associated fee(s).
- Receive a registration acknowledgment with exam authorization number, authorization window, and instructions on how to schedule an exam.
- Schedule your exam appointment with Prometric.
  - ▸ See www.prometric.com/ICMA for a list of test sites.
- Exam(s) must be taken within the assigned authorization window.

The Association of
Accountants and
Financial Professionals
in Business

WCMALS Exam Testing Windows

- Both exams (Parts 1 and 2):
  - ▸ January and February
  - ▸ May and June
  - ▸ September and October
- Scores are not available immediately, because the essay response section of the exam must be corrected manually.

The Association of
Accountants and
Financial Professionals
in Business

How to Use the Wiley CMAexcel Learning System

- Read the self-study book.
- Use the participant guide to take notes.
- **Use the Online Test Bank.**
  - ‣ Multiple-choice questions.
  - ‣ Essay questions in Resources section.

The Association of
Accountants and
Financial Professionals
in Business

WCMALS Book Content Features: Helpful Symbols

- Key terms appear in **boldface** where they are defined in text.

- Key formulas highlighted with a "key" symbol.

- Study tips highlighted with "book" symbol.

- Knowledge checks highlighted with "lightbulb" symbol.

- Practice questions highlighted with "question mark" symbol.

The Association of
Accountants and
Financial Professionals
In Business

Online Test Bank

- Integrate the online tests throughout your study program.
- Use the grade book function to track your progress over time.
- Check the Resources section for any additional study documents.
- Practice tests are drawn from a large bank of questions. Be sure to repeat the tests many times to ensure you have seen all questions.
- Be sure to understand all concepts—don't just memorize questions and answers.

The Association of
Accountants and
Financial Professionals
In Business

How to Access the Online Test Bank

- Use the Wiley CMAexcel Web site to access your online practice test. Visit www.wileycma.com

The Association of
Accountants and
Financial Professionals
in Business

Topic 1: Financial Statements

- Income Statement
- Statement of Changes in Shareholders' Equity
- Balance Sheet
- Statement of Cash Flows
- Limitations of Financial Statements
- Financial Statement Footnotes and Disclosures
- Users of Financial Statements

The Association of
Accountants and
Financial Professionals
in Business

LOS P1.A.1.b and c.

Income Statement

- Aka profit and loss (P&L) statement
- Measures earnings over a given time period
- Used to measure profitability, creditworthiness, and entity valuation
- Major components: revenues, gains, expenses, losses, and other comprehensive income
- Two presentation formats:
  - ‣ Single-step format
  - ‣ Multiple-step format (more commonly used)

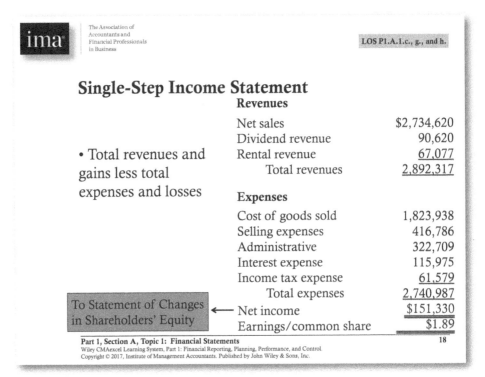

Single-Step Income Statement

Revenues

• Total revenues and gains less total expenses and losses	Net sales	$2,734,620
	Dividend revenue	90,620
	Rental revenue	67,077
	Total revenues	2,892,317

Expenses

Cost of goods sold	1,823,938
Selling expenses	416,786
Administrative	322,709
Interest expense	115,975
Income tax expense	61,579
Total expenses	2,740,987

To Statement of Changes in Shareholders' Equity ← Net income $151,330

Earnings/common share $1.89

Part 1, Section A, Topic 1: **Financial Statements**
Wiley CMAexcel Learning System, Part 1: Financial Reporting, Planning, Performance, and Control.
Copyright © 2017, Institute of Management Accountants. Published by John Wiley & Sons, Inc.

LOS P1.A.1.c., g., and h.

18

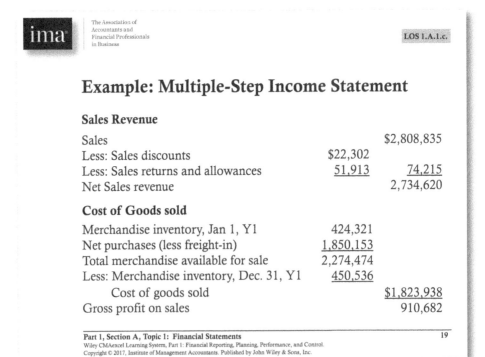

Example: Multiple-Step Income Statement

Sales Revenue

Sales		$2,808,835
Less: Sales discounts	$22,302	
Less: Sales returns and allowances	51,913	74,215
Net Sales revenue		2,734,620

Cost of Goods sold

Merchandise inventory, Jan 1, Y1	424,321	
Net purchases (less freight-in)	1,850,153	
Total merchandise available for sale	2,274,474	
Less: Merchandise inventory, Dec. 31, Y1	450,536	
Cost of goods sold		$1,823,938
Gross profit on sales		910,682

Part 1, Section A, Topic 1: **Financial Statements**
Wiley CMAexcel Learning System, Part 1: Financial Reporting, Planning, Performance, and Control.
Copyright © 2017, Institute of Management Accountants. Published by John Wiley & Sons, Inc.

LOS 1.A.1.c.

19

The Association of
Accountants and
Financial Professionals
in Business

LOS P1.A.1.c., g., and h.

Example: Multiple-Step Income Statement (cont.)

Operating Expenses

Selling expenses	$416,786	
Administrative expenses	322,709	739,495
Income from operations		171,187

Other Revenues and Gains

Dividend and rental revenue	157,697
	328,884

Other Expenses and Losses

Interest on bonds and notes	115,975
Income before income tax	212,909
Income tax	61,579
Net income for the year	$151,330
Earnings per common share	$1.89

To Statement of Changes in Shareholders' Equity ←

Part 1, Section A, Topic 1: Financial Statements
Wiley CMAexcel Learning System, Part 1: Financial Reporting, Planning, Performance, and Control.
Copyright © 2017, Institute of Management Accountants. Published by John Wiley & Sons, Inc.

20

The Association of
Accountants and
Financial Professionals
in Business

LOS 1.A.1.c.

Presentation of Discontinued Operations

- Located below income from continuing operations
- Shown net of tax

Net Sales
 − Cost of goods sold
    Gross profit on sales
 − Operating expenses
    Operating income
 +/− Other gains and losses
    Earnings before tax
 − Tax expenses
    Income from continuing operations
 +/− **Discontinued operations**
    Net income

Part 1, Section A, Topic 1: Financial Statements
Wiley CMAexcel Learning System, Part 1: Financial Reporting, Planning, Performance, and Control.
Copyright © 2017, Institute of Management Accountants. Published by John Wiley & Sons, Inc.

21

The Association of
Accountants and
Financial Professionals
in Business

LOS 1.A.1.e.

Question: Income Statement

In the preparation of a multiple-step income statement, all of the following would be part of income from operations with the except of:

a. gross profit
b. selling expenses
c. interest expense
d. cost of goods sold

Answer: **c. Interest expense. In a multiple-step income statement, interest expense is shown below income from operations as part of "other expenses and losses"**

The Association of
Accountants and
Financial Professionals
in Business

LOS 1.A.1.b. and c.

Statement of Changes in Shareholders' Equity

- FASB requirement when balance sheet is issued
- Includes: capital stock (common and preferred at par value), additional paid-in capital, retained earnings, accumulated other comprehensive income.
- Format of financial information includes in statement:
  - Beginning balance for the period
  - Additions
  - Deductions
  - Ending balance for the period

The Association of Accountants and Financial Professionals in Business

LOS P1.A.1.c., e., and g.

Example: Statement of Changes in Shareholders' Equity

	Common Stock, $1Par	Additional Paid-In Capital	Retained Earnings	Total
Balance, Jan. 1, Y1	$24,680	$345,520	$90,251	$460,451
Net income →	To Statement of Changes in Shareholders' Equity	From Income Statement →	151,330	151.330
Cash dividends paid			(33,330)	(33,330)
Common stock issued	1,000	14,800		15,800
Balance, Dec. 31, Y1	$25,680	$360,320	$208,251	$594,251

To Balance Sheet

The Association of Accountants and Financial Professionals in Business

LOS 1.A.1.b.

Balance Sheet

- Aka "Statement of Financial Position"
- Assets = Liabilities + Shareholders' Equity
- "Snapshot"
- Helps users evaluate an entity's capital structure and assess liquidity, solvency, financial flexibility, and operating capability.
- Three sections: Assets, Liabilities, and Shareholders' Equity
  - Assets and liabilities are further categorized as "current" or "long-term"
  - Assets presented in order of liquidity; liabilities listed in the order in which they come due; equity items are listed in order of those that have most claim to the equity down to those with the least claim to equity

The Association of
Accountants and
Financial Professionals
in Business

LOS I.A.1.c.

Major Components and Classifications of the Balance Sheet

Assets	• Current assets (cash, A/R, inventory) • Long-term investments • Property, plant, and equipment (PP&E) • Intangible assets • Other assets
Liabilities	• Current liabilities (A/P, interest payable, current portion of long-term debt) • Long-term liabilities (bonds, mortgages) • Other liabilities
Shareholders, equity	• Capital stock • Additional paid-in capital • Retained earnings • Treasury stock • Accumulated other comprehensive income

The Association of
Accountants and
Financial Professionals
in Business

LOS P1.A.1.c., g., and h.

Format of Balance Sheet

Asset		Liabilities & Equity	
Current assets:		Current liabilities:	
Cash, cash equivalents	$24,628	A/P	$175,321
Receivables	552,249	Current portion of L/T debt	36,000
Other Receivables	18,941	Other current liabilities	147,500
Note Receivable	80,532	Total current liabilities	358,821
Inventory	252,567	L/T debt	117,343
Prepaid insurance	7,500	Total liabilities	476,164
Total current assets	936,417	Shareholders' equity:	
Fixed assets:		Common stock, par	25,680
PP&E	209,330	APIC	360,320
Less: Account, depreciation	(75,332)	Retained earnings	208,251
Net fixed assets	133,998	Total shareholders' equity	594,251
Total assets	$1,070,415	Total liabilities and equity	$1,070,415

From Statement of Changes in Shareholders' Equity

The Association of
Accountants and
Financial Professionals
in Business

LOS 1.A.1.e.

Question: Balance Sheet

Celio Products, Ltd. was incorporated on January 1 of Year 1 with $500,000 from the issuance of common stock and borrowed funds of $75,000. During the first year of operations, Celio had net income of $25,000 and paid a $2,000 cash dividend. As of December 31 Year 1, liabilities had increased to $94,000. In Celio's December 31 Year 1 balance sheet, how much are total assets?

Answer: Assets = Liabilities + Shareholders' Equity

Liabilities at December 31 = $94,000
Shareholders' Equity at December 31 = Common Stock ($500,000) + *Retained earnings ($23,000) = $523,000

Assets = Liabilities + Shareholders' equity, or $94,000 + $523,000 = **$617,000**

*Note: Retained earnings = Beginning retained earnings + Net income – Dividends = Ending retained earning, or $0 + $25,000 – $2,000 = $23,000

Part 1, Section A, Topic 1: Financial Statements   28
Wiley CMAexcel Learning System, Part 1: Financial Reporting, Planning, Performance, and Control.
Copyright © 2017, Institute of Management Accountants. Published by John Wiley & Sons, Inc.

The Association of
Accountants and
Financial Professionals
in Business

LOS 1.A.1.b.

Statement of Cash Flows Overview

- Reports cash inflow and outflows and net change in cash
- Three major components:
  - ‣ Operating activities.
  - ‣ Investing activities
  - ‣ Financing activities

- Measures cash flows over a period of time
- Purpose: Helps financial statement users assess whether an entity requires external financing or is generating cash flows, meeting obligations, and paying dividends
- Uses the income statement and comparative balance sheet information in its preparation

Net cash inflow/outflow can be used to calculate end of year cash balance
+ Cash balance at beginning of year
+/ – Net cash inflow (outflow) during the year
= Cash balance (end of year)

Part 1, Section A, Topic 1: Financial Statements   29
Wiley CMAexcel Learning System, Part 1: Financial Reporting, Planning, Performance, and Control.
Copyright © 2017, Institute of Management Accountants. Published by John Wiley & Sons, Inc.

Cash Flow Statement: Indirect Method

Start with Net Income

Add Non-cash expenses (e.g., depreciation, amortization)

Subtract Gains from investing and financing activities

Add Losses from investing and financing activities

Add Decreases in current assets

Subtract Increases in current assets

Add Increases in current liabilities

Subtract Decreases in current liabilities

Add Amortization of discounts on bonds

<u>Subtract Amortization of premiums on bonds</u>

Operating cash flow

Statement of Cash Flows: Non-Cash Items

- Net income includes non-cash items that impact current income, but are the result of prior-period costs incurred and do not affect current period cash flows. Net income, therefore, requires adjustments for those items in deriving operating cash flows. Examples include:
    - Depreciation expense (on PP&E); amortization expense (on intangible assets)
    - Amortization of deferred costs (e.g., bond issue costs)
    - Amortization of premium or discount on bonds payable
- Gains/losses on investing and financing activities also require income adjustments in order to derive operating cash flows; gains/losses part of net income, but sales proceeds from these transactions presented in investing and/or financing activities as applicable.
- Net income includes certain accrual-related items that have no cash impact in the current period; these also require adjustments to net income in deriving operating cash flows. Examples include:
    - Accrued sales (uncollected)
    - Accrued expenses (unpaid)

The Association of
Accountants and
Financial Professionals
in Business

LOS P1.A.1.c., e., g., and h.

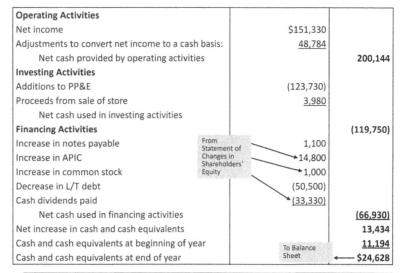

Operating Activities		
Net income	$151,330	
Adjustments to convert net income to a cash basis:	48,784	
Net cash provided by operating activities		**200,144**
Investing Activities		
Additions to PP&E	(123,730)	
Proceeds from sale of store	3,980	
Net cash used in investing activities		
Financing Activities		**(119,750)**
Increase in notes payable	1,100	
Increase in APIC	14,800	
Increase in common stock	1,000	
Decrease in L/T debt	(50,500)	
Cash dividends paid	(33,330)	
Net cash used in financing activities		**(66,930)**
Net increase in cash and cash equivalents		**13,434**
Cash and cash equivalents at beginning of year		**11,194**
Cash and cash equivalents at end of year		**$24,628**

From Statement of Changes in Shareholders' Equity

To Balance Sheet

Part 1, Section A, Topic 1: Financial Statements   32
Wiley CMAexcel Learning System, Part 1: Financial Reporting, Planning, Performance, and Control.
Copyright © 2017, Institute of Management Accountants. Published by John Wiley & Sons, Inc.

The Association of
Accountants and
Financial Professionals
in Business

LOS 1.A.1.e.

Question: Classification of Cash Flow Transactions (#1)

According to ASC Topic 230, *Statement of Cash Flows,* all of the following should be classified under the operating activities section of the Statement of Cash Flows *except:*

a. Purchase of land and building.

b. Decrease in prepaid insurance.

c. Decrease in inventory.

d. Depreciation expense.

Answer: a. Purchase of land and building.

Part 1, Section A, Topic 1: Financial Statements   33
Wiley CMAexcel Learning System, Part 1: Financial Reporting, Planning, Performance, and Control.
Copyright © 2017, Institute of Management Accountants. Published by John Wiley & Sons, Inc.

The Association of
Accountants and
Financial Professionals
in Business

LOS 1.A.1.e.

Question: Classification of Cash Flow Transactions (#2)

ASC Topic 230, *Statement of Cash Flows,* classifies cash receipts and cash payments by operating, investing, and financing activities. Which one of the following transactions should be classified as a financing activity?

a. Purchase of treasury stock.

b. Payment of interest on a mortgage note.

c. Purchase of equipment.

d. Sale of trademarks.

Answer: a. Purchase of treasury stock.

Part 1, Section A, Topic 1: Financial Statements   34
Wiley CMAexcel Learning System, Part 1: Financial Reporting, Planning, Performance, and Control.
Copyright © 2017, Institute of Management Accountants. Published by John Wiley & Sons, Inc.

The Association of
Accountants and
Financial Professionals
in Business

LOS 1.A.1.e.

Question: SOCF—Operating Activities

At the end of the current fiscal year, XM Company reported net income of $40,000. In addition, the XM experienced the following changes in account balances from the beginning to the end of the fiscal year:

- Increase in accounts receivable: $3,000
- Decrease in inventory: $4,500
- Increase in Prepaid expenses: $1,500
- Increase in accounts payable: $7,500
- Decrease in long-term debt: $12,000

What amount should be reported as cash flow from operating activities on XM's statement of cash flows for the current fiscal year?

a. $47,500

b. $49,500

c. $32,500

d. $34,500

Answer: a. $47,500

Part 1, Section A, Topic 1: Financial Statements   35
Wiley CMAexcel Learning System, Part 1: Financial Reporting, Planning, Performance, and Control.
Copyright © 2017, Institute of Management Accountants. Published by John Wiley & Sons, Inc.

The Association of
Accountants and
Financial Professionals
in Business

LOS 1.A.1.e.

Question: SOCF—Investing Activities

Bernstein & Power Corporation (B&P) had the following activities in Year 1:

- Acquired 2,000 shares of stock in Weis & Salute, Inc. for $26,000. B&P intends to hold the stock as a long-term investment.
- Sold an investment in Manganelli Motors for $35,000, when the carrying value was $33,000, thereby recognizing a gain on the sale of $2,000.
- Acquired a $50,000, four-year certificate of deposit from a bank.
- Collected dividends on $1,200 on stock investments.

In B&P's Year 1 statement of cash flows, net cash flows from investing activities should be:

a. $37,200

b. $38,050

c. $39,800

d. $41,000

Answer: d. **$41,000**

Part 1, Section A, Topic 1: Financial Statements   36
Wiley CMAexcel Learning System, Part 1: Financial Reporting, Planning, Performance, and Control.
Copyright © 2017, Institute of Management Accountants. Published by John Wiley & Sons, Inc.

The Association of
Accountants and
Financial Professionals
in Business

LOS 1.A.1.e.

Question: SOCF—Financing Activities

During the current year, Grandoff Corporation had the following activities related to its financial operations:

• Principal repayment on debt:	$425,000
• Dividend payment on common stock:	$50,000
• Purchase of fixed assets:	$30,000
• Proceeds from sale of treasury stock	$20,000

How much should Grandoff report as net cash used in financing activities in its current year statement of cash flows?

a. $495,000

b. $475,000

c. $455,000

d. $425,000

Answer: c. **$455,000**

Part 1, Section A, Topic 1: Financial Statements   37
Wiley CMAexcel Learning System, Part 1: Financial Reporting, Planning, Performance, and Control.
Copyright © 2017, Institute of Management Accountants. Published by John Wiley & Sons, Inc.

The Association of
Accountants and
Financial Professionals
In Business

LOS 1.A.1.d.

Limitations of Financial Statements

- Historical cost
- Different accounting methods
- Omit non-objective items of value
- Use of estimates and judgments
- Off-balance-sheet information
- Non-cash transactions

The Association of
Accountants and
Financial Professionals
in Business

LOS 1.A.1.f.

Financial Statement Footnotes and Disclosures

- Used when parenthetical explanations would not suffice to fully describe certain events or situations that are important and/or material enough to users in making decisions about a particular entity.
- Common disclosures revolve around:
  - ▸ Contingencies
  - ▸ Contractual situations
  - ▸ Accounting policies
  - ▸ Subsequent events

The Association of
Accountants and
Financial Professionals
in Business

LOS 1.A.1.a.

Users of Financial Statements and Their Needs

- Internal users
  - Executives, managers, management accountants, employees who have vested interests in company (i.e., through stock option plans, etc.)
  - Internal decision-making

- External users
  - Creditors and investors
    - Creditors—interested in entity's ability to repay debt and comply with debt covenants
    - Investors—need to assess investment return and make decisions about buying, holding, or selling an entity's securities
  - Investment decisions
  - Other external users include: stock exchanges, unions, analysts, regulatory agencies

The Association of
Accountants and
Financial Professionals
in Business

Section A, Topic 2: Recognition, Measurement, Valuation, and Disclosure

- Accounts and Notes Receivable
- Inventory

Accounts Receivable (A/R)

- Claims against customer, debtors
- Classifications
  - ▸ Balance sheet
    - Current
    - Noncurrent
  - ▸ Source
    - Trade—accounts receivable, some notes receivable
    - Nontrade—interest receivable, dividends receivable, etc.

Trade and Cash Discounts

- Trade discounts
  - ▸ Also known as "volume or quantity discounts"
  - ▸ Sales and receivables should be recorded net of trade discounts

- Cash discounts
  - ▸ Incentives for early or prompt payment.
  - ▸ Example: 2/10, net 30
  - ▸ Discounts not taken represent an opportunity cost.
  - ▸ Two methods for accounting for cash discounts:
    - Gross method
    - Net method

The Association of
Accountants and
Financial Professionals
in Business

Question—Cash Discounts: Opportunity Costs

A vendor offers cash discount terms of 1/15, n/30. What would be the opportunity cost of not taking this discount?

a. 1.01%
b. 16.67%
c. 24.58%
d. 37.25%

Answer: c.

$$\text{Effective Cost of Discount} = \frac{\text{Discount \%}}{(100-\text{Discount \%})} \times \frac{365}{(\text{Net Period} - \text{Discount Period})}$$

$$= \frac{0.01}{0.99} \times \frac{365}{(30-15)} = 0.101 \times 24.3333 = 24.58\%$$

Part 1, Section A, Topic 2: Recognition, Measurement, Valuation, and Disclosure   44
Wiley CMAexcel Learning System, Part 1: Financial Reporting, Planning, Performance, and Control.
Copyright © 2017, Institute of Management Accountants. Published by John Wiley & Sons, Inc.

The Association of
Accountants and
Financial Professionals
in Business

Question—Receivables Reporting

According to FASB ASC Topic 835, *Interest*, how should long-term receivables and trade receivables be recorded?

Answer:

• Long-term receivables recorded at present value

• Trade receivables recorded at maturity value

▸ Net realizable value (NRV) for trade receivables

Part 1, Section A, Topic 2: Recognition, Measurement, Valuation, and Disclosure   45
Wiley CMAexcel Learning System, Part 1: Financial Reporting, Planning, Performance, and Control.
Copyright © 2017, Institute of Management Accountants. Published by John Wiley & Sons, Inc.

A/R Valuation and Uncollectible Accounts

- Direct write-off method
  - ▸ Recognize bad debts when they occur
  - ▸ Not GAAP (cash basis accounting)

- Allowance method = GAAP
  - ▸ Estimate bad debts in advance
    - Balance sheet approach, or
    - Income statement approaches

LOS 1.A.2.a and b.

A/R Valuation and Uncollectible Accounts

Allowance method, balance sheet approach:
- Percentage of outstanding A/R method—determine uncollectible A/R balance
  - ▸ Measuring uncollectible accounts
    - Single percentage applied to outstanding A/R
    - $150,000 × 3% = $4,500 ending balance in allowance
    - If beginning allowance = $2,000, then expense = $2,500

- Aging of A/R method
  - ▸ Percentage uncollectible varies with age of account

LOS 1.A.2.a and b.

Balance Sheet Approach: Aging of A/R Method

Customer	Dec. 31 Balance	Under 60 Days	61–90 Days	91–120 Days	Over 120 Days
East Inc.	$ 54,880	$44,800	$10,080		
West Inc.	210,000	179,200			$30,800
North Inc.	41,440	33,600		$7,840	
Total	$306,320	$257,600	$10,080	$7,840	$30,800

Age	Amount	Uncollectible Estimate (%)	Required Balance in Allowance
Under 60 days old	$257,600	5%	$12,880
60–90 days old	10,080	15%	1,512
91–120 days old	7,840	20%	1,568
Over 120 days	30,800	25%	7,700
Year-end balance of allowance for doubtful accounts			$23,660

LOS 1.A.2.a and b.

A/R Valuation and Uncollectible Accounts

Allowance method, income statement approach:

- Percentage of sales method (matching principle)

% of Bad Debt × Total Sales = Bad Debt Expense

$$2.5\% \times \$200,000 = \$5,000$$

- Percentage of net credit sales method

% of Bad Debt × Net Credit Sales = Bad Debt Expense

$$3\% \times \$175,000 = \$5,250$$

The Association of
Accountants and
Financial Professionals
in Business

LOS 1.A.2.a and b.

Question—A/R Valuation and Uncollectible Accounts

Which of the following are true of the income statement approach to calculating the allowance for uncollectibles?

I. Based on value of sales

II. Based on value of accounts receivable

III. Calculates allowance for uncollectible accounts, bad debt expense is the adjustment to the allowance

IV. Calculates bad-debt expense and increases the allowance by that amount

a. I and III
b. I and IV
c. II and III
d. II and IV

Answer: **b**

The Association of
Accountants and
Financial Professionals
in Business

LOS 1.A.2.c.

Disposition of Accounts and Notes Receivable

Factoring:
- Factors buy receivables and assume collection risks
- Credit approval

Securitization:
- Bundle similar receivables into investment fund
- Sellers service receivables

Sale:
- Without recourse—purchaser assumes risk of bad debts (factoring)
- With recourse—seller retains risk of bad debts

LOS I.A.2.c.

Disposition of Accounts and Notes Receivable

Sale with recourse: Financial components approach

- $100,000 sale of receivables
- 2% finance charge
- 3% collateral (holdback) for bad debt
- Recourse obligation has a fair value of $4,000

Net Proceeds Calculation

Cash received		
$100,000 – (2% + 3%)	$95,000	
Due from factor	3,000	$98,000
Less: Allowance for doubtful accounts		(4,000)
Net proceeds		$94,000

Loss on Sale Calculation

Finance Charge (2% x $100,000)	$2,000
Recourse Obligation	4,000
Loss on sale of receivables	$6,000

LOS I.A.2.a.

A/R Disclosure Requirements: Partial Balance Sheet

Current Assets		
Cash and equivalents		$1,383,985
Accounts receivable*	$6,643,478	
Less: Allowance for doubtful accounts	370,167	
	6,273,311	
Notes receivable—trade*	2,973,930	9,247,241
Total current assets		10,631,226
Noncurrent Receivables		
Notes receivable from officers and key employees		278,307
Claims receivable (settlement collected over five years)		432,900

*Note on accounts and notes receivable; In July Y1, the firm refinanced part of its indebtedness evidenced by an 8% note payable. The note is secured by substantially all the A/R and is payable on demand.

LOS 1.A.2.d.

Inventory—Three Types

▸ Finished goods or merchandise inventory

  • Goods held for sale

▸ Work-in-process inventory

  • Goods created during the production process

▸ Raw materials inventory

  • Materials used in production

LOS 1.A.2.d.

Inventory Valuation—Goods

What goods to include?

• Goods held on consignment—exclude (no title)
• Goods in transit—include if purchased FOB shipping point; exclude if FOB destination
• Sale agreements (high returns, instalment sales)—include if estimable
  ▸ Sales with buyback agreements

LOS 1.A.2.d.

Inventory Valuation—Costs

What costs to include?
- Manufacturing overhead, acquisition (freight-in), and production costs—include; non-production admin., selling expenses—exclude
  - ▸ e.g., include product costs, exclude period costs
- Minus purchase (cash) discounts
- Minus purchase returns and allowances

LOS 1.A.2.g.

Perpetual Inventory Systems

Continuous updating of inventory balances on a computer-based system

- Cost of goods sold measured at sale
- Periodic physical counts for comparison still necessary

Beginning Inventory + Purchases – Cost of Goods Sold = Ending Inventory

The Association of
Accountants and
Financial Professionals
in Business

LOS 1.A.2.g.

Periodic Inventory Systems

Use a "Purchases" account to record inventory purchases

- Cost of goods sold measured at end of period
- A physical count is required to determine ending inventory

Beginning Inventory + Purchases Account –
Ending Inventory (from physical count) =
Cost of Goods Sold

The Association of
Accountants and
Financial Professionals
in Business

LOS 1.A.2.g.

Cost of Goods Sold

What is the total cost of goods available for sale and the cost of goods sold for a firm with $350,000 in beginning inventory and $400,000 in ending inventory for a period that also had a cost of goods acquired or produced of $670,000?

Beginning inventory, Jan. 1	$350,000
Cost of goods acquired or produced during the year	670,000
Total cost of goods available for sale	1,020,000
Ending inventory, Dec. 31	(400,000)
Cost of goods sold during the year	$620,000

The Association of
Accountants and
Financial Professionals
in Business

LOS 1.A.2.f.

Lower of Cost or Market (LCM)

- When market values decline, inventory is written down and cost of goods sold increased
- Market = replacement cost, subject to a

  ‣ Ceiling (net realizable value)
  ‣ Floor (net realizable value less normal profit)

- LCM applied to either individual items, product categories, or the whole inventory

The Association of
Accountants and
Financial Professionals
in Business

LOS 1.A.2.f.

Data for Sportway Co.'s inventory:

Per Unit	Skis	Ski Boots	Parkas
Historical Cost	$190.00	$106.00	$53.00
Selling Price	217.00	145.00	73.75
Cost to Distribute	19.00	8.00	2.50
Current Replacement Cost	203.00	105.00	51.00
Normal Profit Margin	32.00	29.00	21.25

(1) The ceiling and floor of the market value that should be used in the LCM comparison of skis are:

a. $217 and $198
b. $217 and $186
c. $198 and $166
d. $185 and $166

(2) "Cost" in LCM for ski boots is:

a. $105
b. $106
c. $108
d. $137

(3) "Market" in LCM for parkas is:

a. $51.00
b. $53.00
c. $71.25
d. $73.75

The Association of
Accountants and
Financial Professionals
in Business

LOS 1.A.2.f.

Data for Sportway Co.'s inventory:

Per Unit	Skis	Ski Boots	Parkas
Historical Cost	$190.00	$106.00	$53.00
Selling Price	217.00	145.00	73.75
Cost to Distribute	19.00	8.00	2.50
Current Replacement Cost	203.00	105.00	51.00
Normal Profit Margin	32.00	29.00	21.25

(1) The ceiling and floor of the market value that should be used in the LCM comparison of skis are:

a. $217 and $198
b. $217 and $185
c. $198 and $166
d. $185 and $166

Answer: c. The ceiling is the net realizable value, or price less costs required to complete the sale: $ 217–$19 = $198. The floor is NRV less the normal profit margin: $198 – $32 = $166.

The Association of
Accountants and
Financial Professionals
in Business

LOS 1.A.2.f.

Data for Sportway Co.'s inventory:

Per Unit	Skis	Ski Boots	Parkas
Historical Cost	$190.00	$106.00	$53.00
Selling Price	217.00	145.00	73.75
Cost to Distribute	19.00	8.00	2.50
Current Replacement Cost	203.00	105.00	51.00
Normal Profit Margin	32.00	29.00	21.25

(2) "Cost" in LCM for ski boots is:

a. $105
b. $106
c. $108
d. $137

Answer: b. Historical cost is used as the "cost" in LCM: $106

LOS 1.A.2.f.

Data for Sportway Co.'s inventory:

Per Unit	Skis	Ski Boots	Parkas
Historical Cost	$190.00	$106.00	$53.00
Selling Price	217.00	145.00	73.75
Cost to Distribute	19.00	8.00	2.50
Current Replacement Cost	203.00	105.00	51.00
Normal Profit Margin	32.00	29.00	21.25

(3) "Market" in LCM for parkas is:

a. $51.00
b. $53.00
c. $71.25
d. $73.75   Answer: a. Market is the normal replacement
              cost in LCM: $51

LOS 1.A.2.e.

Inventory Cost Flow Assumptions

- Specific identification
  - Tracks the actual cost of each specific item sold to determine cost of goods sold
- Average cost
  - Uses an average cost to price both COGS and ending inventory
- First-in, first-out (FIFO)
  - The oldest costs are assigned to COGS, and the most recent to ending inventory
- Last-in, first-out (LIFO)
  - The most recent costs are assigned to COGS, and the oldest to ending inventory

The Association of
Accountants and
Financial Professionals
in Business

LOS 1.A.2.e.

Moving Average Cost

July 1, beginning inventory	1,000 units @ $40	$40,000
July 7, purchases	1,000 units @ $60	60,000
July 7, balance	2,000 units @ $50	$100,000
July 15, sales	(1,000) units @ $50	(50,000)
July 15, balance	1,000 units @ $50	$50,000
July 20, purchases	500 units @ $56	28,000
July 20, balance	1,500 units @ $52	$78,000
July 28, sales	(300) units @ $52	(15, 600)
July 31, balance (ending inventory)	1,200 units @ $52	$62,400
Cost of goods sold (1,300 units)	$50,000 + $15,600	$65,600

The Association of
Accountants and
Financial Professionals
in Business

LOS 1.A.2.e.

Perpetual FIFO

First-In, First-Out Inventory Cost Flow Assumption (Perpetual)	
Cost of goods sold (1,300 units):	
July 15 1,000 units @ $40	$40,000
July 28 300 units @ $60	18,000
Total	$58,000
Ending inventory (1,200 units):	
Beginning Inventory + Purchases – COGS = Ending Inventory $40,000 + $88,000 – $58,000 = $70,000*	

*700 units @ $60 = $42,000
500 units @ $56 =   28,000
$70,000

The Association of
Accountants and
Financial Professionals
in Business

LOS 1.A.2.e.

Perpetual LIFO

Last-In, First-Out Inventory Cost Flow Assumption (Perpetual)	
Cost of goods sold (1,300 units):	
July 15 1,000 units @ $60	$60,000
July 28 300 units @ $56	16,800
Total	$76,800
Ending inventory (1,200 units):	
Beginning Inventory + Purchases – COGS = Ending Inventory $40,000 + $88,000 – $76,800 = $51,200*	

*1,000 units @ $40 = $40,000
  200 units @ $56 = 11,200
               $51,200

The Association of
Accountants and
Financial Professionals
in Business

LOS 1.A.2.g.

Impact of Inflation

When inventory prices are rising (inflation), LIFO results in lower income and FIFO results in higher inventory valuation

Effects of Inventory Cost Assumptions

Cost Flow Assumption	Cost of Goods Available for Sale	Cost of Goods Sold	Ending Inventory
FIFO, Perpetual	$128,000	$58,000	$70,000
LIFO, Perpetual	128,000	76,800	51,200

The Association of
Accountants and
Financial Professionals
in Business

LOS 1.A.2.e.

Adapted from ICMA question, used with permission.

Jensen Company uses a perpetual inventory system. The purchases and sales made during the month of May are shown on the right.

Date	Activity	Units (u)
May 1	Balance	100 u @ $ 10/u
May 9	Purchase	200 u @ $ 10/u
May 16	Sale	190 u
May 21	Purchase	150 u @ $ 12/u
May 29	Sale	120 u

If Jensen Company uses the first-in, first-out (FIFO) method of inventory valuation, the May 31 inventory would be:

a. $1,460
b. $1,493
c. $1,562
d. $1,680

Answer: d. The FIFO method makes the accounting assumption that goods purchased earlier are used or sold before goods purchased later. May 1 inventory value: 100 × $10 = $1,000. May 9: $1,000 + (200 × $10) = $3,000. May 16: $3,000 − (190 × $10) = $1,100. May 21: $1,100 + (150 × $12) = $2,900. May 29: $2,900 − 110 × $10) − (10 × $12) = $1,680.

The Association of
Accountants and
Financial Professionals
in Business

LOS 1.A.2.e.

Adapted from ICMA question, used with permission.

Jensen Company uses a perpetual inventory system. The purchases and sales made during the month of May are shown on the right.

Date	Activity	Units (u)
May 1	Balance	100 u @ $ 10/u
May 9	Purchase	200 u @ $ 10/u
May 16	Sale	190 u
May 21	Purchase	150 u @ $ 12/u
May 29	Sale	120 u

If Jensen Company uses the last-in, first-out (LIFO) method of inventory valuation, the May 31 inventory would be:

a. $1,460
b. $1,493
c. $1,562
d. $1,680

Answer: a. Under the LIFO method, the cost of the last goods bought are assigned to cost of goods sold and the ending inventory. May include the cost of the earliest purchases. May 1 inventory value: 100 × $10 = $1,000. May 9: $1,000 + (200 × $10) = $3,000. May 16: $3,000 − (190 × $10) = $1,100. May 21: $1,100 + (150 × $12) = $2,900. May 29: $2,900 − (120 × $12) = $1,460.

LOS 1.A.2.e.

LIFO Liquidation

Year 4 beginning inventory: 12,000 pounds raw rubber

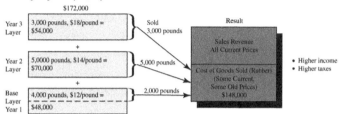

$172,000

Year 3 Layer	3,000 pounds, $18/pound = $54,000	Sold 3,000 pounds	Result
Year 2 Layer	5,0000 pounds, $14/pound = $70,000	5,000 pounds	Sales Revenue All Current Prices
Base Layer Year 1	4,000 pounds, $12/pound = $48,000	2,000 pounds	Cost of Goods Sold (Rubber) (Some Current, Some Old Prices) $148,000

• Higher income
• Higher taxes

During Year 3, 10,000 pounds raw rubber used;
none available for purchase due to shortage.

* If 7,000 additional pounds of rubber were purchased in Year 4 at $18/lb, then COGS (rubber) would be $180,000,
resulting in lower income and taxes.

LOS 1.A.2.e.

Adapted from ICMA question, used with permission.

Wright Hardware adopted the dollar-value LIFO method of inventory valuation at Dec. 31, Y1. Inventory balances and price indices are shown in the table.

Dec. 31	Ending Inventory at End of Year Prices	Price Index at Dec. 31
Y1	$240,000	100
Y2	275,000	110
Y3	300,000	120

Wright Hardware's ending inventory as of Dec. 31, Y2, computed by the dollar-value LIFO method was:

a. $240,000
b. $250,000
c. $251,000
d. $275,000
e. $300,000

Answer: b $275,000/1.1 = $250,000

LOS 1.A.2.e.

Adapted from ICMA question, used with permission.

Wright Hardware adopted the dollar-value LIFO method of inventory valuation at Dec. 31, Y1. Inventory balances and price indices are shown in the table.

Dec. 31	Ending Inventory at End of Year Prices	Price Index at Dec. 31
Y1	$240,000	100
Y2	275,000	110
Y3	300,000	120

Wright Hardware's ending inventory as of Dec. 31, Y3, computed by the dollar-value LIFO method would be:

a. $240,000
b. $250,000
c. $251,000
d. $300,000
e. $275,000

Answer: b $300,000/1.2 = $250,000

LOS 1.A.2.e.

LOS 1.A.2.h.

Inventory Errors

- On the exam, you may face questions addressing two main types of inventory errors
  - Misstated ending inventory
  - Misstated purchases <u>and</u> inventory
- These errors may impact:
  - Balance sheet
  - Income statement
  - Key financial ratio metrics

LOS P1.A.1.d., e., g., and j.

Session 1 Exercise

Inventory Valuation, LIFO to FIFO
Section A, Topic 2: Recognition, Measurement, Valuation, and Disclosure

Session 1 Exercise: Inventory Valuation, LIFO to FIFO

Section A, Topic 2: Recognition, Measurement, Valuation, and Disclosure

Background Information:

Welltronics was founded in Year 1 (Y1) and specializes in the design and manufacture of hand-held electronic games. The company quickly earned a reputation for creativity and introduced a number of new products annually, resulting in several highly profitable years. Welltronics became a public company in Y3 and expanded rapidly by capturing a large share of the growing electronic games market.

In Y7, the chief design engineer retired, and two other design engineers took positions with other companies, which resulted in a decline in new product development and a corresponding decline in market share and profits. Earnings for the past two years have been disappointing and the net income for Y9 is not expected to improve. The Y9 net income is estimated to be $80,000, yielding approximately one percent return on sales and two percent return on shareholders' equity.

During Y9, Welltronics was finally able to assemble a highly capable design team. Several new products have already been tested and will be introduced in Y10. As a result, profit expectations for the future are much improved.

In the meantime, Welltronics' bank and its securities advisor have suggested that the company change its method of reporting inventory. Since its inception, Welltronics has used the first-in, first-out (FIFO) inventory method for internal reporting and the last-in, first-out (LIFO) inventory method for external financial reporting. A change to the FIFO method for external purposes would report inventory balances that more clearly represent actual value and should improve Welltronics' financial statements.

Presented in the following exhibit are the Y8 actual and Y9 pro forma Balance Sheets for Welltronics with the inventory stated on the LIFO basis. Additional information about the statements and the company is as follows.

- If the FIFO method of inventory valuation had been used, inventory would have been higher by $620,000 and $730,000 on December 31, Y8 and Y9, respectively.
- There have not been any dividends paid to common shareholders since Y7.
- Welltronics has an effective income tax rate of 40 percent.

	Welltronics	
	Balance Sheet	
	December 31, Y8 and Y9	
	(in thousands)	
	Y9 Pro Forma	**Y8 Actual**
Cash	$100	$120
Accounts receivable (net)	450	430
Inventory	600	510
Property, plant, & equipment (net)	4,640	4,380
Goodwill (net)	400	430
Total assets	$6,190	$5,870
Current portion of long-term debt	$120	$70
Accounts payable	650	620
Accrued liabilities	340	360
Income taxes payable	60	55
Long-term debt	1,100	925
Common stock	3,000	3,000
Retained earnings	920	840
Total liabilities and shareholders' equity	$6,190	$5,870

Question 1: On December 31, Y9, Welltronics decides to change to the FIFO method of inventory valuation for external financial reporting. Calculate the revised net income for Y9.

Question 2: Present the journal entry that would be required to eliminate the LIFO allowance account, including the tax effect, as of December 31, Y9.

Question 3: Discuss the effects the change in inventory valuation method will have on Welltronics' cash position at December 31, Y9 and Y10.

Session 1 Exercise Solution: Inventory Valuation, LIFO to FIFO

Question 1: On December 31, Y9, Welltronics decides to change to the FIFO method of inventory valuation for external financial reporting. Calculate the revised net income for Y9.

Welltronics' revised net income for Y9 due to the change from the LIFO inventory method to the FIFO method is $146,000, calculated as follows.

Net income reported under LIFO		$80,000
Y9 effect of LIFO to FIFO change:		
Y8 LIFO reserve	$620,000	
Y9 LIFO reserve	730,000	
Before tax income	110,000	
Income tax (40%)	44,000	
Net income effect		66,000
Net income after change to FIFO		$146,000

Question 2: Present the journal entry that would be required to eliminate the LIFO allowance account, including the tax effect, as of December 31, Y9.

The journal entry that would be required to eliminate the LIFO allowance account, including the tax effect, as of December 31, Y9, is as follows.

	Debit	Credit
LIFO reserve (inventory)	$730,000	
Tax expense ($110,000 × 0.40 for Y9)	44,000	
Retained earnings [($730,000 – $110,000) × 0.60]		$372,000
Taxes payable ($730,000 × 0.40)		292,000
Cost of goods sold (Y9 difference)		110,000

Question 3: Discuss the effects the change in inventory valuation method will have on Welltronics' cash position at December 31, Y9 and Y10.

As a result of the change in Welltronic's inventory valuation method, there will be no immediate effect on cash in Y9. However, because the additional $292,000 tax liability will be due in the following year, cash will be affected in Y10.

Session 1 Wrap-Up

Session 1 Wrap-Up

Content covered in Session 1
- Introduction to CMA Credential and Wiley CMAexcel Learning System
- Section A, Topic 1: Financial Statements
- Section A, Topic 2: Recognition, Measurement, Valuation, and Disclosure:
  - ▸ Accounts and Notes Receivable
  - ▸ Inventory
    - ▪ Exercise: Inventory Valuation, LIFO to FIFO

Session 1 Wrap-Up (cont.)

Content to be covered in Session 2
- Study Tips
- Section A, Topic 2 (cont.): Recognition, Measurement, Valuation, and Disclosure:
  - ▸ Investments
    - ▪ Exercise: Investments
  - ▸ Intangibles
  - ▸ Short-Term Debt
  - ▸ Deferred Income Taxes
  - ▸ Leases
  - ▸ Equity Transactions
  - ▸ Revenue Recognition
  - ▸ Comprehensive Income
  - ▸ Discontinued Operations
  - ▸ IFRS versus GAAP

Session 2

The Association of
Accountants and
Financial Professionals
in Business

Wiley
CMAexcel Learning System
Exam Review 2017

Part 1: Financial Reporting, Planning, Performance, and Control

Session 2

Learning Outcome Statements (LOS) identifiers appear on the
slides as applicable to highlight where we address each LOS
within the material.

The Association of
Accountants and
Financial Professionals
in Business

Session 1 Recap

- Introduction to CMA Credential and Wiley CMAexcel Learning System
- Section A, Topic 1: Financial Statements
- Section A, Topic 2: Recognition, Measurement, Valuation, and Disclosure:
  - Accounts and Notes Receivable
  - Inventory
    - Exercise: Inventory Valuation, LIFO to FIFO

The Association of
Accountants and
Financial Professionals
in Business

Session 2 Overview

- Study Tips
- Section A, Topic 2 (cont.): Recognition, Measurement, Valuation, and Disclosure:
  - Investments
    - Exercise 2: Investments
  - Intangibles
  - Short-Term Debt
  - Deferred Income Taxes
  - Leases
  - Equity Transactions
  - Revenue Recognition
  - Comprehensive Income
  - Discontinued Operations
  - IFRS versus GAAP

The Association of
Accountants and
Financial Professionals
in Business

Study Tips

- Create a study plan.
- Schedule regular study times.
- Break study times into small segments.
- Highlight key ideas.
- Create mnemonics.
- Create flash cards of key terms and concepts.
    - Carry cards with you to take advantage of any study opportunity.
    - Use a flash card partner.
- Use other resources to augment study.

The Association of
Accountants and
Financial Professionals
in Business

Study Tips (cont.)

- Use knowledge checks to assess understanding of key points.
- **Test yourself with the Online Test Bank.**
    - Multiple-choice questions—no penalty for incorrect answers.
    - Allow self-checking of answers.
    - Include explanation of correct answers.
    - Can be used to simulate exam experience.
    - Tests can be repeated as often as you like within subscription period.
- Revise and adjust study plan as needed.

The Association of
Accountants and
Financial Professionals
in Business

LOS 1.A.2.k.

Section A, Topic 2: Recognition, Measurement, Valuation, and Disclosure (cont.)

Investments: Debt Securities

- Examples: loans to other entities, federal and municipal securities, commercial paper, corporate notes and bonds, convertible debt.
- Three categories:
  - ▸ Held-to-maturity securities—report at amortized cost
  - ▸ Trading securities—report at fair value
  - ▸ Available-for-sale securities—report at fair value

- Recognition of unrealized gains and/or losses is dependent upon security's categorization

The Association of
Accountants and
Financial Professionals
in Business

LOS 1.A.2.k.

Accounting for Unrealized Holding Gains and Losses

Security	Unrealized Holding Gains and Losses	Balance Sheet Valuation
Held-to-maturity	Not recognized	Amortized cost (acquisition cost +/− premium or discount)
Trading	Recognized in net income	Fair value
Available-for-sale	Recognized in other comprehensive income and accumulated other comprehensive income	Fair value

LOS 1.A.2.k.

Question: Investment in Debt Securities

MV Co. had no investments until it purchased the following debt securities in June, Year 1:

	As of May 31, Year 2		As of May 31, Year 3	
	Amortized cost (AC)	Fair Value (FV)	AC	FV
Cleary bonds	$164,526	$168,300	$152,565	$147,600
Beau bonds	204,964	205,200	193,800	204,500
More bonds	305,785	285,200	289,130	291,400
Total	$675,275	$658,700	$635,495	$643,500

Part 1, Section A, Topic 2: Recognition, Measurement, Valuation, and Disclosure   8
Wiley CMAexcel Learning System, Part 1: Financial Reporting, Planning, Performance, and Control.
Copyright © 2017, Institute of Management Accountants. Published by John Wiley & Sons, Inc.

LOS 1.A.2.k.

Question: Investment in Debt Securities

If the securities are properly classified as "available-for-sale securities," the unrealized gain or loss as of May 31, Year 3 would be:

a. Recognized as a separate component of shareholders' equity with a year-end credit balance of $8,005 in the Unrealized Holding Gain/Loss account.
b. Recognized as a $24,580 unrealized holding loss on the income statement.
c. Recognized as a separate component of shareholders equity with a year-end debit balance of $8,005 in the Unrealized Holding Gain/Loss account.
d. Not recognized

Part 1, Section A, Topic 2: Recognition, Measurement, Valuation, and Disclosure   9
Wiley CMAexcel Learning System, Part 1: Financial Reporting, Planning, Performance, and Control.
Copyright © 2017, Institute of Management Accountants. Published by John Wiley & Sons, Inc.

The Association of Accountants and Financial Professionals in Business

LOS 1.A.2.k.

Question: Investment in Debt Securities

If the securities are properly classified as "held-to-maturity securities", the unrealized gain or loss as of May 31, Year 3 would be:

a. Recognized as a separate component of shareholders' equity with a year-end credit balance of $8,005 in the Unrealized Holding Gain/Loss account.
b. Recognized as a $24,580 unrealized holding loss on the income statement.
c. Recognized as a separate component of shareholders equity with a year-end debit balance of $8,005 in the Unrealized Holding Gain/Loss account
d. Not recognized

The Association of Accountants and Financial Professionals in Business

LOS 1.A.2.l.

Equity Securities

Ownership	Interest	Valuation method?
Less than 20%	Passive	Fair Value
20%–50%	Significant	Equity method
Greater than 50%	Controlling	Consolidated financial statements

The Association of
Accountants and
Financial Professionals
in Business

LOS 1.A.2.1.

Less than 20% Ownership

Fair value method

- Available-for-sale

  ‣ Unrealized gains (losses) on portfolio—reported in other comprehensive income (OCI)
  ‣ Realized gains (losses)—reported in net income and reclassification adjustment made to OCI

- Trading

  ‣ Unrealized gains (losses) on portfolio—reported in net income

The Association of
Accountants and
Financial Professionals
in Business

LOS 1.A.2.1.

Between 20% and 50% Ownership

- "Significant influence"
- Equity method
- Carrying value is adjusted based on the proportionate share of ownership
  ‣ Increase carrying value—net income
  ‣ Decrease carrying value—net loss, dividends, and amortization/depreciation of excess investment over book value of net assets acquired that relates to amortizable/depreciable assets
- Intercompany transactions are eliminated to the extent of investor ownership

The Association of
Accountants and
Financial Professionals
in Business

LOS 1.A.2.1.

Between 20% and 50% Ownership
Calculation of Investment Carrying Amount

Acquisition cost, 1/1/Year 1 (Y1)	$20,000,000	
Plus: Share of Y1 income before dividends and amortization	1,380,000	$21,380,000
Less: Dividends received 6/30 and 12/31	(630,000)	
Amortization of undervalued depreciable assets	(100,000)	(730,000)
Carrying amount, 12/31/Y1		$20,650,000

Part 1, Section A, Topic 2: Recognition, Measurement, Valuation, and Disclosure 14
Wiley CMAexcel Learning System, Part 1: Financial Reporting, Planning, Performance, and Control.
Copyright © 2017, Institute of Management Accountants. Published by John Wiley & Sons, Inc.

The Association of
Accountants and
Financial Professionals
in Business

LOS 1.A.2.1.

Greater than 50% Ownership

- Controlling interest; parent and subsidiary relationship
- Consolidated financial statements—"single entity"
- Purchase accounting is required:
  - ▸ Record acquired firm at fair value (FV) of consideration given (or at EMV of net assets acquired if more reliable)
  - ▸ Goodwill initially computed as the total fair value of consideration given up to acquire the Subsidiary + Fair value of any non-controlling interest + Fair value of any previously held equity interests in the subsidiary – Fair value of net assets acquired
  - ▸ No amortization of goodwill allowed

Part 1, Section A, Topic 2: Recognition, Measurement, Valuation, and Disclosure 15
Wiley CMAexcel Learning System, Part 1: Financial Reporting, Planning, Performance, and Control.
Copyright © 2017, Institute of Management Accountants. Published by John Wiley & Sons, Inc.

The Association of
Accountants and
Financial Professionals
in Business

LOS 1.A.2.k. and 1.

Question: Investments

K Co. has debt and equity investments in B Inc. with carrying values of $100,000 and $200,000, respectively. B recently included K's debt in a filing for bankruptcy. The net realizable value of the equity securities is $60,000. B is expected to regain much of its value after the bankruptcy. Which of the following would be the best way to record these investments?

I.   Debt: Record unrealized loss of $100,000, do not write down
II. Debt: Write down realized loss of $100,000, include in net income
III. Equity: Record unrealized loss of $140,000, do not write down
IV. Equity: Write down realized loss of $140,000 in net income

    a. I and III

    b. II and IV

    c. II and III

    d. I and IV

The Association of
Accountants and
Financial Professionals
in Business

Session 2 Exercise

Investments

Section A, Topic 2: Recognition, Measurement, Valuation, and Disclosure: Investments

Session 2 Exercise: Investments

Section A, Topic 2: Recognition, Measurement, Valuation, and Disclosure

Background Information:

Generally accepted accounting principles through FASB ASC Topic 320, *Investments—Debt and Equity Securities* (formerly addressed in FASB Statement No. 115), provides guidance for reporting the value of different investment securities. Plancker Company is preparing its year-end Year 10 (Y10) financial statement using FASB ASC Topic 320 based on the data provided below. The company uses the straight-line method for recording interest revenue.

The investment securities for Plancker include:

- *Studler Company bonds*—100 Studler Company bonds purchased on January 1, Y8 at 90 percent of their face value of $1,000 per bond. Management intends and will be able to keep these bonds until they are paid off by the issuer on December 31, Y12. The market value for these bonds at the Y10 year end is 102 percent of face value, and at the Y9 year end, it was 100 percent of face value. The annual coupon rate of interest on these bonds is eight percent.
- *Gen Company bonds*—50 Gen Company bonds purchased on July 1, Y9 at 100 percent of their face value of $1,000 per bond. Management intends to hold these bonds for a few years and then sell them prior to their maturity date of December 31, Y20. The market value for these bonds at the Y10 year end is 102 percent of face value, and at the Y9 year end, it was 101 percent of face value. The annual coupon rate of interest on these bonds is nine percent.
- *McCann Company common stock*—2,000 shares of McCann Company common stock, purchased at $10 per share in Y1, with a Y10 year-end market value of $30 per share, and a Y9 year-end market value of $29 per share. In Y10, this stock paid dividends at a quarterly rate of $0.20 per share. Management intends to sell this security in the next few weeks. McCann has several million shares outstanding.
- *Glenn Inc. common stock*—400,000 of the one million shares outstanding of Glenn Inc. common stock, purchased at $5 per share in Y1, with a Y10 year-end market value of $20 per share, and a Y9 year-end market value of $21 per share. In Y10, this stock paid dividends at a quarterly rate of $0.20 per share. Management intends to hold this security indefinitely.

Question 1: Describe the three categories of marketable securities identified in FASB ASC Topic 320, explaining the characteristics a security would have in order to be placed in each of the three categories.

Question 2: Using the data for Plancker Company, and ignoring any securities that do not fit into one of the three categories identified in FASB ASC Topic 320, for each security,

1. Identify the appropriate category for each security.
2. Compute the value to be reported on the December 31, Y10 Balance Sheet.
3. Compute the amount of revenue and/or expense to be reported on the Income Statement for the year ended December 31, Y10.

Security	Category	Balance Sheet	Income Statement

Session 2 Exercise Solution: Investments

Question 1: Describe the three categories of marketable securities identified in FASB ASC Topic 320, explaining the characteristics a security would have in order to be placed in each of the three categories.

Depending on the intentions and abilities of management with respect to marketable securities, the securities identified in FASB ASC Topic 320 are placed into one of the following three categories:

- **Trading.** Securities held with the intention of selling in a short period of time to generate profits from frequent buying and selling transactions. These securities are reported on the financial statements at fair value with unrealized gains and losses included in earnings.
- **Held-to-Maturity.** Debt securities that management has the intent and ability to hold long term to maturity. These securities are reported on the financial statements at amortized cost.
- **Available-for-Sale.** Securities that are in neither the Trading nor the Held-to-Maturity categories. These securities are reported on the financial statements at fair value with unrealized gains and losses reported in the shareholders' equity section and are excluded from earnings.

Question 2: Using the data for Plancker Company, and ignoring any securities that do not fit into one of the three categories identified in FASB ASC Topic 320, for each security:

1. Identify the appropriate category for each security.
2. Compute the value to be reported on the December 31, Y10 Balance Sheet.
3. Compute the amount of revenue and/or expense to be reported on the Income Statement for the year ended December 31, Y10.

The appropriate category, the balance sheet value, and the amount of revenue or expense on the income statement for each of the securities held by Plancker Company, for the year ended December 31, Y10, is summarized in the chart below.

Security	Category	Balance Sheet	Income Statement
Studler Company	Held-to-maturity	$96,000	$10,000
Gen Company	Available-for-sale	51,000	4,500
McCann Company	Trading	60,000	1,600 dividend
			2,000 gain
Glenn Inc.	Not applicable	Full equity	Full equity

1. Category of Marketable Security

Studler Company bonds are classified as held-to-maturity because management intends and is able to keep them until they mature. Gen Company bonds are classified as available-for-sale because they do not fit into either of the other two categories as they are not being traded on a regular basis, and Plancker does not intend to hold them to maturity. McCann Company common stock is classified as trading since management intends to trade the stock in the next few weeks. Glenn, Inc. common stock is not included as it is treated under the equity method since Plancker owns 40 percent of the company.

2. Financial Statement Valuation

The value to be reported on the Statement of Financial Position at December 31, Y10, is as follows.

Studler Company bonds:	
Discount to be amortized	
Face value	$100,000
Purchased at 90%	90,000
Discount	10,000
Amortization per year ($10,000/5 years)	$2,000
$2,000 × 3 years = $6,000 amortized up to Dec. 31, Y10	
Book value:	
Cost	$90,000
Amortization	6,000
Value at Dec. 31, Y10	$96,000
Gen Company bonds:	
50 bonds × $1,000 par × 102%	$51,000
McCann Company common stock:	
2,000 shares × market value of $30 per share	$60,000
Glenn Inc. common stock:	
Plancker owns 40 percent of Glenn's shares (400,000/1,000,000).	
FASB ASC Topic 320 does not apply. Plancker should use the equity method	

3. Calculations of Revenue and/or Expense

The amount of revenue and/or expense to be reported on the Income Statement for the year ended December 31, Y10, is as follows.

Studler Company bonds:	
Interest revenue (100 bonds × $1,000 × 0.08)	$8,000
Amortization of discount ($10,000/5 years)	2,000
Total interest revenue	$10,000
Gen Company bonds:	
Interest revenue (50 bonds × $1,000 × 0.09)	$4,500
McCann Company common stock:	
Dividend revenue ($0.20/quarter × 4 quarters × 2,000 shares)	$1,600
Unrealized gain [2,000 shares × ($30 − $29)]	$2,000

The Association of
Accountants and
Financial Professionals
in Business

LOS 1.A.2.m.

Long-Term Assets and Depreciation

Allocates cost over the life of an asset
Example: $1,000,000 machine with a $150,000 salvage value

To calculate depreciation, determine:

- Depreciable base (e.g., $850,000)
- Useful life (e.g., estimated at 70,000 units or 7 years)
- Method of depreciation:
  - ▸ Activity method
  - ▸ Straight-line method
  - ▸ Accelerated methods: sum–of–the–years' digits, declining balance

The Association of
Accountants and
Financial Professionals
in Business

LOS 1.A.2.m.

Activity Method of Depreciation

- Allocates cost in accordance with asset use
- Estimates total expected usage (units produced, hours run, miles driven)

Depreciation Charge per Unit = Depreciable Base / Estimated Lifetime Usage

= $850,000 / 70,000 units

= $12.14 (rounded) per unit

Depreciation Expense = Actual Usage × Depreciation charge per unit

= 9,500 units × $12.14 (rounded per unit)

= $115,330

LOS 1.A.2.m.

Straight-Line Method of Depreciation

- Time-based: provides a consistent amount of depreciation expense
- Depreciation expense will remain the same for each full year of asset use

$$\text{Depreciation charge} = \frac{\text{Depreciable Base}}{\text{Estimated Service Life}}$$

$$= \frac{\$850,000}{7} = \$121,428.57$$

LOS 1.A.2.m.

Sum-of-the-Years' Digits Method of Depreciation
Formulaic Approach

$$\text{Depreciation charge} = \frac{\text{Years of Useful Life Remaining}}{\text{Sum of All Years of Useful Life}}$$

$$\text{Sum of All Years of Useful Life} = \frac{n(n+1)}{2}, \ n = \text{All Years of Useful Life}$$

Intuitive Approach

For a 5-year asset, the sum of the years' digits is:

$$1 + 2 + 3 + 4 + 5 = 15$$

List the years, reverse the orders of the digits, divide by sum of the years' digits:

Year	Reverse Order	Depreciation
Year 1	5	5/15 = 33%
Year 2	4	4/15 = 27%
Year 3	3	3/15 = 20%
Year 4	2	2/15 = 13%
Year 5	1	1/15 = 17%

The Association of
Accountants and
Financial Professionals
in Business

LOS 1.A.2.m.

Sum-of-the-Years' Digits Method Example

Year	Depreciable Base	Years of Life Remaining	Depreciation Fraction	Depreciation Expense	End of Year Book Value
0	$850,000				$1,000,000
1	$850,000	7	7/28	$212,500	$787,500
2	$850,000	6	6/28	$182,143	$605,357
3	$850,000	5	5/28	$151,786	$453,571
4	$850,000	4	4/28	$121,429	$332,142
5	$850,000	3	3/28	$91,071	$241,071
6	$850,000	2	2/28	$60,714	$180,357
7	$850,000	1	1/28	$30,357	$150,000

The Association of
Accountants and
Financial Professionals
in Business

LOS 1.A.2.m.

150% Declining Balance Method of Depreciation

150% declining balance and 7-yr. depreciation = 14.29% × 150% = 21.43% / year

Year	Book Value at Beginning of Year	Rate	Depreciation Charge	Book Value at End of Year
1	$1,000,000	21.43%	$214,300	$785,700
2	785,700	21.43%	168,376	617,324
3	617,324	21.43%	132,293	485,031
4	485,031	21.43%	103,942	381,089
5	381,089	21.43%	81,667	299,422
6	299,422	21.43%	64,166	235,256
7	235,256	21.43%	50,415	184,841
8	$184,841	21.43%	$34,841	$150,000

The Association of
Accountants and
Financial Professionals
in Business

LOS 1.A.2.m. and n.

Impact of Straight-Line versus 150% Declining Balance Depreciation

Year 1 Impact	Straight-Line	150% Declining Balance
Depreciation Expense	$121,429	$214,300
Income Tax Benefit (40%)	$48,572	$85,720
Net Income	$72,857 decrease	$128,580 decrease
Assets	$121,429 decrease	$214,300 decrease

Part 1, Section A, Topic 2: Recognition, Measurement, Valuation, and Disclosure
Wiley CMAexcel Learning System, Part 1: Financial Reporting, Planning, Performance, and Control.
Copyright © 2017, Institute of Management Accountants. Published by John Wiley & Sons, Inc.

24

The Association of
Accountants and
Financial Professionals
in Business

LOS 1.A.2.m.

Question: Depreciation Methods

Kruse Company acquired a company airplane on June 3, Year 1. The following information relates to this purchase:

Airplane cost	$123,750
Estimated useful life in years	6
Estimated useful life in operating hours	15,000
Estimated residual value	$11,250

Actual hours flown in the year ended May 31.

Year 1	1,984
Year 2	2,800
Year 3	1,690
Year 4	1,824

Part 1, Section A, Topic 2: Recognition, Measurement, Valuation, and Disclosure
Wiley CMAexcel Learning System, Part 1: Financial Reporting, Planning, Performance, and Control.
Copyright © 2017, Institute of Management Accountants. Published by John Wiley & Sons, Inc.

25

The Association of
Accountants and
Financial Professionals
in Business

LOS 1.A.2.m.

Question: Depreciation Methods (cont.)

The depreciation expense for the scale year ended May 31, Year 4, using the activity method for all years would be:

a. $13,680
b. $14,110
c. $15,048
d. $18,750

Answer: a. Computations are provided as follows:

1) Find Depreciable Base = Airplane Cost – Estimated Residual (or Salvage) Value
$$= \$123,750 - \$11,250$$
$$= \$112,500$$
2) Find Depreciation Charge per Unit = Depreciable Base/Lifetime Usage
$$= \$112,500/15,000 \text{ hours}$$
$$= \$7.50 \text{ per hour}$$
3) Compute Depreciation Expense = Actual Usage × Depreciation Charge per Unit
$$= 1,824 \text{ hours} \times \$7.50 \text{ per hour}$$
$$= \$13,680$$

The Association of
Accountants and
Financial Professionals
in Business

LOS 1.A.2.m.

Question: Depreciation Methods (cont.)

The depreciation expense for the scale year ended May 31, Year 2, using the double-declining-balance method for all years would be:

a. $17,188
b. $25,000
c. $27,500
d. $37,500

Answer. c.
Straight-line depreciation rate = 1/6 = 16.6666%/year
Double-declining rate = 2 × 16.6666% = 33.3333%/year
Year 1 depreciation = $123,750 × 33.3333% = $41,250
Year 2 depreciation = ($123,750 – $41,250) × 33.3333% = $27,500

The Association of
Accountants and
Financial Professionals
in Business

LOS 1.A.2.o.

PP&E Valuation

- Fixed assets are valued at historical cost less accumulated depreciation
- When the value of PP&E cannot be recovered through expected future cash flows to be derived from the asset, the asset is deemed to be impaired
- Impaired assets should be written down to their fair value

The Association of
Accountants and
Financial Professionals
in Business

LOS P1.A.1.e. and f.

PP&E Financial Statement Presentation and Disclosure Requirements

- Basis of valuation (i.e., historical cost)
- Depreciation expense for the period
- Balances of major classes of assets
- Accumulated depreciation
- General description of methods used to calculate depreciation for major asset classes

Intangibles

Lack physical substance and are not financial instruments

Categories:	Valuation:
• Marketing	• Purchased
• Customer	▸ On balance sheet at cost (indefinite life) or amortized cost (finite life)
• Artistic	
• Contract	• Internally created
• Technological	▸ R&D costs expensed
• Goodwill	▸ Some costs (e.g., legal and registration fees) incurred to obtain intangibles, capitalized

Question: Acquisition Accounting

In a business combination that is accounted for as a purchase, the acquiring company records the net assets of the acquired company at their:

a. Replacement cost
b. Fair value
c. Book value
d. Original cost

Answer: b.

Under the acquisition method, the acquiring company allocates the acquisition purchase price to all tangible and identifiable intangible assets acquired, and liabilities assumed, based on their fair values.

The Association of
Accountants and
Financial Professionals
in Business

LOS 1.A.2.p.

Goodwill

- Not amortized
- Tested for impairment
    - ▸ Potential impairment exists when fair value (FV) of reporting unit < its carrying value (including existing goodwill)
    - ▸ Implied FV of goodwill as of impairment assessment date needs to be determined
- Measurement of impairment loos
    - ▸ Loss = Excess of implied fair value of goodwill over its carrying value.
    - ▸ Implied fair value of goodwill = Fair value of reporting unit – Fair value of reporting unit's identifiable net assets (excluding existing goodwill)

The Association of
Accountants and
Financial Professionals
in Business

LOS 1.A.2.p.

Question: Treatment of R&D Costs

To comply with FASB ASC Topic 730, *Research and Development* (formerly addressed in FASB Statement No. 2), expenditures for R&D:

a. Must be capitalized in the period incurred and amortized over the estimated life of the asset
b. May be expensed or capitalized in the period incurred
c. May be either capitalized or expensed depending on the amount and useful life of the expected cash receipts
d. Must be expensed in the period incurred, unless the costs have alternate future uses, in which case, that portion of the costs may be capitalized.

Answer: d.

All R&D costs are expensed as incurred, unless they have future alternate uses outside of R&D. In these cases, that portion of the costs can be capitalized and depreciated/amortized.

The Association of
Accountants and
Financial Professionals
in Business

LOS 1.A.2.q.

Current Liabilities (or Short-Term Debt)

- Liabilities

  ▸ "Probable future sacrifices of economic benefits arising from present obligations"

- Current liabilities

  ▸ "Obligations whose liquidation is reasonably expected to require use of existing ... Current assets or the creation of other current liabilities"

The Association of
Accountants and
Financial Professionals
in Business

LOS 1.A.2.r.

Types of Current Liabilities

- <u>General</u>: Accounts payable, current maturities of long-term debt, dividends payable, returnable deposits and advances, unearned or deferred revenues, taxes payable
- <u>Employee-related</u>: Payroll taxes, compensated absences, bonus obligations
- <u>Estimated</u>: Warranties, premiums, and coupons

The Association of
Accountants and
Financial Professionals
in Business

LOS 1.A.2.r.

Estimated Liabilities

- Warranties, premiums, coupons

  ▸ Record estimated cost in period that product is
    sold
  ▸ Employs "matching principle"

- Warranties accounted for in two basic ways:

  ▸ Cash basis
  ▸ Accrual basis (which includes expense warranty
    approach, and sales warranty approach)

The Association of
Accountants and
Financial Professionals
in Business

LOS 1.A.2.r.

Question: Estimated Liabilities

**Perfect Co. manufactures the Perfect Juice Extractor, which is to be
sold with a full, two-year consumer warranty. Perfect has no
previous experience manufacturing juice extractor machines or
selling products to customers. Perfect is unable to reasonably
estimate the amount of future warranty costs related to the
machines, and should:**

a. Set up an estimated warranty liability
b. Use the cash basis method to account for warranty costs
c. Use the accrual method to account for warranty costs
d. Use an estimated warranty expense account

The Association of
Accountants and
Financial Professionals
in Business

LOS 1.A.1.e.

Presentation and Disclosure Requirements for Current Liabilities

- Valued at maturity amount
- Ordered by
  - ▸ Liquidation preference
  - ▸ Maturity data

(in thousands)	Y2	Y1
Current liabilities		
Short-term borrowings	$4	$18
A/P	1,930	1,269
Accrued payroll	1,331	809
Accrued liabilities	2,884	2,075
Deferred service revenues	1,081	678
Income taxes payable	1,031	483
Note payable	60	102
Total current liabilities	$8,321	$5,434

The Association of
Accountants and
Financial Professionals
in Business

LOS 1.A.2.t., v., and w.

Deferred Income Taxes

Result when events are recognized in different years for book and tax purposes

- Temporary differences
- Permanent differences
- Asset and liability method
  - ▸ Measures deferred tax liability or asset when carrying amount of assets or liabilities differ for book and tax purposes
  - ▸ Tax effect is measured based upon future enacted tax rates (e.g., those rates that will be in effect when the difference reverses)

The Association of
Accountants and
Financial Professionals
in Business

LOS 1.A.2.t. and u.

Example: Deferred Tax Calculations

Depreciation creates taxable differences that
result in a deferred tax liability

Taxable Difference	Book	Tax
Asset cost	$1,500	$1,500
Depreciation to date	(300)	(500)
Basis at balance sheet date	$1,200	$1,000
Deferred Tax Liability		
Taxable difference in book-tax basis		$200
Tax rate		40%
Deferred tax liability		$80

The Association of
Accountants and
Financial Professionals
in Business

LOS 1.A.2.t. and v.

Question: Deferred Taxes

A temporary difference that would result in a deferred tax liability is

a. Interest revenue on municipal bonds
b. Accrual of warranty expense
c. Excess of tax depreciation over financial accounting
   (book) depreciation
d. Subscriptions received in advance

The Association of
Accountants and
Financial Professionals
in Business

LOS 1.A.2.x. and y.

Deferred Income Taxes

Financial statement impact:

- Balance sheet classification
  - ▸ Current or noncurrent depending on classification of account producing temporary difference
  - ▸ Report net of current asset and liability, and net of long-term asset and liability
- Note disclosure includes
  - ▸ Total of all deferred tax assets and liabilities
  - ▸ Approximate tax effect of significant differences
  - ▸ Components of tax expense
  - ▸ Reconciliation between effective and statutory tax rates

The Association of
Accountants and
Financial Professionals
in Business

LOS 1.A.2.z. and cc.

Question: Operating Lease

What is a lease, and what are some distinguishing features of an operating lease?

Answer:

Lease: Contract giving the lessee the right to use the lessor's property for a period of time in exchange for a rent payment

Operating leases:

- No substantial transfer of benefits and risks of ownership
- Rental expense for the lessee, and rental revenue for the lessor

The Association of
Accountants and
Financial Professionals
in Business

LOS 1.A.2.z., bb., and cc.

Capital Leases

- Transfers substantially all risks and benefits of ownership
- Conditions for capitalization (meet one)
    - Transfer of title
    - Bargain purchase option
    - Lease term ≥ 75% of asset's estimated useful life
    - PV of minimum lease payments (MLP) ≥ 90% fair value of property

- Lessor recognizes sale and lease receivable and removes asset from its books during the lease term
- Lessee records leased asset and lease liability and depreciates the asset and reports interest on the long-term liability over the lease term

Part 1, Section A, Topic 2: Recognition, Measurement, Valuation, and Disclosure   44
Wiley CMAexcel Learning System, Part 1: Financial Reporting, Planning, Performance, and Control.
Copyright © 2017, Institute of Management Accountants. Published by John Wiley & Sons, Inc.

The Association of
Accountants and
Financial Professionals
in Business

LOS 1.A.2.dd.

Common Stock Issuance

Par value stock:

- Par value recorded in a preferred or common stock account (as is stated value on no-par stock)
- Amount paid in excess of par credited to additional-paid-in-capital

How would 1,000 shares at $6 par value, sold for $10,000 be recorded?

Dr. Cash	$10,000	
Cr. Common stock		$6,000
Cr. Paid-in capital in excess of par		$4,000

Part 1, Section A, Topic 2: Recognition, Measurement, Valuation, and Disclosure   45
Wiley CMAexcel Learning System, Part 1: Financial Reporting, Planning, Performance, and Control.
Copyright © 2017, Institute of Management Accountants. Published by John Wiley & Sons, Inc.

LOS 1.A.2.dd.

Other Stock Issuance Matters

- Lump-sum sales/issuances
  - ‣ Various classes of stock sold for a lump-sum price—allocation to each class of stock needs to be made
    - Proportional method
    - Incremental method
    - When fair value cannot be determined for any of the securities, allocate based on appraisal or estimate.
  - ‣ Stock issued in noncash exchange
    - Recorded at either the market value of stock issued or noncash items received, whichever is more readily determinable.
    - If neither market value determinable, appraisal or estimate is required.
  - ‣ Stock issuance costs
    - If directly related to the issuance, debit/reduce paid-in capital in excess of par
    - If not directly related, expense

LOS 1.A.2.dd.

10,000 shares of common stock and 5,000 shares of preferred stock are issued for a lump-sum price of $180,000. On that date the common stock was selling for $14 per share and the preferred stock for $10 per share.

What is the allocation to common and to preferred?

Proportional Method Allocation

Fair market value of common (10,000 × $14)	= $140,000
Fair market value of preferred (5,000 × $ 10)	= <u>50,000</u>
Aggregate fair market value	$ 190,000

Allocated to common:

$$\frac{\$140,000}{\$190,000} \times \$180,000 = \$132,632$$

Allocated to preferred:

$$\frac{\$50,000}{\$190,000} \times \$180,000 = \underline{47,368}$$

Total allocation	$180,000

The Association of
Accountants and
Financial Professionals
in Business

LOS 1.A.2.dd.

Preferred Stock

- Dividend preference
    - % of par value or as $ per share
    - Cumulative
- No voting rights allowed
- Preference in liquidation:
    - Creditors, then preferred, then common stock

- Redeemable preferred stock
    - Mandatory redemption = due date
    - Equity in form, debt in substance, liability on balance sheet

The Association of
Accountants and
Financial Professionals
in Business

LOS 1.A.2.dd.

Treasury Stock Overview

- Shares of stock reacquired by an organization. Reasons include:
    - Prevent hostile takeover
    - Increase earnings per share
    - Availability of shares for exercise of stock options
    - Availability of shares to issue in a business combination transaction
    - Make a market in company's stock and stabilize or increase stock price
- A reduction of stockholders' equity; not an asset
- Have no voting or dividend rights
- Accounted for by either the cost method or par value method; cost method more commonly used in practice.

The Association of
Accountants and
Financial Professionals
in Business

LOS 1.A.2.dd.

Recording Treasury Stock: Cost Method

On Jan. 5, Y1, Nord Co. issued 5,000 shares of common stock with a par value of $100. The proceeds received were at the issue price of $120/share. On June 4, Y2, the firm reacquired 500 shares at $115/share. Under the cost method, the amount recorded in the Treasury Stock account is:

a. $7,500
b. $10,000
c. $57,500
d. $60,000

Answer: c

In the cost method, the treasury stock account is debited for the cost of the shares reacquired. The cost is 500 × $115= $57,500.

Based on ICMA question, used with permission

Part 1, Section A, Topic 2: Recognition, Measurement, Valuation, and Disclosure
Wiley CMAexcel Learning System, Part 1: Financial Reporting, Planning, Performance, and Control.
Copyright © 2017, Institute of Management Accountants. Published by John Wiley & Sons, Inc.

50

The Association of
Accountants and
Financial Professionals
in Business

LOS 1.A.2.dd.

Retiring Treasury Stock

10,000 shares, $9 cost, $5 par, $3 APIC:

Cost method

Dr. Common stock	$50,000	
Dr. APIC—Common stock	$30,000	
Dr. Retained earnings	$10,000	
Cr. Treasury stock		$90,000

Par value method

Dr. Common stock	$50,000	
Cr. Treasury stock		$50,000

Part 1, Section A, Topic 2: Recognition, Measurement, Valuation, and Disclosure
Wiley CMAexcel Learning System, Part 1: Financial Reporting, Planning, Performance, and Control.
Copyright © 2017, Institute of Management Accountants. Published by John Wiley & Sons, Inc.

51

The Association of
Accountants and
Financial Professionals
in Business

LOS 1.A.1.c.

Balance Sheet Presentation of Paid-In Capital

Disclosure for each class of stock:

- Nature
- Par value
- Preferred stock characteristics
- Dividends in arrears

The Association of
Accountants and
Financial Professionals
in Business

LOS 1.A.1.c.

Contributed Capital: Stockholder's Equity (Partial Balance Sheet)

Contributed capital:	
Preferred stock, $70 par (9% cumulative, 10,000 shares authorized, 5,5000 issued and outstanding)	$385,000
Common stock $4 par (70,000 shares authorized, 46,500 shares issued and outstanding)	186,000
Common stock subscribed, $4 par (4,600 shares at a subscription price of $42 per share)	18,400
Additional paid-in capital	652,093
Total contributed capital	$1,241,493

The Association of
Accountants and
Financial Professionals
in Business

LOS 1.A.2.dd.

Question—Retained Earnings

Which of the following has the greatest effect on retained earnings?

a. Net income/loss
b. Prior period adjustments
c. Dividends
d. Certain treasury stock transactions

The Association of
Accountants and
Financial Professionals
in Business

LOS 1.A.2.dd.

Warrants and Rights

- **Warrants**—allow a holder to acquire shares of stock at a certain price and within a stated time duration.
  - Can be non-detachable or detachable (can be sold separately on an exchange)
    - If non-detachable, not separately recorded on the books
    - If detachable and can be sold separately, recorded on books through additional paid-in capital account
- **Stock rights** (also referred to as "preemptive rights")—give current stockholders the right to purchase newly issued shares in proportion to those currently held

---

The Association of
Accountants and
Financial Professionals
in Business

LOS 1.A.2.dd.

Dividends

- Distributions, typically made from earned capital
  (e.g., retained earnings)
- May be restricted
- Do not have to be paid; earned capital may be retained to fund future growth
- Types of dividends:
  - ▸ Cash dividends
  - ▸ Property dividends
  - ▸ Liquidating dividends
  - ▸ Cumulative dividends
  - ▸ Scrip dividends
  - ▸ Stock dividends and stock splits

The Association of
Accountants and
Financial Professionals
in Business

LOS 1.A.2.dd.

Cash and Property Dividends

- Cash dividends
  - ▸ Fixed and stated either as a percentage of par (typical of preferred stock dividends) or as a per-share amount (typical of common stock dividends)
  - ▸ Three important dates:
    - Date of declaration: liability for dividend payment is established
    - Date of record: date stockholder is eligible for dividend
    - Date of payment: dividend is paid
- Property dividends
  - ▸ Dividends payable in property, merchandise, or investments
  - ▸ Accounted for at fair value of assets transferred on date of declaration

Liquidating Dividends

Dividend declared exceeds retained earnings. Excess dividend is consider a return of the investment.

For example:

$750,000 retained earnings balance at date of declaration

$1,000,000 dividend declared

Treatment:

$750,000 from retained earnings

$250,000 return of investment (reduction of paid in capital)

Stock Dividends

- Stock dividends
  - ▸ Nonreciprocal transfer of company's stock to its shareholders on a pro-rata basis
  - ▸ No impact on total stockholders' equity; reallocation of retained earnings to paid-in capital
  - ▸ Two types:
    - Small stock dividend—report at market value
    - Large stock dividend—report at par value

The Association of
Accountants and
Financial Professionals
in Business

LOS 1.A.2.ee.

Stock Splits

- Stock splits
  - ‣ Tool to reduce market price per share without changing ownership proportions
  - ‣ Change the number of shares outstanding with a corresponding reduction in par value; same impact on market price per share
  - ‣ Reverse stock split has opposite effect

The Association of
Accountants and
Financial Professionals
in Business

LOS 1.A.2.dd.

Dividend Question #1

A company declared a cash dividend on its common stock on December 15, Y1, payable on January 12, Y2. How would this dividend affect stockholders' equity on the following dates?

December 15, Y1	December 31, Y1	January 12, Y2
a. Decrease	No effect	Decrease
b. Decrease	No effect	No effect
c. No effect	Decrease	No effect
d. No effect	No effect	Decrease

Answer: **b**

Dec 15, Y1: date of declaration (dividend liability established and retained earnings reduced)

Dec 31, Y1: not enough information on this date

Jan 12, Y2: date of payment (no impact on retained earnings/stockholders' equity at this time).

The Association of
Accountants and
Financial Professionals
in Business

LOS 1.A.2.ee.

Dividend Question #2

Which of the following dividends has no impact on total stockholders' equity?

a. Scrip dividends
b. Property dividends
c. Liquidating dividends
d. Stock dividends

The Association of
Accountants and
Financial Professionals
in Business

LOS 1.A.2.gg. and nn.

Revenue Recognition

Revenue is recognized if it is realized or realizable, and earned

Revenue recognition points

- Before sale
  - ‣ Market exists with established prices (agriculture, commodities)
  - ‣ Long-term construction contracts (percentage of completion)
- At time sale is made or services provided
  - ‣ Most common point

- After sale—collectibililty uncertain
  - ‣ Instalment sales accounting method
  - ‣ Cost recovery method

The Association of
Accountants and
Financial Professionals
in Business

LOS 1.A.2.hh.

Revenue Recognition—Point of Sale

For the following three types of transactions that raise point-of-sale revenue recognition issues, explain whether a sale should be recorded in each case and why:

Answers:

Sales with buyback agreements	• Have not transferred the risks of ownership to the seller; record no sale
Sales including a right of return	• Record sale less estimated returns when certain conditions met
Trade loading or channel stuffing	• Discouraged as window-dressing, causes future revenues to drop unless practice continued

The Association of
Accountants and
Financial Professionals
in Business

LOS 1.A.2.ll.

Revenue Recognition After Delivery: Installment Sales Method

- Used when collection of sales price is not reasonably assured
- Profit recognized as cash is collected; thus, revenue recognition takes place at point of collection rather than point of sale
  - ▸ Realized gross profit each year = Gross profit from relevant sales period × Cash collections in current period from relevant sales period

The Association of
Accountants and
Financial Professionals
in Business

LOS 1.A.2.ll.

Revenue Recognition After Delivery: Cost Recovery Method

- Used when the uncertainty of collection is so great that even the use of the installment sales method is precluded.
- No profit is recognized until the cumulative receipts/collections exceed the cost of the asset sold.

The Association of
Accountants and
Financial Professionals
in Business

LOS 1.A.2.jj. and pp.

Revenue Recognition Before Delivery: Percentage-of-Completion Method

- Condition for use:
  - ▸ Contract is legal enforceable
  - ▸ Contract revenues, costs, and extent of progress toward completion are reasonably estimable
  - ▸ Buyer can be expected to satisfy obligations; seller can be expected to perform
- Recognize revenues and/or gross profit based on estimate of percentage completed
  - ▸ Use of cost-to-cost ratio = Total costs incurred to date / Total estimated costs (as of that date)
- Contract losses:
  - ▸ Overall contract still expected to be profitable, current period "loss" adjustment
  - ▸ Overall contract expected to be unprofitable—report entire loss in the period, adjusting all previously recognized gross profit

The Association of
Accountants and
Financial Professionals
in Business

LOS 1.A.2.jj.

DC Construction Inc. uses the percentage-of-completion method of accounting. In Y1, the firm started job #34 with a contract price of $5,000,000. Other data:

	Year 1	Year 2
Costs incurred during year	$900,000	$2,350,000
Estimated costs to complete	2,700,000	0
Billings during the year	1,000,000	4,000,000
Collections during the year	700,000	4,300,000

The amount of gross profit to recognized Y1 is:

a. $350,000
b. $700,000
c. $766,667   Answer: a
d. $1,250,000

Part 1, Section A, Topic 2: Recognition, Measurement, Valuation, and Disclosure   68
Wiley CMAexcel Learning System, Part 1: Financial Reporting, Planning, Performance, and Control.
Copyright © 2017, Institute of Management Accountants. Published by John Wiley & Sons, Inc.

The Association of
Accountants and
Financial Professionals
in Business

LOS 1.A.2.jj.

1. **Total estimated contract costs** = Costs incurred during the period +
Estimated costs to complete
= $900,000 + $2,700,000
= $3,600,000

2. **Total estimated gross profit on contract** = Contract price − Total
estimated contract costs
= $5,000,000 − $3,600,000
= $1,400,000

3. **Gross profit recognized** = % complete (based on cost-to-cost ratio) ×
Estimated gross profit
= *25% × $1,400,000
= **$350,000**

*Note that % complete is calculated by dividing total costs incurred to date ($900,000) by total estimated contract costs ($3,600,000)

Part 1, Section A, Topic 2: Recognition, Measurement, Valuation, and Disclosure   69
Wiley CMAexcel Learning System, Part 1: Financial Reporting, Planning, Performance, and Control.
Copyright © 2017, Institute of Management Accountants. Published by John Wiley & Sons, Inc.

The Association of
Accountants and
Financial Professionals
in Business

LOS 1.A.2.jj.

Revenue Recognition Before Delivery: Completed-Contract Method

- No recognition of revenue or profit during period of construction—deferred and recognized when contract is complete
- Used for contracts in which reasonable estimates of critical contract components cannot be estimated (e.g., cannot reasonably estimate contract costs), or the criteria for use of the percentage-of-completion method have not been met.
- Contract losses—recognized in full in period first identified

The Association of
Accountants and
Financial Professionals
in Business

LOS 1.A.2.jj.

DC Construction, Inc. uses the completed-contract method of accounting. In Y1, the firms started Job #34 with a contract price of $5,000,000. Other data is presented below:

	Year 1	Year 2
Costs incurred during year	$900,000	$2,350,000
Estimated costs to complete	2,700,000	0
Billings during the year	1,000,000	4,000,000
Collections during the year	700,000	4,300,000

The amount of gross profit that DC Construction will recognize in Y2 is:

a. $700,000
b. $1,400,000   Answer: c
c. $1,750,000
d. $2,300,000

The Association of Accountants and Financial Professionals in Business

LOS 1.A.2.jj.

Contract is complete in Y2

Total revenue : $5,000,000

Total costs : Y1 ($900,000) + Y2 ($2,350,000) = $3,250,000.

Y2 gross profit recognized: $5,000,000 – $3,250,000 =
$1,750,000

The Association of Accountants and Financial Professionals in Business

LOS 1.A.2.ss.

Comprehensive Income

- Broad measure of all changes in equity over a period other than owner investments and distributions.
- Comprehensive income = Net income +/– Items of other comprehensive income
- Two acceptable methods of presentation:
    ‣ In a combined statement of income and comprehensive income
    ‣ Separate comprehensive income statement

The Association of
Accountants and
Financial Professionals
in Business

LOS 1.A.2.ss.

Question: Comprehensive Income

During the year, a company reports income from continuing operations of $100,000, an unrealized gain of $8,000 in other comprehensive income, and a $6,000 loss on discontinued operations. Ignoring income taxes, the company will report:

a. net income of $94,000 and comprehensive income of $102,000

b. net income of $99,000 and comprehensive income of $107,000

c. net income of $105,000 and comprehensive income of $107,000

d. net income of $107,000 and comprehensive income of $8,000

Answer: a.

The Association of
Accountants and
Financial Professionals
in Business

LOS 1.A.2.ss.

Question: Comprehensive Income (cont.)

Net income = Income from continuing operations +/– Discontinued operations

Comprehensive income is the sum of net income plus (or minus) the Items of other comprehensive income

Net income = $100,000 – $6,000 = $94,000.
Comprehensive income = Net income + Other
Comprehensive income = $94,000 + $8,000 = $102,000

The Association of
Accountants and
Financial Professionals
in Business

LOS 1.A.2.oo. and ss.

Comprehensive Income

Combined income statement:

- Net income shown as subtotal
- Comprehensive income final total

Combined Statement of Comprehensive Income	
Sales revenue	$1,120,000
Cost of goods sold	840,000
Gross profit	280,000
Operating expenses	126,000
Net income	154,000
Unrealized holding gain, net of tax	42,000
Comprehensive income	$196,000

The Association of
Accountants and
Financial Professionals
in Business

LOS 1.A.2.oo. and ss.

Comprehensive Income—Separate Statements

Income Statement	
Sales revenue	$1,120,000
Cost of goods sold	840,000
Gross profit	280,000
Operating expenses	126,000
Net income	$154,000

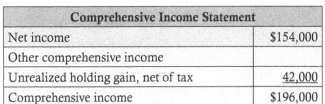

Comprehensive Income Statement	
Net income	$154,000
Other comprehensive income	
Unrealized holding gain, net of tax	42,000
Comprehensive income	$196,000

The Association of
Accountants and
Financial Professionals
in Business

LOS 1.A.2.tt.

Discontinued Operations

- Segment, reporting unit or asset group
  - ▸ Distinguishable operations and cash flows
  - ▸ Disposed of, or held-for-sale category
- Discontinued unit on income statement
  - ▸ Gain/loss on operations during year (net of tax)
  - ▸ Gain/loss on disposal (net of tax)
  - ▸ Separate component of income or in notes to financial statements

The Association of
Accountants and
Financial Professionals
in Business

LOS 1.A.2.uu.

International Financial Reporting Standards (IFRS)

- The International Accounting Standards Board (IASB) was established in 2001.
- The IASB is responsible for approving IFRS.
- The primary objective of the IASB is to bring about convergence in accounting standards globally.
- It works closely with FASB to harmonize with U.S. GAAP.
- Details at www.iasb.org.

The Association of
Accountants and
Financial Professionals
in Business

LOS 1.A.2.uu.

IFRS: Significant Departures from U.S. GAAP

- Revenue recognition
- Intangibles
- Inventory
- Leases

The Association of
Accountants and
Financial Professionals
in Business

LOS 1.A.2.uu.

IFRS—GAAP: Revenue Recognition

- General (e.g., sale of goods)
- Construction contracts
- Special industry guidance
- Discounting of revenues

IFRS—GAAP: Intangibles

Intangible assets—non-physical assets that include copyrights, trademarks, franchises, patents, and goodwill. Also discussed within the context of differences between IFRS and as it relates to intangible assets is R&D costs

- IFRS
  - Development costs may be capitalized, but stringent requirements for doing so
  - May use cost model or revaluation model to report intangible assets
- GAAP
  - Development costs expensed, except in certain cases such as software development costs; special guidance depending on whether the software is for internal use or for sale
  - Revaluation model is prohibited

IFRS versus GAAP: Inventory

- IFRS
  - Does not permit use of the LIFO method
  - Inventory is carried at the lower of cost or net realizable value
  - Previous write-downs of inventory can be reversed if the impairment no longer exists
- GAAP
  - Permits use of the LIFO method
  - Inventory is carried at the lower of cost or market
  - Any write-downs of inventory become the new cost basis and cannot be reversed

IFRS versus GAAP: Leases

- IFRS
  - ▸ Finance leases or operating leases for both the lessee and lessor
  - ▸ Substance over form
  - ▸ Lease classification by the lessor and lessee typically symmetrical
- GAAP
  - ▸ Capital leases (similar to IFRS finance leases) and operating leases for the lessee; and as operating, direct-financing, sales-types, and sometimes leveraged leases for the lessor
  - ▸ Specific "bright-line" rules in classifying leases as capital leases
  - ▸ Two additional criteria for a lessor to classify a lease as a direct-financing or sales-type lease

Section A Conclusion

- Section A content represents 25% of the multiple-choice questions on the Part 2 exam.
- This content may also be tested in essay question format.

To reinforce your learning:

- Study all the LOS for the section.
- Study all material for Section A in the WCMALS self-study book.
- Use the practice test questions in the WCMALS self-study book.
- Take the Section A practice test in the Online Test Bank for a wider range of questions on all topics in the section.

Section A Practice Questions

The Association of
Accountants and
Financial Professionals
in Business

Section A Practice Questions

We will now review Practice Questions from the WCMALS
self-study book, Section A.

- Questions identified by topic.
- More questions on each topic and a full section test are included
  in the Online Test Bank.

The Association of
Accountants and
Financial Professionals
in Business

Session 2 Wrap-Up

Content covered in Session 2

- Study Tips
- Section A, Topic 2 (cont.): Recognition, Measurement, Valuation, and Disclosure:
    - Investments
        - Exercise 2: Investments
    - Intangibles
    - Short-Term Debt
    - ▸ Deferred Income Taxes
    - ▸ Leases
    - ▸ Equity Transactions
    - ▸ Revenue Recognition
    - ▸ Comprehensive Income
    - ▸ Discontinued Operations
    - ▸ IFRS versus GAAP

The Association of
Accountants and
Financial Professionals
in Business

Session 2 Wrap-Up (cont.)
Content to be covered in Session 3

- Section B, Topic 1: Strategic Planning
- Section B, Topic 2: Budgeting Concepts

Session 3

The Association of
Accountants and
Financial Professionals
in Business

Wiley
CMAexcel Learning System
Exam Review 2017

Part 1: Financial Reporting, Planning, Performance, and Control

Session 3

Learning Outcome Statements (LOS) identifiers appear on the
slides as applicable to highlight where we address each LOS
within the material.

Session 2 Recap

The Association of
Accountants and
Financial Professionals
in Business

Session 2 Recap

- Study Tips
- Section A, Topic 2 (cont.): Recognition, Measurement, Valuation, and Disclosure:
  - ➢ Investments
  - ➢ Exercise 2: Investments
  - ➢ Intangibles
  - ➢ Short-Term Debt
  - ➢ Deferred Income Taxes
  - ➢ Leases
  - ➢ Equity Transactions
  - ➢ Revenue Recognition
  - ➢ Comprehensive Income
  - ➢ Discontinued Operations
  - ➢ IFRS versus GAAP

Part 1: Financial Reporting, Planning, Performance, and Control   2
Wiley CMAexcel Learning System, Part 1: Financial Reporting, Planning, Performance, and Control.
Copyright © 2017, Institute of Management Accountants. Published by John Wiley & Sons, Inc.

The Association of
Accountants and
Financial Professionals
in Business

Session 3 Overview

- Section B, Topic 1: Strategic Planning
- Section B, Topic 2: Budgeting Concepts

Part 1: Financial Reporting, Planning, Performance, and Control   3
Wiley CMAexcel Learning System, Part 1: Financial Reporting, Planning, Performance, and Control.
Copyright © 2017, Institute of Management Accountants. Published by John Wiley & Sons, Inc.

The Association of
Accountants and
Financial Professionals
in Business

Section B: Planning,
Budgeting, and Forecasting

- Topic 1: Strategic Planning
- Topic 2: Budgeting Concepts
- Topic 3: Forecasting Techniques
- Topic 4: Budget Methodologies
- Topic 5: Annual Profit Plan and Supporting Schedules
- Topic 6: Top-Level Planning and Analysis

The Association of
Accountants and
Financial Professionals
in Business

Topic 1: Strategic Planning

- Strategy and strategic planning
- Analysis of external factors affecting strategy
- Analysis of internal factors affecting strategy
- S.W.O.T. analysis
- Long-term vision, mission, goals, and objectives
- Alignment of tactics with long-term strategic goals
- Characteristics of successful strategic/tactical planning
- Contingency planning
- Other planning tools and techniques.

The Association of
Accountants and
Financial Professionals
in Business

LOS 1.B.1.a.

Strategy

- Strategy:
  - ‣ Way(s) to achieve organizational goals
  - ‣ Incorporated into the Strategic Plan

- Strategies are commonly developed for three levels in the organization:
  1. Corporate (multiple business units)
  2. Competitive (a business unit)
  3. Functional (within a business)

The Association of
Accountants and
Financial Professionals
in Business

LOS 1.B.1.a. and b.

Strategic Planning

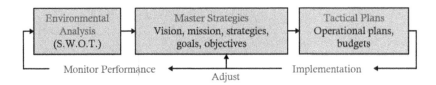

What's the appropriate time frame for strategic planning?

- Generally long term, so 5–10 years
- Depends on:
  - the industry
  - any changes

The Association of
Accountants and
Financial Professionals
in Business

Analysis of External Factors Impacting Strategy

External factors that shape organizational strategy
include:

a. Legal and regulatory

b. Market forces, industry trends, and competition

c. Technological changes

d. Stakeholder groups and their social concerns

e. Globalization trends, emerging markets, and
nongovernmental organizations, e.g., United
Nations, World Bank, etc.

The Association of
Accountants and
Financial Professionals
in Business

a. Legal and Regulatory Factors

- Legal factors

  ‣ Rules of legal entities enforced by threat of punishment

  ‣ Examples: Patents, copyrights, trademarks, antitrust laws, etc.

- Regulatory factors

  ‣ Principles designed to control or govern behavior enforced by self-
    regulation, threat of fines, or disenfranchisement

  ‣ Examples:

    ✓ <u>Social</u>: Environmental Protection Agency (EPA) standards, Occupational Safety
      and Health Administration (OSHA) standards, Federal Trade Commission (FTC)
      regulations

    ✓ <u>Industry</u>: Federal Aviation Administration (FAA) requirements, Federal
      Communications Commission (FCC) regulations, Food and Drug Administration
      (FDA) requirements

The Association of
Accountants and
Financial Professionals
in Business

LOS 1.B.1.c.

Linking Legal and Regulatory Factors to Strategic Planning

- Impact on organization strategy
  - ▸ Influence choice of competition
  - ▸ Limit global operations
  - ▸ Thwart or promote technological innovations
  - ▸ Impact human resource practices
  - ▸ Restrict marketing campaigns
  - ▸ Force environmental accountability
  - ▸ Increase capital requirements

- Impact on management accounting
  - ▸ SEC laws and rules
  - ▸ Sarbanes-Oxley and internal controls
  - ▸ Internal Revenue Service code
  - ▸ Minimum wage requirements and/or overtime compensation
  - ▸ State-regulated insurance and banking commission regulations

Part 1, Section B, Topic 1: Strategic Planning

10

Wiley CMAexcel Learning System, Part 1: Financial Reporting, Planning, Performance, and Control.
Copyright © 2017, Institute of Management Accountants. Published by John Wiley & Sons, Inc.

The Association of
Accountants and
Financial Professionals
in Business

LOS 1.B.1.h.

Porter's Three Generic Strategies to Gain Competitive Advantage

1. **Cost Leadership Strategy**—gain market share by having lowest prices
2. **Differentiation Strategy**—differentiating product or service when competing in a saturated market
3. **Focus Strategy**—focus on a few target/niche markets

Part 1, Section B, Topic 1: Strategic Planning

11

Wiley CMAexcel Learning System, Part 1: Financial Reporting, Planning, Performance, and Control.
Copyright © 2017, Institute of Management Accountants. Published by John Wiley & Sons, Inc.

The Association of
Accountants and
Financial Professionals
in Business

LOS 1.B.1.i.

b. Market Forces, Industry Trends, and Competition
Porter's *Five* Forces Driving Profitability

The Association of
Accountants and
Financial Professionals
in Business

LOS 1.B.1.i.

1. Threat of New Competitors: Barriers to Entry

- New competitors bring new capacity and resources to market
- May have profitability impact on existing market participants
- The threat depends on magnitude of barriers to entry:
  - Existing market participants' cost advantages
  - Economies of scale
  - Production/service differentiation
  - Switching costs
  - Channel crowding
  - Expected reactions from existing market participants

2. Threat of Substitutes

- Substitute products or services—provide same functions and benefits
- Squeezes average price and profit margin
- Limits product or service value
- Low-cost substitutes

Bargaining Power of:

3. Buyers

- Bargaining leverage—exploitable strategic or tactical advantage
- Price sensitivity—importance of lower prices

4. Suppliers

- Size of supplier relative to customer
- Customer's reliance on product/service
- Threat of forward integration

The Association of
Accountants and
Financial Professionals
in Business

LOS 1.B.1.i.

5. Rivalry Among Existing Competitors

Factor	Positive Situation	Negative Situation
Structure of competition	Small competitors escape notice of bigger firms	Few balanced competitors fight/retaliate; no net gain
Structure of costs	Capacity utilization with high fixed costs	Excess capacity leads to price cutting/matching
Product/service differentiation	Sustainable; perceived differentiation suppresses rivalry	Absence intensities rivalry
Customer switching costs	Costs tying buyer to one supplier	Lack of costs opens to raids by rivals
Competitors' strategy/objective diversity	Similar companies easier to predict	Foreign/government/small companies difficult to anticipate strategies
High exit barriers	To keep market share	Emotional rationale

The Association of
Accountants and
Financial Professionals
in Business

LOS 1.B.1.i.

Question: Strategy Formulation and Strategic Planning

What are the key elements at the core of strategic planning and strategy formulation?

Answer:
- External factors
- Internal factors
- S.W.O.T. analysis
- Long-term vision, mission, and goals
- Tactics to achieve long-term goals

LOS 1.B.1.c.

c. Strategic Implications of Technology

- Creation of industry substitutes
- Reduce need for large-scale distribution
- Accelerate new product design/facilitate shorter production runs
- Create shift in the balance of power between an organization and a supplier or buyer
- Change industry structure and impact profitability

LOS 1.B.1.c.

Technology Assessment Steps

1. Identify key technologies
2. Analyze potential changes in current and future technologies
3. Analyze competitive impact of technologies
4. Analyze organization's technical strengths and weaknesses
5. Establish organization's technology priorities

The Association of
Accountants and
Financial Professionals
in Business

LOS 1.B.1.c.

Linking Technology Assessment to Strategic Planning

- Insights gained from technology assessment evolve into an organizational technology strategy
- A sound technology strategy will:
  - ✓ Enhance technology's strategic role in the organization
  - ✓ Support the organization's corporate and competitive strategies
  - ✓ Develop plans for attaining short- and long-term objectives/major projects
  - ✓ Allocate resources more efficiently
  - ✓ Align with financial plan/budget
  - ✓ Provide metrics for measuring accomplishment

The Association of
Accountants and
Financial Professionals
in Business

LOS 1.B.1.c.

Question: Strategic Implications of Technology

What are three strategic implications that technology can have on an organization, and that an organization must be cognizant of in gaining and sustaining competitive advantage?

Answer: Technology can:
1. Result in creation of industry substitutes
2. Reduce the need for large-scale distribution and open a market up to new competition
3. Accelerate new product designs, which can lead to intense rivalry.

LOS 1.B.1.c.

d. Stakeholder Groups and Their Social Concerns

- Stakeholders are

  ▸ Executives, managers, employees, board of directors, stockholders, customers, competitors, suppliers, creditors, unions, regulatory bodies, etc.

- Challenges to balancing the maximization of shareholder value and social responsibility are

  ▸ Accounting practices, advertising, corporate restructuring, diversity issues, employee privacy issues, harassment issues, environmental issues, international operations, competition

LOS 1.B.1.c.

Assessing Challenges: Stakeholder Analysis

1. Identify stakeholders; brainstorm list of main participants
2. Determine stakeholder needs; collect input through interviews, focus groups, surveys
3. Develop matrix of organization's objectives and stakeholder needs
4. Code the effect of organization's objectives versus stakeholder needs using a plus (+) or minus (-) sign or question mark
5. Make decision based on effects recorded

The Association of
Accountants and
Financial Professionals
in Business

LOS 1.B.1.c.

Stakeholder Analysis Example: Automating a Produce Warehouse

(+ or –)	Organization	Employees	Consuming Public	Suppliers	Government Inspectors
Harm and benefits	– Higher costs + Higher profits	+ More free time – Fewer hours, potential layouts	+ Lower costs + Quick time to market; less spoilage	– New hardware	+ Power and influence
Rights and responsibilities	+ Value + Profits for owners and share-holders	+ Competitive market position	? Possible quality concerns ? Public good	? Ability to meet demand	+ Protect public + Regulate Industry

The Association of
Accountants and
Financial Professionals
in Business

LOS 1.B.1.c.

Linking Stakeholder Analysis to Strategic Planning

- Identifies the role good citizenship plays in business
- Balance striving to achieve profitability for shareholders, while remaining socially responsive for the benefit all stakeholders
- Stakeholder analysis enables an organization to learn:

  ‣ How people feel about the organization and industry it is in

  ‣ What issues the organization might reevaluate its position on

  ‣ What the organization might do differently to improve its position

The Association of
Accountants and
Financial Professionals
in Business

LOS 1.B.1.c.

Question: Strategy and Stakeholder Considerations

A telescope manufacturer plans to build an automated warehouse and invest in expensive technology upgrades. Who are four stakeholders potentially impacted by this decision/strategy/plan?

Answer:

1. Shareholders—increased production, increased sales/higher profits; but risk of payback on high upfront costs/significant investment
2. Employees—less need for manual labor, potential layoffs
3. Customers—economies of scale achieved through automation = possible lower prices; quick time to market; quality risks
4. Suppliers—ability to meet demand; possible consolidation of suppliers

---

Part 1, Section B, Topic 1: Strategic Planning

26

Wiley CMAexcel Learning System, Part 1: Financial Reporting, Planning, Performance, and Control.
Copyright © 2017, Institute of Management Accountants. Published by John Wiley & Sons, Inc.

The Association of
Accountants and
Financial Professionals
in Business

LOS 1.B.1.c.

e. Steps to Globalization

- Export
- Establish international division and/or sales subsidiaries
- Multinational corporation (MNC)
- Global organization
- Alliances, partnerships, joint ventures

Part 1, Section B, Topic 1: Strategic Planning

27

Wiley CMAexcel Learning System, Part 1: Financial Reporting, Planning, Performance, and Control.
Copyright © 2017, Institute of Management Accountants. Published by John Wiley & Sons, Inc.

The Association of
Accountants and
Financial Professionals
in Business

LOS 1.B.1.c.

Linking Globalization to Strategic Planning

* Steps to globalization can differ for different organizations
* Additional skills and competence are required as an organization moves through the globalization stages (e.g., international finance and tax knowledge skills)
* Considerable investment in resources is needed

The "how to" and inclusion of additional resources needed at each step have to be factored into the strategic plan.

The Association of
Accountants and
Financial Professionals
in Business

LOS 1.B.1.d.

Analysis of Internal Factors Affecting Strategy

* Resources
* Skills
* Processes

Internal analysis techniques:
* Baldrige
* ISO 9001 and 14000
* Benchmarking
* Competitive analysis
* Employee competency assessments
* Training needs analysis
* Employee surveys
* Audits

The Association of
Accountants and
Financial Professionals
in Business

LOS 1.B.1.d.

Linking Internal Capability Analysis to Strategic Planning

- Internal capability analysis has two phases:
    1. Snapshot of present state—identify gaps
    2. Making decisions to close critical gaps to desired state

    Both are key to strategic planning

- Some gaps are simple to close; some require costly capital expenditures
- Cost of developing new capabilities must be weighed against potential payoffs
- Future success depends on development of the necessary and "right" capabilities

The Association of
Accountants and
Financial Professionals
in Business

LOS 1.B.1.i.

S.W.O.T. Analysis

- **S**trengths: What is the firm good at?
- **W**eaknesses: What needs to improve or be created?
- **O**pportunities: What events/trends help firm meet goals and grow?
- **T**hreats: What events/trends are barriers to firm's growth?

The Association of
Accountants and
Financial Professionals
in Business

LOS 1.B.1.i.

Example: S.W.O.T. Analysis Matrix

Strengths	Weaknesses
Internal factors such as strong leadership, financial soundness, organizational learning, R&D, technology, a strong distribution channel, etc.	Internal factors such as technology or other skills, capabilities, and competencies a firm lacks
Opportunities	**Threats**
External factors such as the chance to expand the customer base, provide new distribution channels, increase appeal of offering, or exploit a competitor's weakness	External factors such as a reduction in customer base, more difficult or costly customer access, reduced product appeal, or a new superior offering

The Association of
Accountants and
Financial Professionals
in Business

LOS 1.B.1.i.

Example: Implementing S.W.O.T. Data Analysis

One key way to implement S.W.O.T. analysis data is through a weighted average approach as follows:

Weishill Company has identified the following factors that can impact market attractiveness and business strength for a product. Each item has a different proportionate weight, all summing to 1.0. The rating scale ranges from 1 (the lowest) to 5 (the highest).

Market Attractiveness	Weight	Rating (1–5)
Market size	0.3	4
Market profitability	0.4	5
Distribution structure	0.2	4
Government regulations	0.1	2
Business Strength	**Weight**	**Rating (1–5)**
Unit costs	0.4	3
Customer loyalty	0.5	2
Brand reputation	0.1	4

The Association of
Accountants and
Financial Professionals
in Business

LOS 1.B.1.i.

Example: Implementing S.W.O.T. Data Analysis (cont.)

The calculated weighted averages for **market attractiveness (4.2)** and **business strength (2.6)** are as follows:

Market attractiveness =
$$(0.3 \times 4) + (0.4 \times 5) + (0.2 \times 4) + (0.1 \times 2) = \textbf{4.2}$$
Business strength $= (0.4 \times 3) + (0.5 \times 2) + (0.1 \times 4) = \textbf{2.6}$

Because the highly attractive market will presumably entice others to enter, strategies that build on the lower business strength (rather than attempting to exploit the higher market attractiveness) would be most beneficial.

The Association of
Accountants and
Financial Professionals
in Business

LOS 1.B.1.i.

Linking S.W.O.T. Analysis to Strategic Planning

- Incorporates both internal and external assessments about a firm into one summary which is important to strategic planning process.
- Opportunities and limitations identified in the analysis provide information for goals and actions in the strategic planning process.
- Outcomes of S.W.O.T. analysis that are important to strategic planning revolve around:
  - Adequacy of resources and capabilities to seize opportunities and neutralize threats.
  - Ability to gain competitive advantage
  - Number of competitors who already have the same resources and competencies
  - Ability of organizational structure to allow taking advantage of its resources and capabilities to support growth/change

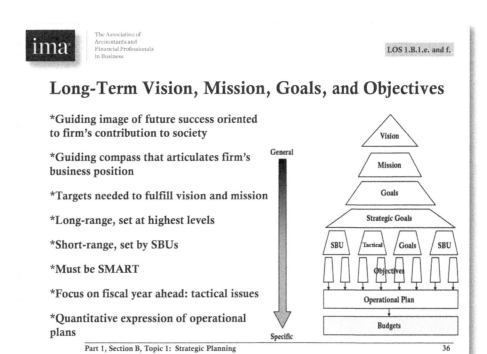

Long-Term Vision, Mission, Goals, and Objectives

*Guiding image of future success oriented to firm's contribution to society

*Guiding compass that articulates firm's business position

*Targets needed to fulfill vision and mission

*Long-range, set at highest levels

*Short-range, set by SBUs

*Must be SMART

*Focus on fiscal year ahead: tactical issues

*Quantitative expression of operational plans

General

Specific

Vision

Mission

Goals

Strategic Goals

SBU | Tactical | Goals | SBU

Objectives

Operational Plan

Budgets

Part 1, Section B, Topic 1: Strategic Planning   36
Wiley CMAexcel Learning System, Part 1: Financial Reporting, Planning, Performance, and Control.
Copyright © 2017, Institute of Management Accountants. Published by John Wiley & Sons, Inc.

Question: Strategic and Operational Plans, and Budgets

What is the hierarchy of budgets, strategic plans, and operational plans?

Answer:
1. Strategic plans
2. Operational plans
3. Budgets

Part 1, Section B, Topic 1: Strategic Planning   37
Wiley CMAexcel Learning System, Part 1: Financial Reporting, Planning, Performance, and Control.
Copyright © 2017, Institute of Management Accountants. Published by John Wiley & Sons, Inc.

The Association of
Accountants and
Financial Professionals
in Business

LOS 1.B.1.e. and f.

Strategic and Operational Plan Comparison

	Strategic Plan	Operational Plan
Focus	Basis for long-short run plans; for budget	Detailed revenue/expense budgets and goals for SBUs
Issues Examined	Identifies and analyzes issues such as: • New global market entrants • Economic conditions • Diversification plans	Identifies and analyzes issues such as: • Quarterly earnings • Inventory levels • Major capital expenditures • Marketing/production plans
Development	Top-down flow; comprehensive internal/ external factor analysis	Bottom-up flow; recommends specific options for the upcoming year
Control	Review/update annually for high-level changes	Review/update through year to address changing needs

The Association of
Accountants and
Financial Professionals
in Business

LOS 1.B.1.g.

Benefits and Limitations of Strategic Planning

Benefits	Limitations
Systematic approach to S.W.O.T. analysis	Effort, time, expense
Sound operating budget framework	Predictions are not exact science; may prove incorrect and fail
Managers learn to implement strategy and align with decisions	Resistance from entrenched ways in firm
Basis for financial/nonfinancial performance measures	Risk that planning can become bureaucratic exercise devoid of fresh ideas and strategic thinking
Communication among all management levels	
Guidance for new situations	

The Association of
Accountants and
Financial Professionals
in Business

LOS 1.B.1.i.

Contingency Planning

- Incorporated into the strategic plan to help cope with changing or turbulent conditions the organization may face
- Preparation of "what-if" situations
- Some conditions for contingency planning include:
    - ✓ Lower sales or profit levels
    - ✓ New entrants who can capture market share
    - ✓ Succession planning for key employee/executives
    - ✓ Disaster recovery
    - ✓ Shrinking capital availability
    - ✓ Mergers, acquisition, takeovers

The Association of
Accountants and
Financial Professionals
in Business

LOS 1.B.1.i.

Steps in Contingency Planning

1. Identify potential scenarios that need a contingency plan (events, "what-ifs," etc.)
2. Estimate potential impact of scenarios identified in terms of financial and/or competitive position, etc.
3. Develop strategies and tactical plans to deal with each possible occurrence
4. Specify trigger points or warning signals
5. Store plans off-site
6. Routinely review plans and revise as warranted, at least as often as strategic planning

LOS 1.B.1.i.

Other Planning Tools and Techniques

- **Situational analysis—a collection of methods**
    - Uses S.W.O.T. analysis; Porter's "five forces" analysis; and a "5C" analysis
    - **"5C"** analysis consists of five mini analyses that focus around:
        1. **C**ompany
        2. **C**ompetitors
        3. **C**ustomers
        4. **C**ollaborators
        5. **C**limate (Business)
    - Business climate analysis or **PEST** analysis assesses environments:
        Political and regulatory
        Economic
        Social/cultural
        Technological

LOS 1.B.1.i.

Other Planning Tools and Techniques (cont.)

- **Scenario planning**: methodology to assist the organization develop flexible strategic plans by simulating plausible alternative trends (**STEEEPA**):
    Social
    Technical
    Economic
    Environmental
    Educational
    Political
    Aesthetic

The Association of
Accountants and
Financial Professionals
in Business

LOS 1.B.1.i.

Other Planning Tools and Techniques

* **Competitive analysis**: focuses on understanding an organization's competition. Recognizing who the competitor is *rather than* who the organization thinks the competitor is
* **BCG (Boston Consulting Group) Growth/Share Matrix**: tool to help organizations analyze business units and/or product lines and ranks them based on Relative Market Share (RMS) and Market Growth Rate (MGR):
    * **Cash Cows**—High RMS / Low MGR
    * **Dogs**—Low RMS / Low MGR
    * **Stars**—High RMS / High MGR
    * **Question Marks**—Low RMS / High MGR

44

The Association of
Accountants and
Financial Professionals
in Business

LOS 1.B.1.i.

Question: Other Planning Tools and Techniques

What are the five mini analyses that comprise the "5C" analysis?

Answer: A *Company* analysis, a *Competitor* analysis, a *Customer* analysis, a *Collaborator* analysis, and a business *Climate* analysis.

45

Section B, Topic 2: Budgeting Concepts

- Reasons for budgeting
- Operations and performance goals
- Characteristics of a successful budget process
- Standard costs
- Resource allocation

Budgeting Terminology

- Budget
- Budgeting
- Budgetary Control
- Pro Forma Statement

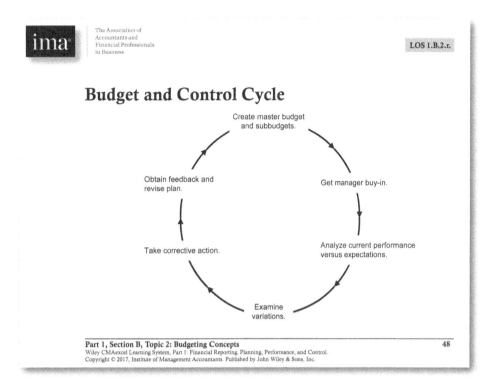

ima® The Association of Accountants and Financial Professionals in Business

LOS 1.B.2.r.

Budget and Control Cycle

ima® The Association of Accountants and Financial Professionals in Business

Four Main Reasons for Budgeting

1. Planning
2. Communication and Coordination
3. Monitoring
4. Evaluation

The Association of
Accountants and
Financial Professionals
in Business

LOS 1.B.2.a.

Question: Budget as Planning Tool

K-Co. currently uses its company budget only as a planning tool. Management has decided also to use budgets for control purposes. To implement this change, the management accountant must

a. develop forecasting procedures.
b. synchronize the budgeting and accounting system with the organizational structure.
c. report daily to operating management any deviations from plan.
d. organize a budget committee.
e. appoint a budget director.

Answer: **b.**
Control is the process of placing checks and balances on the actions of those responsible for aspects of a budget. Control also is linked to company strategy; managers must have incentives to make decisions that benefit the short-term and long-term strategies. Aligning the budgeting and accounting system with the organizational structure will help ensure that budget incentives work toward organizational goals.

Based on ICMA question, used with permission

Part 1, Section B, Topic 2: Budgeting Concepts
Wiley CMAexcel Learning System, Part 1: Financial Reporting, Planning, Performance, and Control.
Copyright © 2017, Institute of Management Accountants. Published by John Wiley & Sons, Inc.

50

The Association of
Accountants and
Financial Professionals
in Business

LOS 1.B.2.a. and b.

Economic Considerations in the Budgeting Process

Managers should consider all economic factors:
- Organizational objectives
- Relationship between organizational objectives and budgeting process
- Competition and the company's differentiating factors
- Effects of competition and marketplace trends
- Organizational risks and the effect on budgeting process
- Organizational opportunities

Part 1, Section B, Topic 2: Budgeting Concepts
Wiley CMAexcel Learning System, Part 1: Financial Reporting, Planning, Performance, and Control.
Copyright © 2017, Institute of Management Accountants. Published by John Wiley & Sons, Inc.

51

The Association of
Accountants and
Financial Professionals
in Business

LOS 1.B.2.a.

Operations and Performance Goals

- Strategic direction provides basis for planning support.
- Budgeting facilitates movement toward goals.

Wiley CMAexcel Learning System, Part 1: Financial Reporting, Planning, Performance, and Control.
Copyright © 2017, Institute of Management Accountants. Published by John Wiley & Sons, Inc.

The Association of
Accountants and
Financial Professionals
in Business

LOS 1.B.2.e.

Characteristics of Successful Budgeting

The budget must:

- Be aligned with the corporate strategy.
- Be separate but flow from strategic planning and forecasting processes.
- Be used to alleviate potential bottlenecks.
- Contain realistic projected numbers.
- Be perceived as a planning, communication, and coordinating tool.
- Be detailed in selling and administrative budgets.
- Achieve buy-in from all levels of management.
- Be reviewed and approved by a higher authority.
- Be flexible but not easily changed.

Wiley CMAexcel Learning System, Part 1: Financial Reporting, Planning, Performance, and Control.
Copyright © 2017, Institute of Management Accountants. Published by John Wiley & Sons, Inc.

The Association of
Accountants and
Financial Professionals
in Business

LOS 1.B.2.i.

Budget Time Period

The budget time period is the length of time appropriate for the purpose of the budget.

Most Detail → Least Detail

Weekly	Monthly	Quarterly	Annual	3–10 Years
Production	Production	Production	Production	Strategic Plans
Purchasing	Purchasing	Purchasing	Purchasing	
Sales	Sales	Sales	Sales	
	Operating	Operating	Operating	
Cash	Cash	Cash	Cash	

The Association of
Accountants and
Financial Professionals
in Business

LOS 1.B.2.j. and k.

Budget Process

Authoritative   -Preparation Approach-   Participative

Five Steps in a combined approach:

1. Identify participants: key employees, expertise
2. Top management communicates strategic direction to participants
3. Participants create first draft of their budget
4. Lower levels submit budgets to next higher level: stress communication
5. Rigorous/fair review: approval sets the final budget

The Association of
Accountants and
Financial Professionals
In Business

LOS 1.B.2.e.

Question: Roles in the Budget Process

Which of the following best describes the role of top management in the budgeting process?

a. Top management should establish strict goals that must be met when the budgets are developed.

b. Top management needs to be involved, including using the budget process to communicate goals.

c. Top management lacks the detailed knowledge of daily operations and should limit its involvement.

d. Top management should be involved only in the approval process.

Answer: **b**.

Top management ultimately is responsible for its budgets, and its primary means of exercising this responsibility is to ensure that all levels of management understand and support the budget and the overall budget control process. Budgets play a role in measuring performance against established goals.

Based on ICMA question, used with permission

Part 1, Section B, Topic 2: Budgeting Concepts
Wiley CMAexcel Learning System, Part 1: Financial Reporting, Planning, Performance, and Control.
Copyright © 2017, Institute of Management Accountants. Published by John Wiley & Sons, Inc.

56

The Association of
Accountants and
Financial Professionals
in Business

LOS 1.B.2.t.

A Budget Issue

- Budget slack
    - Extra money in budget to accommodate unexpected
    - Budgeting to fail
    - Cumulative for sublevels leads to inaccurate master budget
    - Top management needs to allow some flexibility or subordinates may make decisions that negate goal congruence

Part 1, Section B, Topic 2: Budgeting Concepts
Wiley CMAexcel Learning System, Part 1: Financial Reporting, Planning, Performance, and Control.
Copyright © 2017, Institute of Management Accountants. Published by John Wiley & Sons, Inc.

57

LOS 1.B.2.m., n., and o.

Cost Standards

A **standard** is any carefully determined price, quantity, service level, or cost.

Authoritative **Standards:** Set by management

Participative **Standards:** Set by dialogue between management and input from involved parties

Standards can be:
Ideal: attainable *only* if everything goes right; no work delays, interruptions, or machine breakdowns.
Reasonably attainable: attainable by operating at a normal pace; allows for delays, work breaks, and machine down time

LOS 1.B.2.p.

Determining Standard Costs

Standard costs are determined by evaluating:

Direct materials
- Quality
- Quantity
- Supply chain costs

Direct labor
- Ideal standards
- Product complexity
- Personnel skill levels
- Type and condition of equipment
- Nature of manufacturing process

The Association of
Accountants and
Financial Professionals
in Business

LOS 1.B.2.p.

Standard Costs for Direct Materials (DM) and Labor (DL)

Standard Cost for DM and DL =
# of Units of Input × Standard Cost per Unit of Input

Standard Type	Units of Input per Unit of Output	Standard Cost per Unit	Standard Cost
DM	8.0	$ 4	$32
DL	0.5	$12	$ 6
Total			$38

The Association of
Accountants and
Financial Professionals
in Business

LOS 1.B.2.l. and q.

Sources for Standard Setting

Source	Advantages	Limitations
Activity analysis	Thorough	Expensive
Historical data	Inexpensive	Less reliable
Market expectations	Realistic price	May be difficult to maintain high standards
Benchmarking	Measures performance against best-in-class	May discourage using new process

The Association of
Accountants and
Financial Professionals
in Business

LOS 1.B.2.h. and c.

Resource Allocation

Every firm has a finite amount of resources. The allocation of these resources is done through:

- **Strategy:** SWOT analysis to determine the strategy that is then applied to the budget

- **Master Budget:** a plan for controlling operations, based on the firm's strategy. Note the master budget is fixed at an expected level of activity,

- **Long-Term Planning:** ensures the strategy gets implemented.

- **Short-Term Objectives:** variations in the LT plan resulting from capital budgeting, past operating results, and expected future results

The Association of
Accountants and
Financial Professionals
in Business

LOS 1.B.2.h.

Master Budget Components

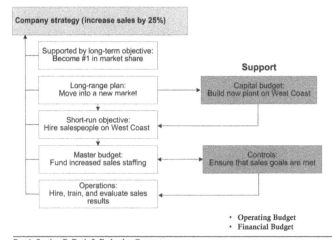

Session 3 Exercise: Preparing Operating Budgets and Pro Forma Income Statement

Section B, Topic 5: Annual Profit Plan and Supporting Schedules

Majestic Furniture Company manufactures two primary products: bar stools and dining chairs. Its upcoming quarter's sales of bar stools and dining chairs are 100,000 and 70,000 units, respectively. Majestic Furniture expects to continue to sell each bar stool for $40 and each dining chair for $100.

Majestic Furniture's products are made with oak and pine, and both products require assembly and painting. The next table provides information on the materials and labor requirement for making each bar stool and dining chair and the costs of the materials and labor.

	Material		Labor	
	Pine	**Oak**	**Assembly**	**Painting**
Bar stool	1.5 ft	2.5 ft	0.5 hr	0.5 hr
Dining chair	5.0 ft	2.0 ft	2.0 hr	1.0 hr
Unit cost	$2.00/ft	$1.50/ft	$10.00/hr	$15.00/hr

In addition to the materials and labor hours needed to manufacture the two products, the company also expects to incur, for the upcoming quarter, $400,000 of indirect factory wages, $90,000 of indirect materials, $60,000 of plant and equipment depreciation, and $60,000 of utilities.

Majestic Furniture uses the LIFO method to value inventory. To ensure a smooth operation, Majestic Furniture wants to hold a certain level of inventories of its two products and the materials needed. The next table provides information related to the company's last quarter's ending inventories, its upcoming quarter's desired inventories, and the costs of the inventories.

	Product		Material	
	Bar Stool	**Dining Chair**	**Pine**	**Oak**
Prior-period ending inventories	10,000	8,000	15,000 ft	10,000 ft
Unit cost for prior period and desired ending inventories	$20.00	$40.00	$2.00	$1.50
Desired inventories	9,000	7,000	10,000 ft	6,000 ft

Majestic Furniture estimates that it will incur $450,000 of selling and administrative expenses and $90,000 of interest expense in the upcoming quarter. The company currently faces a 30% tax rate.

Majestic does not distinguish between fixed and variable costs in its overhead budget. Use planned direct labor hours as the denominator level of production and round the resulting overhead rate to the nearest penny.

Majestic uses the FIFO method of valuing its inventory.

Using the information provided, create the next nine budgets for Majestic Furniture for the upcoming quarter:

a. Sales budget
b. Production budget
c. Direct materials purchase budget
d. Direct materials usage budget
e. Direct labor budget
f. Overhead cost budget
g. Overhead rate and product cost sheets
h. Cost of goods sold budget
i. Pro forma income statement

ANSWER CHECKS:

a. Sales Budget = $11,000,000
b. Bar Stool = 99,000 units
   Dining Chair = 69,000 units

c. Pine = $977,000
   Oak = $572,250

d. Pine = $987,000
   Oak = $578,250

e. Assembly = $1,875,000
   Painting = $1, 777,500

f. Overhead Cost Budget = $610,000
g. Bar Stool $21.24 Dining Chair $53.97
h. Cost of Goods Sold Budget = $5,778,800
i. Net Income = $3,276.840

Session 3 Exercise Solution: Preparing Operating Budgets and Pro Forma Income Statement

a. Sales budget

	Sales in Units	Price per Unit	Revenue
Bar stool	100,000	$ 40	$ 4,000,000
Dining chair	70,000	$100	$ 7,000,000
Total revenue			$11,000,000

b. Production budget

	Bar Stool	Dining Chair
Budgeted sales (in units)	100,000	70,000
Add: Desired ending inventory	9,000	7,000
Total units needed	109,000	77,000
Less: Beginning inventory	10,000	8,000
Total production	99,000	69,000

c. Direct materials purchase budget

	Pine	Oak
Materials needed for production*		
Bar stool	148,500	247,500
Dining chair	345,000	138,000
Add: Desired ending inventory	10,000	6,000
Total direct materials needed	503,500	391,500
Less: Beginning inventory	15,000	10,000
Direct materials purchased	488,500	381,500
Unit cost of direct materials	$ 2.00	$ 1.50
Total cost of direct materials purchased	$ 977,000	$ 572,250

* Bar stool: Pine needed = 99,000 (from production budget) × 1.5 = 148,500; Oak needed = 99,000 × 2.5 = 247,500

Dining chair: Pine needed = 69,000 (from production budget) × 5.0 = 345,000; Oak needed = 69,000 × 2.0 = 138,000

d. Direct materials usage budget

	Pine	Oak	Total
Beginning direct materials inventory	15,000	10,000	
Unit cost of direct materials	$2.00	$1.50	
Cost of beginning inventory	$ 30,000	$ 15,000	
Add: Cost of direct materials purchased	977,000	572,250	
Cost of materials available for production	$1,007,000	$587,250	
Desired direct materials ending inventory	10,000	6,000	
Unit cost of direct materials	$2.00	$1.50	
Cost of desired ending inventory	20,000	9,000	
Cost of direct materials used	$987,000	$578,250	$1,565,250

e. Direct labor budget

	Assembly	Painting	Total
Labor hours needed for production*			
Bar stool	49,500	49,500	
Dining chair	138,000	69,000	
Total direct labor hours needed	187,500	118,500	
Unit cost of direct labor hour	$10	$15	
Total cost of direct labor hours used	$1,875,000	$1,777,500	$3,652,500

* Bar stool: Assembly hours needed = 99,000 (from production budget) × 0.5 = 49,500;
  Painting hours needed = 99,000 × 0.5 = 49,500
Dining chair: Assembly hours needed = 69,000 (from production budget) × 2.0
  = 138,000; Painting hours needed = 69,000 × 1.0 = 69,000

f. Overhead cost budget

Indirect factory wages	$ 400,000
Indirect materials	90,000
Depreciation of plant and equipment	60,000
Utilities	60,000
Total overhead cost	$610,000

g. Overhead rate and product cost sheets

Total overhead	$610,000	
/Total direct labor hours needed	306,000	
=Total overhead rate	$1.99	(rounded to two decimals)

Product Cost Sheets

		Bar Stool		Dining Chair	
		Resource Units	Resource Cost	Resource Units	Resource Cost
Resource	Cost/Unit	/Unit of Product	/Unit of Product	/Unit of Product	/Unit of Product
Pine	$2.00 /ft.	1.5 ft.	$3.00	5.0 ft.	$10.00
Oak	1.50 /ft.	2.5 ft.	3.75	2.0 ft.	3.00
Assembly Labor	10.00 /hr.	0.5 hr.	5.00	2.0 hr.	20.00
Paint Labor	15.00 /hr.	0.5 hr.	7.50	1.0 hr.	15.00
Variable Cost			$19.25		$48.00
Overhead	1.99 /hr.	1.0 hr.	1.99	3.0 hr.	5.97
Full Cost			$21.24		$53.97

h. Cost of goods sold budget

	Bar Stool	Dining Chair	Total
Beginning inventory	10,000	8,000	
Unit cost of inventory	$20.00	$40.00	
Cost of beginning inventory	$200,000.00	$320,000.00	$520,000.00
Cost of direct materials used			$1,565,250.00
Add: Cost of direct labor hours used			3,652,500.00
Add: Overhead cost			610,000.00
Cost of goods manufactured			$5,827,750.00
Costs of goods available for sale			$6,347,750.00
Desired ending inventory	9,000.00	7,000.00	
Unit cost of inventory	$21.24	$53.97	
Cost of desired ending inventory	$191,160.00	$377,790.00	$568,950.00
Cost of goods sold			$5,778,800.00

i. Pro forma income statement

Sales revenue	$11,000,000.00
Less: Cost of goods sold	5,778,800.00
Gross margin	$5,221,200.00
Less: S&A expenses	450,000.00
Operating income (EBIT)	$4,771,200.00
Less: Interest expense	90,000.00
Earnings before taxes (EBT)	$4,681,200.00
Less: Taxes (30%)	1,404,360.00
Net income	$3,276,840.00

The Association of
Accountants and
Financial Professionals
in Business

Session 3 Wrap-Up

Content covered in Session 3

- Section B, Topic 1: Strategic Planning
- Section B, Topic 2: Budgeting Concepts

Content to be covered in Session 4

- Section B, Topic 5: Annual Profit Plan and Supporting Schedules
- Exercise 1: Preparing Operating Budgets and Pro Forma Income Statement
- Exercise 2: Preparing a Cash Budget

Session 4

The Association of
Accountants and
Financial Professionals
in Business

Wiley
CMAexcel Learning System
Exam Review 2017

Part 1: Financial Reporting, Planning, Performance, and Control

Session 4

Learning Outcome Statements (LOS) identifiers appear on the
slides as applicable to highlight where we address each LOS
within the material.

The Association of
Accountants and
Financial Professionals
in Business

Session 3 Recap

- Section B, Topic 1: Strategic Planning
- Section B, Topic 2: Budgeting Concepts

The Association of
Accountants and
Financial Professionals
in Business

Session 4 Overview

- Section B, Topic 5: Annual Profit Plan and Supporting Schedules
- Exercise 1: Preparing Operating Budgets and Pro Forma Income Statement
- Exercise 2: Preparing a Cash Budget

Section B: Planning, Budgeting, and Forecasting

- Topic 1: Strategic Planning
- Topic 2: Budgeting Concepts
- Topic 3: Forecasting Techniques
- Topic 4: Budget Methodologies
- Topic 5: Annual Profit Plan and Supporting Schedules
- Topic 6: Top-Level Planning and Analysis

Topic 5: Annual Profit Plan and Supporting Schedules

- Operating budgets
- Financial budgets

LOS 1.B.5.a.

Master Budget

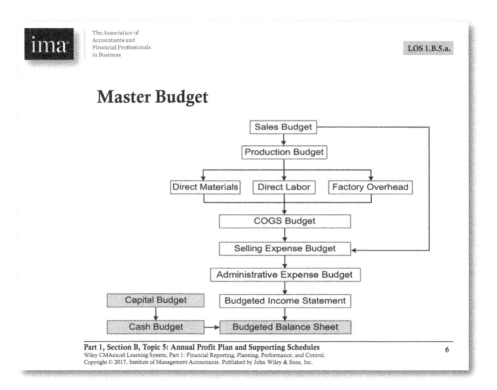

LOS 1.B.5.a.

Operating Budgets

- Sales forecast
  - ▸ Accuracy of sales forecast affects all other budgets
- Sales budget
- Production/inventory budget
- Direct materials budget
- Direct labor budget
- Overhead budget
- Cost of goods sold budget
- Selling and administrative expense budgets
- Pro forma income statement

The Association of
Accountants and
Financial Professionals
in Business

LOS 1.B.5.b.

Sales Forecast—Factors to Consider

- Historical trends
- Economic conditions
- Industry conditions
- Competitors' actions
- Product costs
- Pricing policies
- Credit policies
- Planned advertising and forecasting expenditures
- Expected sales from targeted new accounts
- Impact on sales from targeted company acquisitions

The Association of
Accountants and
Financial Professionals
in Business

LOS 1.B.5.a. and c.

Sales Budget

Sales budget defines capacity needed.

Sales Budget	
Sales in units	158,000 (a)
Selling price per unit	$148
Total sales	$23,384,000 (b)

The Association of
Accountants and
Financial Professionals
in Business

LOS 1.B.5.d. and e.

Production Budget

- Is prepared in units
- Defines the production capacity needed
- Based on the budgeted sales units
- Takes into account the desired *ending* finished goods inventory
- Considers the *beginning* finished goods inventory in units

Finished Goods Inventory Budget

- Based on:
  - Management directives, or
  - Calculated as a percentage of future sales

The Association of
Accountants and
Financial Professionals
in Business

LOS 1.B.5.f.

Production/Inventory Budget

Production Budget	
Budgeted sales in units	158,000 (a)
Add: Desired ending inventory of finished goods (units)	16,000
Total units needed	174,000
Less: Beginning inventory of finished goods (units)	14,000
Budgeted production in units	160,000 (c)

LOS 1.B.5.i.

Direct Materials Usage Budget

AA Models Direct Materials Usage Budget	
Production budget in units	160,000 (c)
Pounds of clay per unit of product	× 3
Total pounds of clay required	480,000 (d)
Cost per pound	× $14 (e)
Cost of clay to be used in production	$6,720,000 (f)

LOS 1.B.5.i.

Direct Materials Purchase Budget

AA Models Direct Materials Purchase Budget	
Total direct materials needed in production (units)	480,000 (d)
Add: Desired ending inventory (units)	48,000
Total direct materials required (units)	528,000
Less: Direct materials beginning inventory	40,000
Direct materials purchases	488,000
Purchase price per unit	$14 (e)
Total cost for direct materials purchases	$6,832,000 (g)

The Association of
Accountants and
Financial Professionals
in Business

LOS 1.B.5.h.

DM Budget

- Based on the budgeted finished good production units
- Takes into account the desired *ending* DM inventory in units
- Considers the *beginning* DM inventory in units
- Incorporates any procurement policies for purchasing decisions made

The Association of
Accountants and
Financial Professionals
in Business

LOS 1.B.5.i.

Question: AA Models' DM Purchases

AA Models has the following finished goods production plan in units:

 January 10,000   February 8,000   March 9,000   April 12,000

Each FG unit contains 3 pounds of raw material; desired raw material ending inventory each month is 120% of the next month's production + 500 pounds (Beginning inventory meets this requirement.)

How much raw material should AA purchase in March?

a. 27,000 pounds
b. 32,900 pounds
c. 37,800 pounds
d. 43,700 pounds

The Association of
Accountants and
Financial Professionals
in Business

LOS 1.B.5.i.

Question: AA Models' DM Purchases

a. 27,000 pounds
b. 32,900 pounds
c. 37,800 pounds
d. 43,700 pounds

Answer: **c.**

1. Calculate the amount of RM needed for March & April Production:

    March Production needs: 9,000 units × 3 lbs. /unit = 27,000 lbs.

    April Production needs: 12,000 units × 3 lbs./unit = 36,000 lbs.

2. Calculate the desired raw material ending inventory for March:

    (36,000 units × 1.2) + 500 lbs. = 43,700 lbs.

3. Calculate the beginning inventory for March (this is February's ending inventory):

    (27,000 lbs. × 1.2) + 500 lbs. = 32,900 lbs.

4. Calculate the raw materials purchased for March:

March Production Needs	27,000 lbs.
+ Desired Ending Inventory	43,700 lbs.
- Beginning Inventory	32,900 lbs.
= March RM Purchases	37,800 lbs.

Based on ICMA question, used with permission   **Part 1, Section B, Topic 5: Annual Profit Plan and Supporting Schedules**   16
Wiley CMAexcel Learning System, Part 1: Financial Reporting, Planning, Performance, and Control.
Copyright © 2017, Institute of Management Accountants. Published by John Wiley & Sons, Inc.

The Association of
Accountants and
Financial Professionals
in Business

LOS 1.B.5.g. and i.

Direct Labor Budget

AA Models Direct Labor Budget	
Budgeted production (units)	160,000 (c)
Direct labor hours required per unit	× 0.4
Direct labor hours needed	64,000 (h)
Hourly rate	× $13
Total wages for direct labor	$832,000 (i)

Part 1, Section B, Topic 5: Annual Profit Plan and Supporting Schedules   17
Wiley CMAexcel Learning System, Part 1: Financial Reporting, Planning, Performance, and Control.
Copyright © 2017, Institute of Management Accountants. Published by John Wiley & Sons, Inc.

The Association of
Accountants and
Financial Professionals
in Business

LOS 1.B.5.j., k., and l.

Factory Overhead Budget

AA Models Factory Overhead Budget		
Total direct labor hours (DLH)		64,000 (h)
Variable factory overhead	Per DLH	Total
Supplies ($11,520/64,000)	$0.30	$19,200
Other ($352,000/64,000)	5.50	352,000
Total variable factory overhead	$5.80	371,200
Fixed factory overhead		
Depreciation		35,000
Plant insurance		1,200
Indirect labor		128,000
Salary supervision		34,000
Total fixed factory overhead		198,200
Total factory overhead		$569,400 (j)

The Association of
Accountants and
Financial Professionals
in Business

LOS 1.B.5.k. and l.

Determination of Fixed Overhead Rate

Fixed Overhead Budget ÷ DLH = Fixed Overhead Rate

$198,200   ÷ 64,000 = $3.10 per DLH

Determination of Total Overhead Rate

Fixed Overhead Rate + Variable Overhead Rate = Total Overhead Rate

$3.10   + $5.68   = $8.78 per DLH

The Association of
Accountants and
Financial Professionals
in Business

LOS 1.B.5.g. and k.

Product Cost Sheet

Cost Component	Qty. of Component/Unit of Production	Cost/Unit of Component	Cost/Unit of Production
DM	3.00 lb./unit	$14.00 /lb.	$42.00
DL	0.40 hr./unit	13.00/hr.	5.20
Variable Overhead	0.40 hr./unit	5.68/hr.	2.27
Total Variable Cost			**$49.47**
Fixed Overhead	0.40 hr./unit	3.10/hr.	1.24
Total Cost per Unit			**$50.71**

The Association of
Accountants and
Financial Professionals
in Business

LOS 1.B.5.n. and p.

Contribution Margin

Both the Cost of Goods Sold and the Selling and Administrative Expenses need to be separated into their variable and fixed components. the Contribution Margin can then be calculated:

Unit Contribution Margin =
        Price per Unit – Variable Cost per Unit

Total Contribution Margin =
        Total Revenue – Total Variable Cost

The Association of
Accountants and
Financial Professionals
in Business

LOS 1.B.5.m.

Cost of Goods Sold Budget

AA Models Cost of Goods Sold Budget	
Beginning finished goods inventory, Jan. 1	$709,940
(f) Direct materials used	$6,720,000
(i) Direct labor	832,000
(j) Manufacturing overhead	561,720
Cost of goods manufactured	8,113,720
Cost of goods available for sale	8,823,660
Less: Ending finished goods inventory	811,360
Cost of goods sold	$8,012,300 (k)

The Association of
Accountants and
Financial Professionals
in Business

LOS 1.B.5.o.

Selling and Administrative Expense Budget

AA Models Selling and Administrative Expense Budget	
Research/design	$348,000
Marketing	972,000
Shipping	510,000
Product support	330,000
Administration	680,400
Total S&A	$2,840,400 (l)

The Association of Accountants and Financial Professionals in Business

LOS 1.B.5.q.

Pro Forma Income Statement

Additional Information:
- Interest expense is $400,000
- Tax rate is 35%

AA Models Pro Forma Income Statement	
Sales	$23,384,000(b)
Less: Cost of goods sold	8,012,300(k)
Gross profit	15,371,700
Less: S&A expenses	2,840,400(l)
Operating income	12,531,300
Less: Interest Expense	$400,000
Earnings before taxes	12,131,300
Less: Taxes	4,245,955
Net income	$7,885,345

The Association of Accountants and Financial Professionals in Business

Question: Master Budget Components

Match the following master budget components to the appropriate descriptions:

I. Uses pro forma data to predict the end result of operations.
II. Helps firms to identify and acquire production resources.
III. Prevents long-term goals from being neglected.

a. Operating budget

b. Financial budget

Answer: I = b, II = a, III = b

The Association of
Accountants and
Financial Professionals
in Business

LOS 1.B.5.c.

Session 4 Exercise 1

Preparing Operating Budgets and Pro Forma Income Statement

Section B, Topic 5: Annual Profit Plan and Supporting Schedules

Session 4 Exercise 1: Preparing Operating Budgets and Pro Forma Income Statement

Section B, Topic 5: Annual Profit Plan and Supporting Schedules

Majestic Furniture Company manufactures two primary products: bar stools and dining chairs. Its upcoming quarter's sales of bar stools and dining chairs are 100,000 and 70,000 units, respectively. Majestic Furniture expects to continue to sell each bar stool for $40 and each dining chair for $100.

Majestic Furniture's products are made with oak and pine, and both products require assembly and painting. The next chart provides information on the materials and labor requirement for making each bar stool and dining chair, along with the costs of the materials and labor.

	Material		Labor	
	Pine	**Oak**	**Assembly**	**Painting**
Bar stool	1.5 ft	2.5 ft	0.5 hr	0.5 hr
Dining chair	5.0 ft	2.0 ft	2.0 hr	1.0 hr
Unit cost	$2.00/ft	$1.50/ft	$10.00/hr	$15.00/hr

In addition to the materials and labor hours needed to manufacture the two products, the company also expects to incur in the upcoming quarter, $400,000 of indirect factory wages, $90,000 of indirect materials, $60,000 of plant and equipment depreciation, and $60,000 of utilities.

Majestic Furniture uses the FIFO method to value inventory. To ensure a smooth operation, Majestic Furniture wants to hold certain levels of inventory of its two products and the materials needed to make them. The next chart provides information related to the company's last quarter's ending inventories, its upcoming quarter's desired inventories, and the costs of the inventories.

	Product		Material	
	Bar Stool	**Dining Chair**	**Pine**	**Oak**
Prior-period ending inventories	10,000	8,000	15,000 ft	10,000 ft
Unit cost for prior period and desired ending inventories	$20.00	$40.00	$2.00	$1.50
Desired inventories	9,000	7,000	10,000 ft	6,000 ft

Majestic Furniture estimates that it will incur $450,000 of selling and administrative expenses and $90,000 of interest expense in the upcoming quarter. The company currently faces a 30% tax rate.

Majestic does not distinguish between fixed and variable costs in its overhead budget. Use planned direct labor hours as the denominator level of production and round the resulting overhead rate to the nearest penny.

Majestic uses the FIFO method of valuing its inventory.

Using the information provided, create the next nine budgets for Majestic Furniture for the upcoming quarter:

a. Sales budget
b. Production budget
c. Direct materials purchase budget
d. Direct materials usage budget
e. Direct labor budget
f. Overhead cost budget
g. Overhead rate and product cost sheets
h. Cost of goods sold budget
i. Pro forma income statement

Session 4 Exercise 1 Solution: Preparing Operating Budgets and Pro Forma Income Statement

a. Sales budget

	Sales in Units	Price per Unit	Revenue
Bar stool	100,000	$ 40	$ 4,000,000
Dining chair	70,000	$100	$ 7,000,000
Total revenue			$11,000,000

b. Production budget

	Bar Stool	Dining Chair
Budgeted sales in units	100,000	70,000
Add: Desired ending inventory	9,000	7,000
Total units needed	109,000	77,000
Less: Beginning inventory	10,000	8,000
Total production	99,000	69,000

c. Direct materials purchase budget

	Pine	Oak
Materials needed for production*		
Bar stool	148,500	247,500
Dining chair	345,000	138,000
Add: Desired ending inventory	10,000	6,000
Total direct materials needed	503,500	391,500
Less: Beginning inventory	15,000	10,000
Direct materials purchased	488,500	381,500
Unit cost of direct materials	$ 2.00	$ 1.50
Total cost of direct materials purchased	$ 977,000	$ 572,250

* Bar stool: Pine needed = 99,000 (from production budget) × 1.5 = 148,500; Oak needed = 99,000 × 2.5 = 247,500

 Dining chair: Pine needed = 69,000 (from production budget) × 5.0 = 345,000; Oak needed = 69,000 × 2.0 = 138,000

d. Direct materials usage budget

	Pine	Oak	Total
Beginning direct materials inventory	15,000	10,000	
Unit cost of direct materials	$2.00	$1.50	
Cost of beginning inventory	$ 30,000	$ 15,000	
Add: Cost of direct materials purchased	977,000	572,250	
Cost of materials available for production	$1,007,000	$587,250	
Desired direct materials ending inventory	10,000	6,000	
Unit cost of direct materials	$2.00	$1.50	
Cost of desired ending inventory	20,000	9,000	
Cost of direct materials used	$987,000	$578,250	$1,565,250

e. Direct labor budget

	Assembly	Painting	Total
Labor hours needed for production*			
Bar stool	49,500	49,500	
Dining chair	138,000	69,000	
Total direct labor hours needed	187,500	118,500	306,000
Unit cost of direct labor hour	$10	$15	
Total cost of direct labor hours used	$1,875,000	$1,777,500	$3,652,500

* Bar stool: Assembly hours needed = 99,000 (from production budget) × 0.5 = 49,500;
Painting hours needed = 99,000 × 0.5 = 49,500

Dining chair: Assembly hours needed = 69,000 (from production budget) × 2.0 = 138,000;
Painting hours needed = 69,000 × 1.0 = 69,000

f. Overhead cost budget

Indirect factory wages	$ 400,000
Indirect materials	90,000
Depreciation of plant and equipment	60,000
Utilities	60,000
Total overhead cost	$610,000

g. Overhead rate and product cost sheets

Total overhead	$610,000
/ Total direct labor hours needed	306,000
= Total overhead rate	$1.99 (rounded to two decimals)

		Product Cost Sheets Bar Stool		Dining Chair	
	Resource	Resource Units	Resource Cost	Resource Units	Resource Cost
Resource	**Cost/Unit**	**/Unit of Product**	**/Unit of Product**	**/Unit of Product**	**/Unit of Product**
Pine	$2.00 /ft.	1.5 ft.	$3.00	5.0 ft.	$10.00
Oak	1.50 /ft.	2.5 ft.	3.75	2.0 ft.	3.00
Assembly Labor	10.00 /hr.	0.5 hr.	5.00	2.0 hr.	20.00
Paint Labor	15.00 /hr.	0.5 hr.	7.50	1.0 hr.	15.00
Variable Cost			$19.25		$48.00
Overhead	1.99 /hr.	1.0 hr.	1.99	3.0 hr.	5.97
Full Cost			$21.24		$53.97

h. Cost of goods sold budget

	Bar Stool	Dining Chair	Total
Beginning inventory	10,000	8,000	
Unit cost of inventory	$20	$40	
Cost of beginning inventory	$200,000	$320,000	$520,000
Cost of direct materials used			$1,565,250
Add: Cost of direct labor hours used			3,652,500
Add: Overhead cost			610,000
Cost of goods manufactured			$5,827,750
Costs of goods available for sale			$6,347,750
Desired ending inventory	9,000	7,000	
Unit cost of inventory	$21.24	$53.97	
Cost of desired ending inventory	$191,160	$377,790	$568,950
Cost of goods sold	$1,875,000		$5,778,800

i. Pro forma income statement

Sales revenue	$11,000,000
Less: Cost of goods sold	5,778,800
Gross margin	$5,221,200
Less: S&A expenses	450,000
Operating income (EBIT)	$4,771,200
Less: Interest expense	90,000
Earnings before taxes (EBT)	$4,681,200
Less: Taxes (30%)	1,404,360
Net income	$3,276,840

Financial Budgets

- Capital budget
- Cash budget
- Pro forma balance sheet
- Pro forma statement of cash flows

LOS 1.B.5.s.

Financial Budget Flow

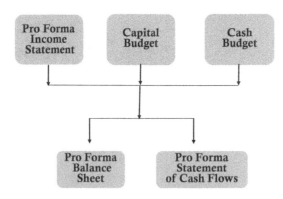

LOS 1.B.5.r.

Capital Expenditures Budget

- Plan to purchase:
    1. Property, plant, or equipment
    2. Company or corporation
    3. Operating capabilities
- The budget includes the timing of all **cash disbursements** for each capital item budgeted
- Capital is usually a scarce resource and so it must be rationed

LOS 1.B.5.v.

Cash Budget

- Plan to maintain liquidity
- Plan for financing needs
- Plan investment decisions, if excess cash
- Three parts:
    1. Cash available
    2. Cash disbursements
    3. Financing needs

The Association of
Accountants and
Financial Professionals
in Business

LOS 1.B.5.u.

Cash Collections Illustration

Assume the pattern of collections is 40% collected in month of sale, 30% is collected in first month following month of sale, 20% is collected in second month following sale, and 10% is collected in third month following sale. Given the following pattern of sales for January through April, determine the amount expected to be collected in the month of April.

	January	February	March	April
Sales	200	220	250	280
Collected in month of sale	80	88	100	112
Collected in first mo following sale		60	66	75
Collected in second mo following sale			40	44
Collected in third mo following sale				20
Total cash collected in April				251

Part 1, Section B, Topic 5: Annual Profit Plan and Supporting Schedules   31
Wiley CMAexcel Learning System, Part 1: Financial Reporting, Planning, Performance, and Control.
Copyright © 2017, Institute of Management Accountants. Published by John Wiley & Sons, Inc.

The Association of
Accountants and
Financial Professionals
in Business

LOS 1.B.5.u.

Question: Calculation of Cash Collections

Estimated sales for a firm's first 3 months of the year:
January: $600,000   February: $650,000   March: $700,000
20% of sales are in cash, the rest in credit. Collection patterns are 30% in month of sale, 40% the following month, and 25% the third month. The amount of cash collected in March from sales will be:

a. $308,000
b. $636,000
c. $700,000
d. $760,000

Based on ICMA question, used with permission

Part 1, Section B, Topic 5: Annual Profit Plan and Supporting Schedules   32
Wiley CMAexcel Learning System, Part 1: Financial Reporting, Planning, Performance, and Control.
Copyright © 2017, Institute of Management Accountants. Published by John Wiley & Sons, Inc.

The Association of
Accountants and
Financial Professionals
in Business

LOS 1.B.5.u.

Question: Calculation of Cash Collections

a. $308,000
b. $636,000
c. $700,000
d. $760,000

Answer: **b**.

Step 1: Calculate total March cash collections:

Cash Sales: $700,000 × 0.2 =	$140,000
Credit Sales: $700,000 × 0.8 × 0.3 =	$168,000

Step 2: Calculate February cash collections in March:

Credit Sales: $650,000 × 0.8 × 0.4 =	$208,000

Step 3 Calculate January cash collections in March:

Credit Sales: $600,000 × 0.8 × 0.25 =	$120,000
Total March cash collections:	$636,000

Based on ICMA question, used with permission

Part 1, Section B, Topic 5: Annual Profit Plan and Supporting Schedules   33
Wiley CMAexcel Learning System, Part 1: Financial Reporting, Planning, Performance, and Control.
Copyright © 2017, Institute of Management Accountants. Published by John Wiley & Sons, Inc.

The Association of
Accountants and
Financial Professionals
in Business

LOS 1.B.5.u.

Pro Forma Schedule of Cash Receipts and Cash Disbursements

Cash Receipts:

- A/R balance patterns/disbursement patterns
- Reflect prior months' activities and thus will not match same month's budget numbers

Cash Disbursements:

- Salaries and wages
- Interest and tax payments
- Depreciation and amortization expense removed from fixed overhead, non-cash transaction

Part 1, Section B, Topic 5: Annual Profit Plan and Supporting Schedules   34
Wiley CMAexcel Learning System, Part 1: Financial Reporting, Planning, Performance, and Control.
Copyright © 2017, Institute of Management Accountants. Published by John Wiley & Sons, Inc.

LOS 1.B.5.u.

Schedule of Cash Disbursements

Expenses to be Paid:	January Expenses	February Expenses	February Cash
Paid in same month			
DL and benefits	$ 994,000	$1,000,000	$1,000,000
Interest and tax	4,619,208	1,000,000	1,000,000
50% in month of purchase, balance next month			
DM purchases	6,832,000	5,080,000	5,956,000
Paid in following month			
Variable factory overhead	353,920	360,000	353,920
Fixed factory overhead	35,200	40,000	35,200
Selling & admin. expense	2,120,000	2,000,000	2,120,000
February Cash Disbursement			$10,465,120

LOS 1.B.5.v.

Cash Budget Example

February Cash balance, beginning (given)	$ 475,000
Collections from customers (given)	20,000,000
Interest received in cash	10,000
Total cash receipts	20,485,000
Less: Disbursements (previous slide)	10,465,120
Cash available	10,019,880
Minimum required	200,000
Cash excess/(deficiency)	9,819,880
Borrowings	0
Repayments	0
February Cash balance, ending	$10,019,880

The Association of
Accountants and
Financial Professionals
in Business

LOS 1.B.5.t.

Relationship Among Cash Budget, Capital Expenditure Budget, and Pro Forma Financial Statements

- **Cash Budget:**
  Combines the results of the cash collections and cash disbursements budgets

- **Capital Expenditure Budget:**
  Shown as a line item in the cash disbursements budget

- **Pro Forma Financial Statements:**
  ➢ Pro Forma Income Statement
     Combines sales and expense budgets
  ➢ Pro Forma Balance Sheet
     Projects an organization's financial position
  ➢ Pro Forma Statement of Cash Flows
     Classifies all cash receipts and disbursements into operating, investing, and financial activities

The Association of
Accountants and
Financial Professionals
in Business

Session 4 Exercise 2

Preparing a Cash Budget

Section B, Topic 5: Annual Profit Plan and Supporting Schedules

Session 4 Exercise 2: Preparing a Cash Budget

Section B, Topic 5: Annual Profit Plan and Supporting Schedules

Fuzzy Toys, Inc., which specializes in making luxury pet toys, is in the process of requesting a line of credit from its bank for the upcoming quarter. The company's May and June sales were $120,000 and $130,000, respectively; and its May and June raw materials and labor costs were $50,000 and $60,000, respectively. Fuzzy Toys estimates that its sales and its raw materials and labor costs for the months of July, August, and September are:

	July	August	September
Sales	$ 220,000	$ 260,000	$ 300,000
Raw materials and labor costs	130,000	150,000	150,000

Based on its past collection practice, Fuzzy Toys expects to collect 10% of a particular month's sale in the month of sale, 70% in the month following the sale, and 20% in the second month following the sale. The company typically makes payments for its raw materials and labor the month following the one in which those costs are incurred.

In addition to the raw materials and labor expenses, Fuzzy Toys also incurred these monthly expenses: (a) general and administrative salaries of $25,000, (b) rent payment of $8,000, (c) depreciation expense of $20,000, and (d) miscellaneous expenses of $3,000. The company will be making a tax payment of $60,000 in July and a scheduled payment of $120,000 in September toward its facility expansion project.

The company has a cash balance of $100,000 at the end of June and will maintain a minimum cash balance of $80,000 a month for the upcoming quarter.

Using the information provided, prepare Fuzzy Toy's cash budget for the months of July, August, and September. Does the company need to secure a line of credit with its bank? If yes, how much does the company need to borrow from its bank during the upcoming quarter?

Session 4 Exercise 2 Solution: Preparing a Cash Budget

The top half of the next table represents the pro forma schedule of cash receipts and cash disbursements of Fuzzy Toys. The bottom half represents the company's cash budget. In this problem, Fuzzy Toys will need to secure a line of credit for September because it needs to borrow $9,000 that month in order to bring its cash balance to the target level of $80,000.

	May (Actual)	June (Actual)	July (Expected)	August (Expected)	September (Expected)
Sales	$ 120,000	$ 130,000	$ 220,000	$ 260,000	$ 300,000
Raw materials and labor costs	50,000	60,000	130,000	150,000	150,000
Cash receipts					
Collection from sales[1]					
10% during month of sale			$ 22,000	$ 26,000	$ 30,000
70% one month after sale			91,000	154,000	182,000
20% two months after sale			24,000	26,000	44,000
Total cash receipts			$ 137,000	$ 206,000	$ 256,000
Cash disbursements[2]					
Payments for raw materials and labor costs[3]					
One month after purchase			$ 60,000	$ 130,000	$ 150,000
General and administrative salaries			25,000	25,000	25,000
Rent payment			8,000	8,000	8,000
Miscellaneous expenses			3,000	3,000	3,000
Tax payment			60,000		
Plant expansion payment					120,000
Total cash disbursements			$ 156,000	$ 166,000	$ 306,000
Beginning cash balance			$ 100,000	$ 81,000	$ 121,000
Add: Cash receipts			137,000	206,000	256,000
Less: Cash disbursements			156,000	166,000	306,000
Available cash balance			$ 81,000	$ 121,000	$ 71,000
Target cash balance			$ 80,000	$ 80,000	$ 80,000
Cash excess (deficiency)[4]			$ 1,000	$ 41,000	$ (9,000)
Financing[5]					
Beginning loan balance			$ 0	$ 0	$ 0
Monthly borrowing			–	–	9,000
Monthly repayment			–	–	–
Ending loan balance			$ 0	$ 0	$ 9,000
Ending cash balance[6]		$ 100,000	$ 81,000	$ 121,000	$ 80,000

Table notes:

1. Cash collection in July comes from three sources (in this problem):

10% from July sales = 0.1 × $220,000 = $22,000
70% from June sales = 0.7 × $130,000 = $91,000
20% from May sales = 0.2 × $120,000 = $24,000

Cash collection in August comes from:

10% from August sales = 0.1 × $260,000 = $26,000
70% from July sales = 0.7 × $220,000 = $154,000
20% from June sales = 0.2 × $130,000 = $26,000

Cash collection in September comes from:

10% from September sales = 0.1 × $300,000 = $30,000
70% from August sales = 0.7 × $260,000 = $182,000
20% from July sales = 0.2 × $220,000 = $44,000

2. Depreciation expense is a noncash expense and is not included in total cash disbursement.
3. Cash payment in July for raw materials and labor costs = $60,000 (i.e., raw materials and labor costs incurred in June)

Cash payment in August for raw materials and labor costs
    = $130,000 (i.e., raw materials and labor costs incurred in July)
Cash payment in September for raw materials and labor costs
    = $150,000 (i.e., raw materials and labor costs incurred in August)

4. Cash Excess (Deficiency) = Beginning Cash Balance + Total Cash Receipts − Total Cash Disbursements − Target Cash Balance
5. The financing section involves the determination of monthly borrowing and monthly repayment. This is influenced by the company's cash excess (or deficiency).
    *   *Cash excess.* A company will use this amount to pay off any outstanding short-term borrowing used to cover cash deficiency, or the company can choose to invest this in a short-term investment.
    *   *Cash deficiency.* A company will borrow this amount using short-term loans to bring the cash balance back to the target cash balance.

    *   In this problem, Fuzzy Toys has excess cash in July and August so no monthly borrowing is necessary. In addition, the company also does not have any outstanding loan balance so the excess cash will not be used to pay off any of the loans. However, the company is facing a cash deficiency of $9,000 in September; it will need to borrow $9,000 to bring its cash balance of $71,000 back to the target cash balance of $80,000.

The formula used to calculate the monthly ending loan balance is:

$$\text{Monthly Ending Loan Balance} = \text{Monthly Beginning Loan Balance} \\ + \text{Monthly Borrowing} \\ - \text{Monthly Repayment}$$

Rationale: Monthly borrowing will add to the outstanding loan balance, and monthly repayment will reduce the outstanding loan balance.

6. The formula used to calculate the ending cash balance is:

$$\text{Ending Cash Balance} = \text{Available Cash Balance} + \text{Monthly Borrowing} \\ - \text{Monthly Repayment}$$

The Association of
Accountants and
Financial Professionals
In Business

Session 4 Wrap-Up

Content covered in Session 4

- Section B, Topic 5: Annual Profit Plan and Supporting Schedules
- Exercise 1: Preparing Operating Budgets and Pro Forma Income Statement
- Exercise 2: Preparing a Cash Budget

Content to be covered in Session 5

- Section B, Topic 3: Forecasting Techniques
- Section B, Topic 4: Budgeting Methodologies

Session 5

The Association of
Accountants and
Financial Professionals
in Business

Wiley
CMAexcel Learning System
Exam Review 2017

Part 1: Financial Reporting, Planning, Performance, and Control

Session 5

Learning Outcome Statements (LOS) identifiers appear on the
slides as applicable to highlight where we address each LOS
within the material.

The Association of
Accountants and
Financial Professionals
in Business

Session 4 Recap

- Section B, Topic 5: Annual Profit Plan and Supporting Schedules
- Exercise 1: Preparing Operating Budgets and Pro Forma Income Statement
- Exercise 2: Preparing a Cash Budget

The Association of
Accountants and
Financial Professionals
in Business

Session 5 Overview

- Section B, Topic 3: Forecasting Techniques
- Section B, Topic 4: Budget Methodologies

The Association of
Accountants and
Financial Professionals
in Business

Topic 3: Forecasting Techniques

- Regression analysis
- Learning curve analysis
- Expected value

The Association of
Accountants and
Financial Professionals
in Business

Quantitative Methods

Quantitative methods help management deal with the uncertainty of forecasting the future to make better decisions:

- **Data analysis**—analyze a given set of date to find relationships and /or patterns
- **Model building**—create a mathematical model to establish the relationship between different factors
- **Decision theory**—looks at potential outcomes and likelihood of the outcomes to deal with uncertainty

The Association of
Accountants and
Financial Professionals
in Business

LOS 1.B.3.a.

Assumptions of Linear Regression

Linear regression assumes:

- A linear relationship between one dependent variable and one or more independent variables.
  - ‣ *Simple regression* assumes only one independent variable.
  - ‣ *Multiple regression* assumes two or more independent variables
- Past relationships between dependent and independent variables hold in the future.
- Linear relationships are valid over a relevant range

The Association of
Accountants and
Financial Professionals
in Business

LOS 1.B.3.a. and c.

Simple Linear Regression Analysis

- The following slides analyzes a simple linear regression using the following example:

- Build & Fix is a retailer trying to forecast sales. It believes that store sales depend on marketing costs.
  - ‣ *Dependent variable* is store sales
  - ‣ *Independent variable* is marketing costs

Data Analysis: Three Years of Sales and Marketing Costs

Quarter	Marketing Costs ($000)	Sales ($000)	Marketing Costs ($000)	Sales ($000)	Marketing Costs ($000)	Sales ($000)
	Year 1		Year 2		Year 3	
Q1	$50	$48,000	$100	$89,000	$40	$62,000
Q2	30	40,000	90	105,000	90	130,000
Q3	40	62,000	80	73,000	70	80,000
Q4	60	75,000	110	105,000	50	50,000

Linear Regression—Plot the Data on a Graph

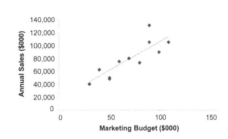

Data points are plotted and a line is drawn

The Association of
Accountants and
Financial Professionals
in Business

LOS 1.B.3.c.

Simple Regression Mathematical Formula

$$y = a + bX$$

y = dependent variable
a = y intercept; the value of y when X = 0
b = slope of the line (also called "regression coefficient")
X = value for the independent variable

The Association of
Accountants and
Financial Professionals
in Business

LOS 1.B.3.c.

Regression Values for Marketing Costs as Predictor of Sales

	Coefficients	T-Value	Standard Error
Intercept	18,444,809	1.48	12,460,201
Marketing costs	861	4.98	173

- T-value should be > 2 to indicate a strong relationship between the independent and dependent variables.

- Standard error measures dispersion around regression line to allow assessment of accuracy of estimates.

$$y = \$18,444,809 + \$861(X)$$

The Association of
Accountants and
Financial Professionals
in Business

LOS 1.B.3.c.

Simple Regression Calculation

Calculate the forecasted sales when marketing costs are budgeted to be $75,000

$$y = \$18,444,809 + \$861(X)$$

$$y = \$18,444,809 + \$861(\$75,000) = \$83,019,809 \text{ Forecasted Sales}$$

Based on ICMA question, used with permission

Part 1, Section B, Topic 3: Forecasting Techniques   12
Wiley CMAexcel Learning System, Part 1: Financial Reporting, Planning, Performance, and Control.
Copyright © 2017, Institute of Management Accountants. Published by John Wiley & Sons, Inc.

The Association of
Accountants and
Financial Professionals
in Business

LOS 1.B.3.c.

Regression Analysis: Three Benchmarks to Evaluate Reliability of Regression Equation

1. **Goodness of Fit:** a value between 0 and 1 is the degree of change in the dependent variable (y) due to changes in independent variable(s)(b). Also called R-squared or coefficient of determination.

2. **T-Value:** measures if an independent variable (b) has valid long-term relationship to the dependent variable. Should be > 2.

3. **Standard Error of the Estimate:** measures dispersion around the regression line

Part 1, Section B, Topic 3: Forecasting Techniques   13
Wiley CMAexcel Learning System, Part 1: Financial Reporting, Planning, Performance, and Control.
Copyright © 2017, Institute of Management Accountants. Published by John Wiley & Sons, Inc.

The Association of
Accountants and
Financial Professionals
in Business

LOS 1.B.3.c.

Question: Regression Analysis for Happy Pet Food

Using monthly information from the last three years, Happy Pet Food is able to estimate the relationship between its overhead cost and direct labor hours (DLH) using a simple regression model. The result is:

> **Overhead Cost = $25,000 + $10.32(DLH)**

Interpret the y-intercept and the slope coefficient.

Answer:

- The y-intercept of $25,000 represents the fixed cost portion of the overhead cost.

- The slope coefficient of $10.32 represents the variable cost per DLH.

Based on ICMA question, used with permission

Part 1, Section B, Topic 3: Forecasting Techniques   14
Wiley CMAexcel Learning System, Part 1: Financial Reporting, Planning, Performance, and Control.
Copyright © 2017, Institute of Management Accountants. Published by John Wiley & Sons, Inc.

The Association of
Accountants and
Financial Professionals
in Business

LOS 1.B.3.b.

Interpreting Coefficient of Determination of a Simple Linear Regression—Build & Fix

> **Coefficient of determination (R-squared): 0.7127**

Interpretation and implication of the coefficient of determination:

- R-squared of 0.7127 indicates that 71.27% of the variation in sales can be explained by changes in marketing costs.

- This means that 28.73% (100% – 71.27%) of the variation in sales is explained by other variables not included in the simple regression model.

- **Recommendation: A multiple regression model should be used**

Based on ICMA question, used with permission

Part 1, Section B, Topic 3: Forecasting Techniques   15
Wiley CMAexcel Learning System, Part 1: Financial Reporting, Planning, Performance, and Control.
Copyright © 2017, Institute of Management Accountants. Published by John Wiley & Sons, Inc.

LOS 1.B.3.b.

Multiple Linear Regression Model

- Build & Fix had 28.73% of sales explained by factors other than marketing costs
- Other factors include:
  - ▸ Economic conditions
  - ▸ Competitors' actions
  - ▸ Build & Fix's pricing strategy

LOS 1.B.3.b.

Multiple Linear Regression Model

$$y = a + b_1X_1 + b_2X_2 + b_3X_3 + \ldots b_nX_n$$

- The interpretation of R-squared, the T-value, and the standard error of the estimate is similar to the simple regression analysis.
- In addition, evaluation of correlation between the independent variables (X) is required
  - Correlation between two independent variables should be < 0.7
  - If > 0.7 eliminate one of the independent variables
- Multiple regressions require a computer program

The Association of
Accountants and
Financial Professionals
in Business

Regression Analysis: Advantage and Limitations

Advantage

- Gives management accountants an objective measure of the estimates.

Limitations

- Outliers can severely affect the regression results.

- A user must evaluate the reasonableness of the relationship between the dependent and independent variables.

- The value of X must fall within a relevant range.

The Association of
Accountants and
Financial Professionals
in Business

Learning Curve Analysis

- Systematic method estimating costs based on increased learning by an employee, group, or business

- Cumulative average-time learning model (Wright method) is the generally accepted method

- Measures increased efficiency due to learning

The Association of
Accountants and
Financial Professionals
in Business

LOS 1.B.3.e.

Cumulative Average-Time Learning Model

80% curve = learning rate of 0.80

Cum. # Of Widgets (X)	Cumulative Average Time Per Widget y (rate × previous y)	Cumulative Total Time ($c = X \times y$)	Individual Unit Time for xth Widget ($c - y$)
1	10 (value of y)	10 (10 × 1)	10
2†	8 (0.8 × 10)	16 (8 × 2)	6 (16 – 10)
4†	6.4 (0.8 × 8)	25.6 (6.4 × 4)	4.54*
8†	5.12 (0.8 × 6.4)	40.96 (5.12 × 8)	3.55*

*Calculated by a formula not shown here.
† Note: Widgets double in each row.

Part 1, Section B, Topic 3: Forecasting Techniques   20
Wiley CMAexcel Learning System, Part 1: Financial Reporting, Planning, Performance, and Control.
Copyright © 2017, Institute of Management Accountants. Published by John Wiley & Sons, Inc.

The Association of
Accountants and
Financial Professionals
in Business

LOS 1.B.3.e.

Question: Cumulative DLH for Reeves, Inc.

Reeves, Inc. has developed a complex new production process that requires workers with a high degree of technical skill. Management believes that current employees will improve as they become more familiar with the production process.

The production of the first unit requires 100 direct labor hours.

With a 70% learning curve, what are the cumulative direct labor hours required to produce a total of eight units?

a. 196 hours
b. 274 hours
c. 392 hours
d. 560 hours

Answer: **b.**

Units	Cumulative Average Time Per Unit	Cumulative Total Time
1	100	100 (100 × 1)
2	70 (0.70 × 100)	140 (70 × 2)
4	49 (0.70 × 70)	196 (49 × 4)
8	34.3 (0.70 × 49)	274.4 (34.3 × 8)

Based on ICMA question, used with permission

Part 1, Section B, Topic 3: Forecasting Techniques   21
Wiley CMAexcel Learning System, Part 1: Financial Reporting, Planning, Performance, and Control.
Copyright © 2017, Institute of Management Accountants. Published by John Wiley & Sons, Inc.

LOS 1.B.3.f.

Learning Curve Analysis: Advantages and Limitations

Advantages

- Can be used to make decisions such as setting prices. Firm may set price lower than initial cost based on assumption that costs will decline as learning increases.
- Learning affects quality and improves productivity.

Limitations

- Not effective or relevant with machine-intensive operations.
- Learning rate is assumed to be constant, but actual declines are not constant.
- Conclusions might be unreliable because observed changes in productivity actually may be due to other factors.

LOS 1.B.3.g.

Expected Value (EV)

- Deals with future uncertainty
- Uses probability distribution of a likely set of outcomes
- Calculates the weighted average of a set of possible outcomes
- Result is the forecast to be used

The Association of
Accountants and
Financial Professionals
in Business

LOS 1.B.3.g.

Expected Value (EV)

Expected value formula is:

$$EV = \Sigma\ S \times (P_x)$$

Where:
EV = expected value
Σ = sum of the variables that follow in the equation
S = amount associated with a specific outcome
P_x = probability associated with each expected outcome

The Association of
Accountants and
Financial Professionals
in Business

LOS 1.B.3.i.

Calculate the Expected Cash Flow for Hardware Haven Using Expected Value

Economic Condition	Cash Flow Forecast	Probability
Boom	$3,000	0.1
Normal	$2,000	0.8
Recession	$600	0.1

Expected Cash Flow = 0.1 ($3,000) + 0.8 ($2,000) + 0.1 ($600)
= $1,960

Based on ICMA question, used with permission

The Association of
Accountants and
Financial Professionals
in Business

Expected Value: Advantages and Limitations

Advantages

- Determines the weighted average outcome of an event when faced with uncertainty.
- Helps management decide if it should take on certain actions.

Limitations

- The calculation is only as good as the estimation of the potential outcome and probability of each scenario.
- Assumes the decision maker is risk neutral.
- May not be appropriate if decision maker is a risk taker or risk averse.

The Association of
Accountants and
Financial Professionals
in Business

Section B, Topic 4: Budget Methodologies

- Activity-based budgeting
- Zero-based budgeting
- Incremental budgeting
- Continuous (rolling) budgeting
- Other budgeting methodologies

The Association of
Accountants and
Financial Professionals
in Business

LOS 1.B.4.a., b., c., and d.

Budgeting Methodologies

- A company chooses a budget methodology that supports and reinforces its management approach. It depends on:
    - ‣ Type of business
    - ‣ Organizational structure
    - ‣ Complexity of operations
    - ‣ Management philosophy
- The annual/master budget preparation will be based on the methodologies used.

The Association of
Accountants and
Financial Professionals
in Business

LOS 1.B.4.a., b., c., and d.

Activity-Based Budgeting (ABB)

- Classifies cost based on activities instead of departments
- Activities are put into cost pools based on its cost driver
- Cost drivers can be
    - ‣ Volume-based (labor hours or square feet)
    - ‣ Activity-based unit (number of setups)
- Fixed costs in one or more pools
- Variable costs in multiple pools
- The cost pools should be evaluated for accuracy when a master budget is prepared.

LOS 1.B.4.a., b., c., and d.

Activity-Based Budgeting versus Traditional Budgeting

ABB	Traditional
Connects resource consumption with output	Focus on resource inputs by functional area (department)
Focus on value-added activities	Focus on historical/past budgets
Emphasis on teamwork, synchronized activity, and customer satisfaction	Emphasis on increasing management performance

LOS 1.B.4.a., b., c., and d.

Cost Determination Using ABB for Robin Manufacturing

	Subcomponent Machining	Final Assembly
Amount to produce in July	720,000 subcomponents	72,000 units
Subcomponents or units per lot	100 subcomponents/lot	100 units/lot
Number of lots to inspect	720,000/100 = 7,200 lots	72,000/100 = 720 lots
Inspection time per lot	0.2 hours/lot	0.3 hours/lot
Total inspection hour	7,200 x 0.2 =1,440 hours	720 x 0.3 = 216 hours

Calculate the amount of inspection labor costs if *subcomponent* inspection labor costs $12 per hour and the *final assembly* inspection costs $15 per hour.

$$1{,}440 \text{ hours} \times \$12 = \$17{,}280$$

$$216 \text{ hours} \times \$15 = \underline{\$\ 3{,}240}$$

$$\text{Total inspection labor costs} = \$20{,}520$$

Based on ICMA question, used with permission

The Association of
Accountants and
Financial Professionals
in Business

LOS 1.B.4.d.

Activity-Based Budgeting (ABB)

- Appropriate for businesses with products having varying complexity or other factors such as setups
- Key advantage is greater precision in determining costs
- Disadvantage is the cost of the ABB and ABC systems
- The cost savings from better planning must outweigh the cost of designing and maintaining the ABB and ABC systems

The Association of
Accountants and
Financial Professionals
in Business

LOS 1.B.4.a., b., c., and d.

Zero-Based Budgeting

- Strength is that it forces a review of each and every expense item in a budget
- Motivates managers to identify and remove items that the costs exceed the benefits
- Useful when new managers are hired

LOS 1.B.4.a., b., c., and d.

Zero-Based Budgeting

- Steps in developing a zero-based budget:
  - ▸ Each department manager ranks all department activities from most to least important. Then assign cost to each.
  - ▸ Upper management review the list and cuts items that lack justification or are less critical
  - ▸ Only activities approved are included in the budget
  - ▸ The zero-based budget becomes the basis for the master budget

LOS 1.B.4.d.

Zero-Based Budgeting

Advantages	Disadvantages
Focuses on every line item	Manager may include budget slack in revenues and/or expenses
More accurate costs	Process is time consuming and expensive
	Ignores lessons learned from prior years

LOS 1.B.4.a., b., c., and d.

Incremental Budgeting

- Starts with the prior year's budget or actual
- Makes changes to determine the future year's budget
- The changes can be increases or decreases to the dollar amounts
- Is the *opposite* of zero-based budgeting

LOS 1.B.4. f. and g.

Incremental Budgeting

- Assume an increase in sales and expenses of 10%

	Prior Year Actual	Increase of 10%	Future Year Budget
Sales	$1,500,000	× 1.10	$1,650,000
Expenses	1,200,000	× 1.10	1,320,000
Net Income	$300,000		$330,000

The Association of
Accountants and
Financial Professionals
in Business

LOS 1.B.4.d.

Incremental Budgeting

Advantages	Disadvantages
Simple to use	Manager may include budget slack in revenues and/or expenses
Less time consuming	Budgets tend to only *increase* over time

The Association of
Accountants and
Financial Professionals
in Business

LOS 1.B.4.a., b., c., and d.

Continuous (Rolling) Budgeting

- Adds a new period onto the budget at the end of each period so there are always the same periods planned for the future
- For example:
    - Assume a twelve-month budget that runs from January through December
    - When January ends, the following January is added after December
- Stays up-to-date with the operating environment
- Becomes the basis for the master budget

The Association of
Accountants and
Financial Professionals
in Business

LOS 1.B.4.d.

Continuous (Rolling) Budgeting

Advantages	Disadvantages
More relevant than a budget prepared once a year	May need to have a budget coordinator *or* the opportunity cost of having managers use part of each month working on the next month's budget
Reflects current events and changes in estimates	
Breaks down a large process into manageable steps	
Promotes a longer-term view of the firm	

Part 1, Section B, Topic 4: Budget Methodologies   40
Wiley CMAexcel Learning System, Part 1: Financial Reporting, Planning, Performance, and Control.
Copyright © 2017, Institute of Management Accountants. Published by John Wiley & Sons, Inc.

The Association of
Accountants and
Financial Professionals
in Business

LOS 1.B.4.e.

Question: Continuous Budgets

Which of the following is true of a continuous (rolling) budget:

a. Works best for a company that can reliably forecast its sales revenue and expenses.

b. Presents the plan for a range of activity so the plan can be adjusted for changes in activity.

c. Is one of the budgets that is part of a long-range strategic plan, unchanged unless the strategy of the company changes.

d. Presents the plan for only one level of activity and does not adjust to changes in the level of activity.

e. Is a plan that is revised monthly or quarterly, dropping one period and adding another.

Answer: **e.**

A continuous budget adds a new period on the end of the budget, at the end of each period, so there are always several periods planned for the future. The budgets remain up to date with the operating environment.

*Based on ICMA
question, used
with permission*

Part 1, Section B, Topic 4: Budget Methodologies   41
Wiley CMAexcel Learning System, Part 1: Financial Reporting, Planning, Performance, and Control.
Copyright © 2017, Institute of Management Accountants. Published by John Wiley & Sons, Inc.

Other Budget Methodologies

- **Project budgeting.** Focuses on a project within an organization.
- **Flexible budgeting.** Performance/control mechanism.

LOS 1.B.4.a., b., c., and d.

Project Budgeting

- Used when a project is completely separate from other elements of a company
- Examples include:
    - Motion picture—crew and costs related only to that movie
    - Road project
    - Major capital asset

LOS 1.B.4.a., b., c., and d.

Project Budgeting (cont.)

- Includes allocations for variable and fixed overhead
- Reports the total cost of the project
- Developed using the same techniques as used for the master budget
- Time frame is the duration of the project. A multi-year project would be broken down by year

LOS 1.B.4.d.

Project Budgeting (cont.)

Advantages	Disadvantages
Includes all the project's costs	Limitation occurs when projects use resources and staff that are not solely dedicated to the project
Works well for both large and small projects	Affected individuals may end up reporting to two or more supervisors
Project management software available to develop and track the project budget	
Promotes a longer-term view of the firm	

LOS 1.B.4.a., b., c., and d.

Flexible Budgeting

- Control mechanism that evaluates managers' performance by comparing actual revenues and expenses to budgeted amounts for the *actual level* of activity

- Only variable cost budgets are adjusted, fixed cost budgets remain the same

LOS 1.B.4.f.

Flexible Budgeting Example for Direct Labor

	Actual	Flexible Budget	Actual – Flexible	Original Budget	Actual – Original
Production	68,000	68,000	0	72,000	4,000F
DLH per unit	× 0.5	× 0.5		× 0.5	
Total DLH	34,000	34,000	0	36,000	2,000F
Hourly rate	$15.50	$15.00	$0.50U	$15.00	$0.50U
Total DL Costs	$527,000	$510,000	**$17,000U**	$540,000	**$13,000F**

It appears that the direct labor costs are favorable by $13,000. In reality the direct labor costs are unfavorable by $17,000 due to an increase in the hourly rate of $0.50!

The Association of Accountants and Financial Professionals in Business

LOS 1.B.4.e.

Question: Budget Methodologies

In which method of budgeting must the cost of each program be justified, starting with the one most vital to the company?

a. Continuous budgeting
b. Flexible budgeting
c. Incremental budgeting
d. Zero-based budgeting

Answer: **d**.

Zero-based budgets, as the name implies, start with zero dollars allocated.

Based on ICMA question, used with permission

Part 1, Section B, Topic 4: Budget Methodologies 48
Wiley CMAexcel Learning System, Part 1: Financial Reporting, Planning, Performance, and Control.
Copyright © 2017, Institute of Management Accountants. Published by John Wiley & Sons, Inc.

The Association of Accountants and Financial Professionals in Business

Session 5 Wrap-Up

Content covered in Session 5

• Section B, Topic 3: Forecasting Techniques
• Section B, Topic 4: Budget Methodologies

Content to be covered in Session 6

• Section B, Topic 6: Top-Level Planning and Analysis
• Session 6 Exercise: Preparing Pro Forma Financial Statements, Determining External Funding Needed, and Performing Sensitivity Analysis
• Section B Exam Practice Questions

Part 1, Financial Reporting, Planning, Performance, and Control 49
Wiley CMAexcel Learning System, Part 1: Financial Reporting, Planning, Performance, and Control.
Copyright © 2017, Institute of Management Accountants. Published by John Wiley & Sons, Inc.

Session 6

The Association of
Accountants and
Financial Professionals
in Business

Wiley
CMAexcel Learning System
Exam Review 2017

Part 1: Financial Reporting, Planning, Performance, and Control

Session 6

Learning Outcome Statements (LOS) identifiers appear on the
slides as applicable to highlight where we address each LOS
within the material.

The Association of
Accountants and
Financial Professionals
in Business

Session 5 Recap

- Section B, Topic 3: Forecasting Techniques
- Section B, Topic 4: Budget Methodologies

The Association of
Accountants and
Financial Professionals
in Business

Session 6 Overview

- Section B, Topic 6: Top-Level Planning and Analysis
- Session 6 Exercise: Preparing Pro Forma Financial Statements, Determining External Funding Needed, and Performing Sensitivity Analysis
- Section B Exam Practice Questions

The Association of
Accountants and
Financial Professionals
in Business

Topic 6: Top-Level Planning and Analysis

- Estimating funding needs
- Assessing anticipated performance
- Performing what-if analysis

The Association of
Accountants and
Financial Professionals
in Business

LOS 1.B.6.a.

The Purpose of the Pro Forma Financial Statements

They are key elements to help a company plan for the future

- Based on the statements a company can:
  - ▸ Determine if predetermined targets are met
  - ▸ Estimate if external funding is needed
  - ▸ Perform sensitivity analysis

The Association of
Accountants and
Financial Professionals
in Business

LOS 1.B.6.a.

The Pro Forma Financial Statements

- **Pro Forma Income Statement**
    - ▸ Use to determine dividends and retained earnings
    - ▸ Use to determine internal funding available
- **Pro Forma Balance Sheet**
    - ▸ Use to determine if external funding is needed
- **Pro Forma Statement of Cash Flows**
- Statements will be *recalculated* based on what-if scenarios

The Association of
Accountants and
Financial Professionals
in Business

LOS 1.B.6.a.

Estimating Funding Needs

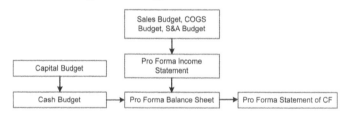

Step 1. Use pro forma income statement to determine internal funding generated.

Step 2. Use pro forma balance sheet to determine external funding needed.

Step 3. Use pro forma statements to prepare pro forma statement of cash flow (CF).

The Association of
Accountants and
Financial Professionals
in Business

LOS 1.B.6.c.

Preparation of Pro Forma Statements

Process should produce a plan that:

- ▸ Is attainable

- ▸ If achieved, will be viewed as acceptable results

- ▸ Is financially viable

The Association of
Accountants and
Financial Professionals
in Business

LOS 1.B.6.e.

Factors to Consider for Medium- and Long-Term Cash Forecasts

- • Internally generated funding
- • External funding needs
- • Timing of capital expenditures
- • Changing economic environment
- • Timing of fixed cash payments

LOS 1.B.6.a.

Preparation of Pro Forma Statements

Statements support three major functions:

1. Assess if anticipated performance is in line with targets

2. Anticipate funding needed to achieve forecasted sales growth

3. Estimate effects of changes in assumptions by performing sensitivity analysis

LOS 1.B.6.b.

Creating Pro Forma Statements Using the Percentage-of-Sales Method

- Simple approach to create the pro forma statements

- Ties many line items on the statements to future sales revenue

- Assumes the relationships between sales revenue and the income statement and balance sheet items remain constant

  - The **income statement** items: COGS and S&A

  - The **balance sheet** items: current assets, net fixed assets, accounts payable, and accruals

- Assumes **financing activities** do not grow proportionately with sales: notes payable, long-term debt, and owners' equity

The Association of
Accountants and
Financial Professionals
in Business

LOS 1.B.6.b.

Percentage of Sale Method Example for Memory Lane, Inc.

The following relationships are based on historical financial statements:

- ▸ Projected sales for coming year: $200,000

- ▸ COGS: 80% of sales

- ▸ S&A expenses: 10% of sales

- ▸ Interest expense: $5,000

- ▸ Tax rate: 35%

- ▸ Dividends: 40% of earnings

Part 1, Section B, Topic 6: Top-Level Planning and Analysis   12
Wiley CMAexcel Learning System, Part 1: Financial Reporting, Planning, Performance, and Control.
Copyright © 2017, Institute of Management Accountants. Published by John Wiley & Sons, Inc.

The Association of
Accountants and
Financial Professionals
in Business

LOS 1.B.6.b.

Projecting a Pro Forma Income Statement

- Dividends:
  $3,900 (= 40% of NI)
- Change in retained earnings:
  $5,850 (= 9,750 − 3,900)

Memory Lane Pro Forma Income Statement		
Sales	$200,000	100%
Less: Cost of goods sold	160,000	80%
Gross margin	40,000	20%
Less: S&A expenses	20,000	10%
EBIT	20,000	10%
Less: Interest (given)	5,000	
EBT	15,000	
Less: Taxes (35%)	5,250	
Net income	$9,750	

Part 1, Section B, Topic 6: Top-Level Planning and Analysis   13
Wiley CMAexcel Learning System, Part 1: Financial Reporting, Planning, Performance, and Control.
Copyright © 2017, Institute of Management Accountants. Published by John Wiley & Sons, Inc.

The Association of
Accountants and
Financial Professionals
in Business

LOS 1.B.6.d.

Memory Lane: Balance Sheet Assumptions

Assets/Liabilities	% of sales
Current assets	30%
Net fixed assets	40%
Current liabilities	25%

Liabilities/Owners' Equity	Amount
Notes payable	$ 5,000
Long-term debt	$40,000
Common stock	$20,000
Retained earnings	$ 4,150
Common stock outstanding	50,000 shares

The Association of
Accountants and
Financial Professionals
in Business

LOS 1.B.6.d.

Projecting Memory Lane's Pro Forma Balance Sheet

- **Projected retained earnings:** $10,000 (= $4,150 current retained earnings + $5,850 change in retained earnings)
- **External funding needed:** $15,000 (= $140,000 − $125,000)

Memory Lane Pro Forma Balance Sheet	
Current assets	$60,000
Net fixed assets	80,000
Total assets	**$140,000**
Current liabilities	$50,000
Notes payable	5,000
Long-term debt	40,000
Common stock	20,000
Retained earnings	10,000
Total liability and owner's equity	**$125,000**

LOS 1.B.6.d.

Projecting Memory Lane's Pro Forma Balance Sheet (cont.)

The company chooses to raise the $15,000 additional funding with long-term debt

Projected long-term debt
= $40,000 + $ 15,000
= $55,000

Memory Lane Pro Forma Balance Sheet	
Current assets	$60,000
Fixed assets	80,000
Total assets	**$140,000**
Current liabilities	$50,000
Notes payable	5,000
Long-term debt	55,000
Common stock	20,000
Retained earnings	10,000
Total liability and owner's equity	**$140,000**

LOS 1.B.6.c.

Financial Ratios as Indicators of Performance:

Current Ratio = CA/CL

ROA = NI/TA

ROE = NI/TE

Debt to TA Ratio = TL/TA

Basic EPS = NI/Weighted avg. common shares outstanding

Where:

CA = Current assets
CL = Current liabilities
NI = Net income

TA = Average total assets
TE = Average total equity
TL = Total liabilities

LOS 1.B.6.c.

Assessing Anticipated Performance

Selected Financial Ratios for Memory Lane		
Current Ratio	1.20:1	(= $60,000/$50,000)
ROA	6.96%	(= $9,750/$140,000)
ROE	32.50%	(= $9,750/$30,000)
Debt to TA Ratio	78.57%	(= $110,000/$140,000)
Basic EPS	$0.20	(= $9,750/50,000 shares)

LOS 1.B.6.d.

Preparing a Pro Forma Statement of Cash Flows

- The following are needed to prepare this statement using the Indirect Method:
    - Pro forma income statement—net income
    - Pro forma and prior years' balance sheet
    - Additional information

The Association of
Accountants and
Financial Professionals
in Business

LOS 1.B.6.d.

Preparing a Pro Forma Statement of Cash Flows

Pro Forma Statement of Cash Flows	
Operating activities	Net Income
Adjust to arrive at net cash provided or (used) by **operating activities**	XXX
Net cash provided /(used) by **investing activities**	XXX
Net cash provided/(used) by **financing activities**	XXX
Net change in cash flow	XXX
Beginning cash	XXX
Ending cash per pro forma balance sheet	XXX

The Association of
Accountants and
Financial Professionals
in Business

LOS 1.B.6.b.

Performing What-If Analysis: Sensitivity Analysis

- Change one assumption and keep all others the same.
- Pro forma financial statements created based on changes.
- Analysis of key ratios and financial positions to determine effect of changes.

The Association of
Accountants and
Financial Professionals
in Business

LOS 1.B.6.b.

What-If Pro Forma Income Statements

Memory Lane Pro Forma Income Statements	COGS @ 75%	COGS @ 80%	COGS @ 85%
Sales	$200,000	$200,000	$200,000
Less: Cost of goods sold	150,000	160,000	170,000
Gross margin	50,000	40,000	30,000
Less: S&A expenses	20,000	20,000	20,000
EBIT	30,000	20,000	10,000
Less: Interest (given)	5,000	5,000	5,000
EBT	25,000	15,000	5,000
Less: Taxes (35%)	8,750	5,250	1,750
Net income	$16,250	$9,750	$3,250
Dividends @40%	$6,500	$3,900	$1,300

Wiley CMAexcel Learning System, Part 1: Financial Reporting, Planning, Performance, and Control.
Copyright © 2017, Institute of Management Accountants. Published by John Wiley & Sons, Inc.

The Association of
Accountants and
Financial Professionals
in Business

LOS 1.B.6.d and f.

What-If Pro Forma Balance Sheets

Memory Lane Pro Forma Balance Sheets			
COGS	@ 75%	@ 80%	@ 85%
Current assets	$60,000	$60,000	$60,000
Net Fixed assets	80,000	80,000	80,000
Total assets	**$140,000**	**$140,000**	**$140,000**
Current liabilities	$50,000	$50,000	$50,000
Notes payable	5,000	5,000	5,000
Long-term debt	40,000	40,000	40,000
Common stock	20,000	20,000	20,000
Retained earnings	13,900	10,000	6,100
Total liability and owner's equity	**$128,900**	**$125,000**	**$121,100**
Addition to Long-term Debt	**$11,100**	**$15,000**	**$18,900**

Wiley CMAexcel Learning System, Part 1: Financial Reporting, Planning, Performance, and Control.
Copyright © 2017, Institute of Management Accountants. Published by John Wiley & Sons, Inc.

LOS 1.B.6.c.

Performing What-If Analysis: Memory Lane

Sensitivity analysis

- The impact on the financial ratios and external funding needed due to the change in COGS %
- Impact of changes to other variables?

Selected Financial Ratios for Memory Lane			
COGS	75%	80%	85%
Current ratio	1.20:1	1.20:1	1.20:1
ROA	11.61%	6.96%	2.32%
ROE	47.94%	32.50%	12.45%
Debt ratio	75.79%	78.57%	81.36%
EPS	$0.30	$0.20	$0.07
Funding Needed	$11,100	$15,000	$18,900

Session 6 Exercise

Preparing Pro Forma Financial Statements, Determining External Funding Needed, and Performing Sensitivity Analysis

Section B, Topic 6: Top-Level Planning and Analysis

Session 6 Exercise: Preparing Pro Forma Financial Statements, Determining External Funding Needed, and Performing Sensitivity Analysis

Section B, Topic 6: Top-Level Planning and Analysis

Wendy Peyton, the owner of Elegant Home Design, expects a 15% boost in the company's revenue in the upcoming year. She needs to know if she must seek out any external funding to support the anticipated growth. The next tables present Elegant Home Design's current income statement and balance sheet.

Elegant Home Design
Current-Year Income Statement

	Current Year
Sales	$1,500,000
COGS	1,050,000
Gross Margin	450,000
S&A Expenses	90,000
Earnings Before Income and Taxes (Operating Income)	360,000
Interest	33,000
Earnings Before Taxes	327,000
Taxes (30%)	98,100
Net Income	$ 228,900

Elegant Home Design
Current-Year Balance Sheet

	Current Year
Assets	
Cash and equivalents	$ 600,000
Receivables	225,000
Inventories	150,000
Total current assets	975,000
Net fixed assets	375,000
Total assets	$ 1,350,000
Liabilities and equity	
Accounts payable	$ 180,000
Accruals	90,000
Notes payable	100,000
Total current liabilities	370,000
Long-term debt	250,000
Total liabilities	620,000
Common stocks	400,000
Retained earnings	330,000
Total equity	730,000
Total liabilities and equity	$ 1,350,000

Peyton decides to use the percentage-of-sale method to project the company's income statement and balance sheet in order to determine if any external funding is needed for the upcoming year. She assumes the relationship between sales and the following items in the current year will continue to hold in the coming year:

COGS

S&A expenses

Cash and equivalent

Accounts receivable

Inventories

Net fixed assets

Accounts payable

Accruals

Peyton plans to maintain the company's current dividend policy of paying out half of its earnings as dividends. In addition, the company is paying 8% interest on notes payable and 10% interest on long-term debt.

a. Prepare Elegant Home Design's pro forma income statement and balance sheet based on a 15% revenue growth (assuming no additional external funding).
b. Determine the amount of external funding needed (if any) to support the projected 15% revenue growth.
c. Determine the amount of external funding needed if the projected revenue growth is (i) 10% and (ii) 20%.

Session 6 Exercise Solution: Preparing Pro Forma Financial Statements, Determining External Funding Needed, and Performing Sensitivity Analysis

In order to prepare the company's pro forma income statement and balance sheet, we need to first determine the relationship between sales and COGS, S&A, cash, receivables, inventories, net fixed assets, payables, and accruals from the current year's financial statements.

Using the information provided in the financial statements, we can express each of the items as a ratio (or percentage) of sales as shown:

COGS	1,050,000/1,500,000	=	0.70
S&A	90,000/1,500,000	=	0.06
Cash	600,000/1,500,000	=	0.40
Receivables	225,000/1,500,000	=	0.15
Inventories	150,000/1,500,000	=	0.10
Net fixed assets	375,000/1,500,000	=	0.25
Payables	180,000/1,500,000	=	0.12
Accruals	90,000/1,500,000	=	0.06

These ratios will now be used to prepare the coming year's pro forma income statement and balance sheet for a projected 15% revenue growth or a projected $1,725,000 revenue (= $1,500,000 × 1.15).

First we prepare Elegant Home Design's pro forma income statement. Given projected sales revenue of $1,725,000:

Elegant Home Design
Coming-Year Pro Forma Income Statement

	Coming Year
Sales	$1,725,000
COGS*	$1,207,500
Gross Margin	$ 517,500
S&A Expenses[†]	$ 103,500
EBIT (Operating Income)	$ 414,000
Interest[‡]	$ 33,000
EBT	$ 381,000
Taxes (30%)	$ 114,300
Net Income	$ 266,700

* COGS = $1,725,000 × 0.70 = $1,207,500
[†] S&A = $1,725,000 × 0.06 = $103,500
[‡] Interest expense is calculated based on the outstanding debt at the beginning of the upcoming year (i.e., at the end of the current year). Interest expense = $100,000 × 0.08 (notes payable) + $250,000 × 0.10 (long-term debt) = $33,000

With a projected net income of $266,700, the company will pay out $133,350 as dividend (per the current dividend policy of paying half the earnings as dividends) and retain $133,350. This $133,350 of retained earnings will now be added to the (cumulative) retained earnings in the pro forma balance sheet, which is prepared next.

The pro forma balance sheet will help a company determine if it requires any external funding to support its projected revenue growth. In order to do so, the pro forma balance sheet initially is created by holding all external funding sources (i.e., notes payable, long-term debt, and common stock for Elegant Home Design) at the same level as the current year. The company's pro forma balance sheet with no additional external funding is:

Elegant Home Design
Coming-Year Pro Forma Balance Sheet

	Coming Year
Assets	
Cash and equivalents[a]	$ 690,000
Receivables[b]	258,750
Inventories[c]	172,500
Total current assets	1,121,250
Net fixed assets[d]	431,250
Total assets	$ 1,552,500
Liabilities and equity	
Accounts payable[e]	$ 207,000
Accruals[f]	103,500
Notes payable	100,000
Total current liabilities	410,500
Long-term debt	250,000
Total liabilities	660,500
Common stocks	400,000
Retained earnings[g]	463,350
Total equity	863,350
Total liabilities and equity	$1,523,850

[a] Cash = $1,725,000 × 0.40 = $690,000
[b] Receivables = $1,725,000 × 0.15 = $258,750
[c] Inventories = $1,725,000 × 0.10 = $172,500
[d] Net fixed assets = $1,725,000 × 0.25 = $431,250
[e] Payables = $1,725,000 × 0.12 = $207,000
[f] Accruals = $1,725,000 × 0.06 = $103,500
[g] Retained earnings = $133,350 (projected retained earnings generated from pro forma income statement) + $330,000 (retained earnings from current year's balance sheet) = $463,350

a. Elegant Home Design's pro forma balance sheet (with no additional external funding) indicates that the company needs $1,552,500 of assets to support the 15% projected revenue growth. However, the company will have only $1,523,850 of liabilities and equity in the coming year, which represents a shortfall of $28,650 (= $1,552,500 − $1,523,850). This means that Peyton will need to seek out an additional $28,650 of external funding to support the projected revenue growth.

b. Using the same procedure as in (a), we can prepare Elegant Home Design's pro forma income statement and balance sheet for:

(i) A projected 10% revenue growth
(ii) A projected 20% revenue growth

Remember that the ratios calculated in (a) will remain the same since they are calculated using the current year's information, not the coming year's information. The pro forma financial statements for the two different projected growth rates are presented in the next tables.

Elegant Home Design
Coming-Year Pro Forma Income Statement

	Growth = 10%	Growth = 20%
Sales	$ 1,650,000	$ 1,800,000
COGS	1,155,000	1,260,000
Gross margin	495,000	540,000
S&A expenses	99,000	108,000
EBIT (operating income)	396,000	432,000
Interest	33,000	33,000
EBT	363,000	399,000
Taxes (30%)	108,900	119,700
Net income	$ 254,100	$ 279,300

Elegant Home Design
Coming-Year Pro Forma Balance Sheet

	Growth = 10%	Growth = 20%
Assets		
Cash and equivalents	$ 660,000	$ 720,000
Receivables	247,500	270,000
Inventories	165,000	180,000
Total current assets	1,072,500	1,170,000
Net fixed assets	412,500	450,000
Total assets	$ 1,485,000	$ 1,620,000
Liabilities and equity		
Accounts payable	$ 198,000	$ 216,000
Accruals	99,000	108,000
Notes payable	100,000	100,000
Total current liabilities	397,000	424,000
Long-term debt	250,000	250,000
Total liabilities	647,000	674,000
Common stocks	400,000	400,000
Retained earnings	457,050	469,650
Total equity	857,050	869,650
Total liabilities and equity	$1,504,050	$ 1,543,650

(i) Projected 10% revenue growth

Total assets needed to support growth is $1,485,000, and the available liabilities and equities is $1,504,050. This represents an excess (rather than a shortfall) of $19,050. This means Elegant Home Design has an excess funding of $19,050, and no additional external funding is required.

(ii) Projected 20% revenue growth

Total asset needed to support growth is $1,620,000, and the available liabilities and equities is $1,543,650. This represents a shortfall of $76,350 and means Elegant Home Design will need to seek out $76,350 of additional external funding.

The Association of
Accountants and
Financial Professionals
in Business

Section B Conclusion

- Section B content represents 30% of the multiple-choice questions on the Part 1 exam.
- This content also may be tested in essay question format.

To reinforce your learning:

- Study all the LOS for the section.
- Study all material for Section B of the WCMALS self-study book.
- Use the practice test questions in the WCMALS self-study book.
- Take the Section B practice test in the Online Test Bank for a wider range of questions on all topics in the section.

The Association of
Accountants and
Financial Professionals
in Business

Section B Exam Practice Questions

We will now review Practice Questions from the WCMALS self-study book, Section B.

- Questions identified by topic
- Not all topics covered in this selection
- More questions on each topic and full section test included in Online Test Bank

The Association of
Accountants and
Financial Professionals
in Business

Session 6 Wrap-Up

Content covered in Session 6

- Section B, Topic 6: Top-Level Planning and Analysis
- Session 6 Exercise: Preparing Pro Forma Financial Statements, Determining External Funding Needed, and Performing Sensitivity Analysis
- Section B Exam Practice Questions

Content to be covered in Session 7

- Section C, Topic 1: Cost and Variance Measures
- Exercise: Current Variance

Session 7

The Association of
Accountants and
Financial Professionals
in Business

Wiley CMAexcel Learning System Exam Review 2017

Part 1: Financial Reporting, Planning, Performance, and Control

Session 7

Learning Outcome Statements (LOS) identifiers appear on the slides as applicable to highlight where we address each LOS within the material.

1

The Association of
Accountants and
Financial Professionals
in Business

Session 6 Recap

- Section B, Topic 6: Top-Level Planning and Analysis
- Session 6 Exercise: Preparing Pro Forma Financial Statements, Determining External Funding Needed, and Performing Sensitivitiy Analysis
- Section B Exam Practice Questions

The Association of
Accountants and
Financial Professionals
in Business

Session 7 Overview

- Section C, Topic 1: Cost and Variance Measures
- Exercise: Current Variance

The Association of
Accountants and
Financial Professionals
in Business

Section C: Performance Management

- Topic 1: Cost and Variance Measures
- Topic 2: Responsibility Centers and Reporting Segments
- Topic 3: Performance Measures

The Association of
Accountants and
Financial Professionals
in Business

Topic 1: Cost and Variance Measures

- Comparison of actual to planned results
- Use of flexible budgets to analyze performance
- Management by exception using variance analysis
- Use of standard cost systems
- Analysis of variation from standard cost expectation

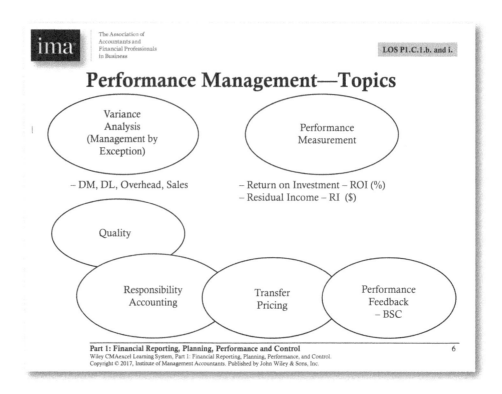

Control Step in Management Cycle Means Feedback

- Essential components are:
  - Profit plan
  - Standards
  - Feedback
- Differences between actual and plan/standard are **variances** and they may be favorable (F) or unfavorable (U)

LOS P1.C.1.j.

Purposes of a Standard Cost System

- Measure performance currently and point to sources of problems
- Value inventory (conveniently) at standard cost
- Measure marketing performance on CM (difference between selling price and standard variable manufacturing cost)

Product Cost Sheet for Tennis Racquet

Input	Units of Input /Unit of Prod.		Cost/Unit of input	Cost/Unit of Prod.
Titanium	1.000	lb./unit	$60.00/lb	$60.00/unit
Direct Labor	2.000	DLH/unit	8.00/DLH	16.00
Variable Overhead	1.200	mach-hr./unit	10.00/mach-hr	12.00
Variable Cost				$88.00/unit
Fixed Overhead				10.00/unit
Total Cost				$98.00/unit

The Association of
Accountants and
Financial Professionals
in Business

LOS P1.C.1.c.

Bounce Income Statement for 2015

	Plan	Actual	Variance	
Unit Sales	30000	24000	6000	U
Revenue	3,600,000	3,000,000	600,000	U
Variable Cost of Goods Sold	2,640,000	2,280,240	359,760	F
Contribution Margin	960,000	719,760	240,240	U
Fixed Mfg. Cost	300,000	294,000	6,000	F
Fixed SG&A Exp.	390,000	390,000	0	
Operating Income	270,000	35,760	234,240	U

The Association of
Accountants and
Financial Professionals
In Business

LOS P1.C.1.e., f., and g.

Bounce Income Statement for 2015, Including Flexible Budget

	Static Budget (1)	Flexible Budget (2)	Actual (3)	Flex. Bud. Variance (4)=(2)-(3)		Overall Variance (5)=(1)-(3)	
Unit Sales	30,000	24,000	24,000	0		6,000	U
Revenue	$3,600,000	$2,880,000	$3,000,000	$120,000	F	$600,000	U
Variable Cost of Goods Sold	2,640,000	2,112,000	2,280,240	168,240	U	359,760	F
Contribution Margin	$960,000	$768,000	$719,760	$48,240	U	$240,240	U
Fixed Mfg. Cost	300,000	300,000	294,000	6,000	F	6,000	F
Fixed SG&A Exp.	390,000	390,000	390,000	0		0	
Operating Income	$270,000	$78,000	$35,760	$42,240	U	$234,240	U

The Bounce Facts

Actual direct labor hours used to produce 24,000 units were 52,800, costing $475,200 (average of $9.00/hour).

25,000 lb. of titanium were purchased for $1,839,840 (average of $73.5936/lb.) and 19,200 lb. were used in production, increasing inventory by 5,800 lb.

$313,200 was spent on variable overhead and 28,000 machine hours were used.

$294,000 was spent on fixed overhead.

LOS P1.C.1.k. and l.

Prime Costs (Direct Labor) Variances

$AH \times (AR - SR)$ 2 types $SR \times (AH - SH)$

P R I C E

Q U A N T I T Y

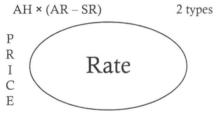

Rate

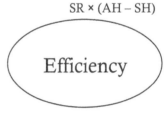

Efficiency

As a result of paying more or less than expected for prime costs items.

Purchase Mgr.

As a result of usage not in line with expected norms.

Production Mgr.

The Association of
Accountants and
Financial Professionals
in Business

LOS P1.C.1.k. and l.

Illustration: Derivation of Direct Labor Variances

Here's a set of symbols and their meanings

AH = Actual Direct Labor Hours, AR = Actual Direct Labor Rate

Q = Actual Quantity of Units Produced

SH/U = Standard Hours/Unit, SR = Standard Rate/Unit

SH = Standard Hours that should have been used to produce Q

DL variances = Actual DL cost – Standard DL cost that can be applied into inventory

$= (AH \times AR) – (Q \times SH/U \times SR)$. Next, subtract and add $AH \times SR$ to right side

$= AH \times AR – AH \times SR + AH \times SR – Q \times SR \times SH/U$. Next, regroup and factor

$= AH \times (AR – SR) + SR \times (AH – Q \times SH/U)$. Next, substitute SH for $Q \times SH/U$

$= [AH \times (AR – SR)] + [SR \times (AH – SH)]$

Finally, call the first term "DL rate variance" and the second term "DL efficiency variance"

DL rate variance $= [AH \times (AR – SR)]$

DL efficiency variance $= [SR \times (AH – SH)]$

The Association of
Accountants and
Financial Professionals
in Business

LOS P1.C.1.k. and l.

Bounce Direct Labor Variances

Bounce actually spent $475,200 for 52,800 direct labor hours (average = $9.00 per hour).

DL rate variance = AH(AR – SR)

$= 52800 \text{ hr.} \times (\$9.00/\text{hr.} – \$8.00/\text{hr.})$

$= 52800 \text{ hr.} \times \$1.00/\text{hr.}) = \$52,800 \text{ U}$

DL efficiency variance = SR(AH – SH)

$= \$8.00/\text{hr.} (52800 \text{ hr.} – 48000 \text{ hr.})$

$= \$8.00/\text{hr.} \times 4800 \text{ hr.} = \$38400 \text{ U}$

Prime Costs (Direct Materials) Variances

LOS P1.C.1.k. and l.

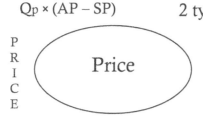

$Q_P \times (AP - SP)$ 2 types $SP \times (AQ_u - SQ)$

P R I C E

Price   Efficiency

Q U A N T I T Y

As a result of paying more or less than expected for Prime Costs items

As a result of usage not in line with expected norms

Purchase Mgr.   Production Mgr.

LOS P1.C.1.k. and l.

Bounce Direct Material Variances Defined

DM price variance = $Q_P (AP - SP)$

DM efficiency variance = $SP (AQ_U - SQ)$

LOS P1.C.1.k. and l.

Bounce DM Variances

25,000 lb. of titanium were purchased for $1,839,840 (average of $73.5936/lb.) and 19,200 lb. were used in production, increasing inventory by 5,800 lb.

DM price variance = Q_P (AP − SP)

$$= 25{,}000 \text{ lb.} \times (\$73.5936/\text{lb.} - \$60.00/\text{lb.})$$

$$= 25{,}000 \text{ lb.} \times \$13.5936/\text{lb.} = \$339{,}840 \text{ U}$$

DM efficiency variance = SP (AQ_U − SQ)

$$= \$60.00/\text{lb.} \times (19{,}200 \text{ lb.} - 24{,}000 \text{ lb.})$$

$$= \$60.00/\text{lb.} \times (- 4{,}800 \text{ lb.}) = \$288{,}000 \text{ F}$$

LOS P1.C.1.m.

Variable OHD Variances

AH × (AR − SR)   2 types   SR × (AH − SH)

P U
R S
I A   Spending*   Efficiency   S
C G   A
E E   G
                                                              E

U
S

USAGE

As a result of paying more or less than expected for OHD items and from excessive usage of OHD items

Controlled by managing the OHD activity cost driver

VOH Rate

* Similar to price variance for the Prime Costs DL and DM

The Association of
Accountants and
Financial Professionals
in Business

LOS P1.C.1.m.

Variable Overhead Variances Defined

VOH Spending Variance = AH (AR – SR)

VOH Efficiency Variance = SR (AH – SH)

The Association of
Accountants and
Financial Professionals
in Business

LOS P1.C.1.m.

Bounce VOH Variances

$313,200 was spent on variable overhead and 28,000 machine hours were used.

VOH Spend. Variance = AH (AR – SR)

$$= 28{,}000 \text{ m.-hr.}(\$11.1857 - \$10.00)/\text{m-hr}$$

$$= 28{,}000 \text{ m.-hr.} \times \$1.1857/\text{m-hr.}$$

$$= \$33{,}200 \text{ U}$$

VOH Efficiency Variance = SR (AH – SH)

$$= \$10.00/\text{m-hr.} \ (28{,}000 - 28{,}800)\text{m-hr.}$$

$$= \$10/\text{m-hr.} \times -800 \text{ m-hr.} = \$8{,}000 \text{ F}$$

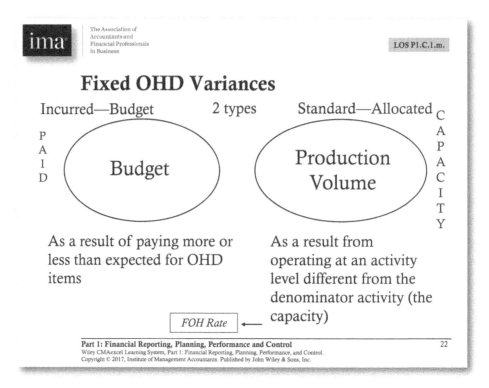

Part 1: Financial Reporting, Planning, Performance and Control
Wiley CMAexcel Learning System, Part 1: Financial Reporting, Planning, Performance, and Control.
Copyright © 2017, Institute of Management Accountants. Published by John Wiley & Sons, Inc.

22

The Association of
Accountants and
Financial Professionals
in Business

LOS P1.C.1.m.

Fixed Overhead Variances Defined

FOH Spending Variance = Actual Fixed Overhead – Budgeted Fixed Overhead

Production Volume Variance = Budgeted Fixed Overhead – Absorbed Fixed Overhead

Part 1: Financial Reporting, Planning, Performance and Control
Wiley CMAexcel Learning System, Part 1: Financial Reporting, Planning, Performance, and Control.
Copyright © 2017, Institute of Management Accountants. Published by John Wiley & Sons, Inc.

23

The Association of
Accountants and
Financial Professionals
in Business

LOS P1.C.1.m.

Bounce Fixed Overhead Variances

$294,000 was spent on fixed overhead

FOH Spending Variance = Actual Fixed Overhead – Budgeted
Fixed Overhead

$$= \$294,000 - \$300,000 = \$6,000 \text{ F}$$

Production Volume Variance = Budgeted Fixed Overhead –
Absorbed Fixed Overhead

$$= \$300,000 - (\$10/\text{unit} \times 24,000 \text{ units})$$

$$= \$300,000 - \$240,000 = \$60,000 \text{ U}$$

The Association of
Accountants and
Financial Professionals
in Business

LOS P1.C.1.m.

Denominator Activity Level—Capacity as Basis for the Predetemined Rate

3,000hrs

1,800hrs

1,500hrs

1,000hrs

Theoretical   Practical   Master-bgt   Normal

Supply-oriented   *Demand-oriented*

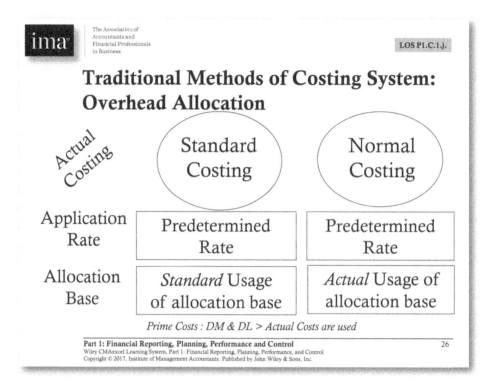

The Association of
Accountants and
Financial Professionals
in Business

LOS P1.C.1.j.

Traditional Methods of Costing System: Overhead Allocation

Actual Costing

Standard Costing

Normal Costing

	Standard Costing	Normal Costing
Application Rate	Predetermined Rate	Predetermined Rate
Allocation Base	*Standard* Usage of allocation base	*Actual* Usage of allocation base

Prime Costs : DM & DL > Actual Costs are used

The Association of
Accountants and
Financial Professionals
in Business

LOS P1.C.1.m.

Variances Analysis Example—Variable and Fixed Overhead

	Variable	Fixed
1. Actual Costs Incurred	11,900	6,000
2. Costs allocated to products	9,000	4,500
3. Flex budget: Budget input allowed for actual output produced × budget rate	9,000	5,000
4. Actual input × budget rate	10,000	5,000

Fill in the blanks: use F or U	Variable	Fixed
1. Spending (price)		
2. Efficiency		
3. Production-volume		
4. Flex budget		
5. Under/Over applied overhead		

The Association of
Accountants and
Financial Professionals
in Business

LOS P1.C.1.m.

Variance Analysis—Variable Overhead

	Variable	Fixed
1. Spending (price/usage)	1,900 U	
2. Efficiency	1,000 U	
3. Production-volume	Never	
4. Flex budget	2,900 U	
5. Under/Over applied overhead	2,900 U	

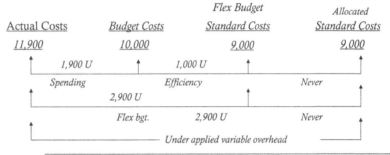

The Association of
Accountants and
Financial Professionals
in Business

LOS P1.C.1.m.

Variance Analysis—Fixed Overhead

	Variable	Fixed
1. Spending (price)		1,000 U
2. Efficiency		Never
3. Production-volume		500 U
4. Flex budget		1,000 U
5. Under/over applied overhead		1,500 U

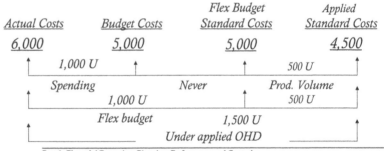

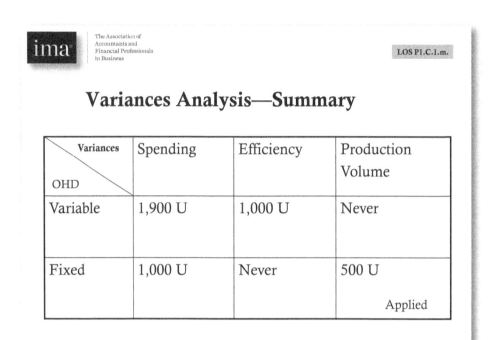

ima°
The Association of
Accountants and
Financial Professionals
in Business

LOS P1.C.1.m.

Variances Analysis—Summary

Variances OHD	Spending	Efficiency	Production Volume
Variable	1,900 U	1,000 U	Never
Fixed	1,000 U	Never	500 U Applied

ima°
The Association of
Accountants and
Financial Professionals
in Business

LOS P1.C.1.m.

Adjustment for Over/Under Applied Overhead

Actual costs incurred: 80
Overhead applied   :   50
Over (<u>under</u>) applied :   (30)

1. Immaterial: charge (under) applied to COGS (debit)
2. Material:

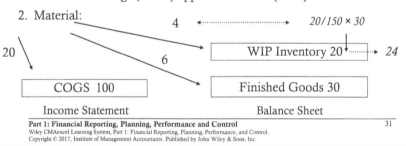

COGS 100	WIP Inventory 20
Income Statement	Finished Goods 30
	Balance Sheet

4 ← .... → *20/150 × 30*

WIP Inventory 20 ....→ *24*

6

The Association of
Accountants and
Financial Professionals
in Business

LOS P1.C.1.m.

Overhead Variances

A company uses standard costing. The following information about overhead was generated during a certain period (month)

Required:
Compute a) the variable overhead spending variance and efficiency variances
and b) the fixed overhead budget and production volume variances.
c) Show also in diagram form ("bridges").

Standard overhead rate	$2 per machine hour
Standard fixed overhead rate	$3 per machine hour
Actual variable costs	$443,200
Actual fixed overhead costs	$698,800
Budgeted fixed overhead costs	$700,000
Standard machine hours per unit produced	12
Goods unit produced	18,940
Actual machine hours	228,400

The Association of
Accountants and
Financial Professionals
in Business

LOS P1.C.1.m.

Variable Overhead Variances

Budget/spending variance:
Budgeted for actual hours
Standard rate × actual hours worked

2	×	228,400	$456,800
Actual incurred			443,200
Budget/spending variance			$ 13,600 (F)

Efficiency variance:
Applied to goods units produced
Standard rate × standard hours allowed

2	×	18,940 × 12	$454,560

Budgeted for actual hours
Standard rate × actual hours worked

2	×	228,400	456,800
Efficiency variance			$ 2,240 (U)

Over (F) /under applied (U):

Budget/spending variance	$ 13,600 (F)
Efficiency variance	2,240 (U)
Under applied	$ 11,360 (U)
Posting: Debit to Cost of Goods Sold	$ 11,360

The Association of
Accountants and
Financial Professionals
in Business

LOS P1.C.1.m.

Fixed Overhead Variances

Budget/spending variance:

Budgeted	$700,000
Actual incurred	698,800
Budget/spending variance	$ 1,200 (F)

Production volume variance:
Applied to goods units produced
Standard rate × standard hours allowed

3 × 18,940 × 12	$861,840
Budgeted	700,000
Volume variance	$ 18,160 (U)

Over (F) /under applied (U):

Budget/spending variance	$ 1,200 (F)
Volume variance	18,160 (U)
Under applied	$ 16,960 (U)

Posting: Debit to Cost of Goods Sold $ 16,960

The Association of
Accountants and
Financial Professionals
in Business

LOS P1.C.1.n.

Sales Mix Variance

	Product A		Product B	
	Budget	Actual	Budget	Actual
Unit sales	5,500	6,000	4,500	6,000
Unit contribution margin$	4.50	4.80	10.00	10.50

Assess the selling dept. performance on revenues.
Sold more/less quantities or selling price more/less than expected

Use : Contribution Margin method (Sales Price – Variable Costs)	
Budgeted Mix Std. CMu	Actual Mix Std. CMu
55% A × 4.50 = 2,475	50% × 4.50 = 2,250
45% B × 10.00 = 4,500	50% × 10.00 = 5,000
CMu = 6,975	CMu = 7,250

Increase in Standard CM = 275
×
Actual units of 12,000 } 3,300 F

The Association of
Accountants and
Financial Professionals
in Business

LOS P1.C.1.n.

The Sales Mix Variance

Given a firm with more than a single product and units that can be meaningfully aggregated, show how a sales mix variance might be constructed. The firm with two products—tennis balls and racquet balls—has planned and actual results as shown below:

| | Per Unit | | Planned | | | Actual | | |
	Tennis	Racquet	Tennis	Racquet	Total	Tennis	Racquet	Total
Units			6,000	4,000	**10,000**	4,800	4,800	**9,600**
Standard Revenue	$9.00	$6.00	$54,000	$24,000	$78,000	$43,200	$28,800	$72,000
Standard Variable Cost	$4.00	$3.00	24,000	12,000	36,000	19,200	14,400	33,600
Standard Contribution Margin	$5.00	$3.00	$30,000	$12,000	$42,000	$24,000	$14,400	$38,400
Average CM/Unit					**$4.20**			**$4.00**

The shift in product mix caused the standard unit CM to decrease by $.20/unit × 9,600 units or $1,920 unfavorable. The decrease in units sold caused standard CM to decrease by 400 units × $4.20/unit or $1,680 unfavorable for a total of $3,600 unfavorable.

Part 1: Financial Reporting, Planning, Performance and Control   36
Wiley CMAexcel Learning System, Part 1: Financial Reporting, Planning, Performance, and Control.
Copyright © 2017, Institute of Management Accountants. Published by John Wiley & Sons, Inc.

The Association of
Accountants and
Financial Professionals
in Business

LOS P1.C.1.o. and p.

Mix Variance with Substitutable Raw Materials

A tennis ball is expected to require 1.6 lb. of a blend of rubber. The blend is normally expected to be 1.0 lb. of synthetic rubber at a cost of $2.00/lb. and 0.6 lb. of natural rubber at a cost of $3.00/lb. Therefore, the standard cost of a lb. of the blend is expected to be $2.375/lb.

1,600 balls are produced, using 988 lb. of synthetic rubber and 532 lb. of natural rubber. What is the mix variance? The efficiency (yield) variance?

Instead of 62.5:37.5 mix, the actual mix is 65:35 for a blended cost of $2.35/lb. The mix variance = $0.025/lb.× 1520 lb. or $38 F. The yield variance is 80 lb. × $2.375/lb. or $190 F.

Part 1: Financial Reporting, Planning, Performance and Control   37
Wiley CMAexcel Learning System, Part 1: Financial Reporting, Planning, Performance, and Control.
Copyright © 2017, Institute of Management Accountants. Published by John Wiley & Sons, Inc.

Mix and Yield Variances

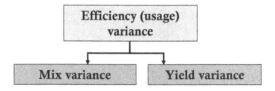

Mix variance (#1 – #2 below) and yield variance (#2 – #3) for a specific substitutable ingredient or labor type:

1. Budgeted Cost/Unit × Actual Total Quantity Used × Actual Mix Ratio
2. Budgeted Cost/Unit × Actual Total Quantity Used × Budgeted Mix Ratio
3. Budgeted Cost/Unit × Budgeted Total Quantity Used × Budgeted Mix Ratio

Session 7 Exercise

Current Variance
Section C, Topic 1: Cost and Variance Measures

Session 7 Exercise: Current Variance

Section C, Topic 1: Cost and Variance Measures

Aunt Molly's Old Fashioned Cookies bakes cookies for retail stores. The company's best-selling cookie is chocolate nut supreme, which is marketed as a gourmet cookie and regularly sells for $8.00 per pound. The standard cost per pound of chocolate nut supreme, based on Aunt Molly's normal monthly production of 400,000 pounds, is shown next.

Cost Item	Quantity	Standard Unit Cost	Total Cost
Direct materials			
Cookie mix	10 oz.	$0.02 /oz.	$0.20
Milk chocolate	5 oz.	0.15 /oz.	0.75
Almonds	1 oz.	0.50 /oz.	0.50
			$1.45
Direct labor			
Mixing	1 min.	$14.40 /hr.	$0.24
Baking	2 min.	18.00 /hr.	0.60
			$0.84
Variable overhead*	3 min.	$32.40 /hr.	$1.62
Total standard cost per pound			$3.91

*Variable overhead is applied based on total direct labor hours.

Aunt Molly's management accountant, Karen Blair, prepares monthly budget reports based on these standard costs. Presented next is April's contribution report that compares budgeted and actual performance.

Contribution Report
April Year 1

	Budget	Actual	Variance
Units (in pounds)	400,000	450,000	50,000 F
Revenue	$3,200,000	$3,555,000	$355,000 F
Direct material	580,000	865,000	285,000 U
Direct labor	336,000	348,000	12,000 U
Variable overhead	648,000	750,000	102,000 U
Total variable costs	1,564,000	1,963,000	399,000 U
Contribution margin	$1,636,000	$1,592,000	$44,000 U

Justine Molly, president of the company, is disappointed with the results. Despite a sizable increase in the number of cookies sold, the product's expected contribution to the overall profitability of the firm decreased. Molly asked Blair to identify the reasons why the contribution margin decreased. Blair has gathered the next information to help in her analysis of the decrease.

Usage Report
April Year 1

Cost Item	Quantity	Actual Cost
Direct materials		
Cookie mix	4,650,000 oz.	$ 93,000
Milk chocolate	2,660,000 oz.	532,000
Almonds	480,000 oz.	240,000
Direct labor		
Mixing	450,000 min.	$ 108,000
Baking	800,000 min.	240,000
Variable overhead		750,000
Total variable costs		$1,963,000

Question 1: Prepare an explanation of the $44,000 unfavorable variance between the budgeted and actual contribution margin for the chocolate nut supreme cookie product line during April Year 1 by calculating the next variances. Assume that all materials are used in the month of purchase.

1. Sales price variance
2. Material price variance
3. Material quantity variance
4. Labor efficiency variance
5. Variable overhead efficiency variance
6. Variable overhead spending variance
7. Contribution margin volume variance

1. Sales price variance =	

2. Material price variance =	

3. Material quantity variance =	

4. Labor efficiency variance =	

5. Variable overhead efficiency variance =	

6. Variable overhead spending variance =	

7. Contribution margin volume variance =			
Summary			
1. Sales price variance			
2. Material price variance			
3. Material quantity variance			
4. Labor efficiency variance			
5. Variable overhead efficiency variance			
6. Variable overhead spending variance			
7. Contribution margin volume variance			

Question 2a: Explain the problems that might arise in using direct labor hours as the basis for allocating overhead.

Question 2b: How might activity-based costing solve the problems described in Question 2a?

Session 7 Exercise Solution: Current Variance

Question 1: Prepare an explanation of the $44,000 unfavorable variance between the budgeted and actual contribution margin for the chocolate nut supreme cookie product line during April Year 1 by calculating the following variances. Assume that all materials are used in the month of purchase.

1. Sales price variance
2. Material price variance
3. Material quantity variance
4. Labor efficiency variance
5. Variable overhead efficiency variance
6. Variable overhead spending variance
7. Contribution margin volume variance

The $44,000 unfavorable variance between budgeted and actual contribution margin for the chocolate nut supreme cookie product line during April Year 1 is explained by the calculations of the next variances. All materials were used in the month of the purchase.

1. Sales Price Variance = Actual Units × (Actual Price − Budgeted Price)

$$\text{Actual: Revenue/Units} = \frac{\$3,555,000}{450,000 \text{ units}} = \$7.90 \text{ /Unit}$$

$$\text{Budgeted: Revenue/Units} = \frac{\$3,200,000}{400,000 \text{ units}} = \$8.00\text{/Unit}$$

Sales Price Variance = 450,000 Units × ($7.90 − $8.00) = $45,000 U

2. Material Price Variance = Actual Quantity Used × (Standard Price − Actual Price)

	Ounces Used		(Standard Price − Actual Price*)			
Cookie Mix	4,650,000	×	($0.02 − $0.02)	=	$	0
Milk chocolate	2,660,000	×	($0.15 − $0.20)	=	133,000	U
Almonds	480,000	×	($0.50 − $0.50)	=	0	
					$133,000	U

* Actual total cost/actual total quantity

Session 7   **239**

3. Material Quantity Variance = Standard Price × [(Standard Usage per Unit × Actual Units Produced) – Actual Quantity Used]

	Standard Price		**Ounces Used***			
Cookie mix	0.02	×	[(10 × 450,000 units) – 4,650,000]	=	$ 3,000	U
Milk chocolate	0.15	×	[(5 × 450,000 units) – 2,660,000]	=	61,500	U
Almonds	0.50	×	[(1 × 450,000 units) – 480,000]	=	15,000	U
					$79,500	U

* Standard Ounces × Actual Units Produced) – Actual Units Used = Variance

4. Labor Efficiency Variance = Standard Hourly Rate × (Standard Hours – Actual Hours)

	Standard Cost		**Minutes Used***			
Mixing	($14.40/hr. 60 minutes)	×	[(1 min. × 450,000 units) – 450,000 min.]	=	$	0
Baking	($18.00/hr. 60 minutes)	×	[(2 min. × 450,000 units) – 800,000 min.]	=	30,000	
					$30,000 F	

* [(Standard Minutes × Actual Units Produced) – Actual Minutes Used] = Variance

5. Variable Overhead Efficiency Variance = Standard Hourly Rate × (Standard Hours – Actual Hours)

$$\frac{\$32.40/hr}{60\ min} \times [(3\ min. \times 450,000\ units) - (450,000\ min. + 800,000\ min.)]$$

$$= \$54,000\ F$$

6. Variable Overhead Spending Variance = (Actual Minutes × Standard Overhead Rate) – Actual Variable Overhead

$$\left[\left(450,000\ min. + 800,000\ min. \right) \times \left(\frac{\$32.40/hr.}{60\ min.} \right) \right] - \$750,000 = \$75,000\ U$$

7. Contribution Margin Volume Variance = Budgeted Unit Contribution* × (Actual Units – Budgeted Units)

$$* \frac{\$1,636,000\ Contribution\ Margin}{400,000\ Budgeted\ Units} = \$4.09$$

$4.09 × (450,000 Units – 400,000 Units) = $204,500 F

	Summary	
1.	Sales price variance	$45,000 U
2.	Material price variance	133,000 U
3.	Material quantity variance	79,500 U
4.	Labor efficiency variance	30,000 F
5.	Variable overhead efficiency variance	54,000 F
6.	Variable overhead spending variance	75,000 U
7.	Contribution margin volume variance	204,500 F
		$44,000 U

Question 2a: Explain the problems that might arise in using direct labor hours as the basis for allocating overhead.

A problem may be that direct labor hours is not an appropriate base for Aunt Molly's Old Fashioned Cookies because it may not be the activity that drives variable overhead. A good indication of this disconnect is shown in the variance analysis. The labor efficiency variance is favorable while the variable overhead spending variance is unfavorable. Another problem is that baking requires considerably more power than mixing, which could distort product costs.

Question 2b: How might activity-based costing solve the problems described in Question 2a?

ACTIVITY-BASED costing (ABC) may solve the problems described in Question 2a and therefore is an alternative that Aunt Molly's should consider, since direct labor does not seem to have a direct cause-and-effect relationship with variable overhead. If the same proportion of these activities is used in all of Aunt Molly's products, ABC may not be beneficial; however, if the products require a different mix of these activities, ABC would be beneficial.

The Association of
Accountants and
Financial Professionals
in Business

Session 7 Wrap-Up

Content covered in Session 7
- Section C, Topic 1: Cost and Variance Measures
- Exercise: Current Variance

Content to be covered in Session 8
- Section C, Topic 2: Responsibility Centers and Reporting Segments
- Section C, Topic 3: Performance Measures
- Section C Practice Questions

Session 8

Wiley
CMAexcel Learning System
Exam Review 2017

Part 1: Financial Reporting, Planning, Performance, and Control

Session 8

Learning Outcome Statements (LOS) identifiers appear on the
slides as applicable to highlight where we address each LOS
within the material.

The Association of
Accountants and
Financial Professionals
in Business

Session 7 Recap

- Section C, Topic 1: Cost and Variance Measures
- Exercise: Current Variance

The Association of
Accountants and
Financial Professionals
in Business

Session 8 Overview

- Section C, Topic 2: Responsibility Centers and Reporting Segments
- Section C, Topic 3: Performance Measures
- Section C Practice Questions

The Association of
Accountants and
Financial Professionals
in Business

Section C: Performance Management

- Topic 1: Cost and Variance Measures
- Topic 2: Responsibility Centers and Reporting Segments
- Topic 3: Performance Measures

Part 1, Section C, Topic 2: Performance Management   4

The Association of
Accountants and
Financial Professionals
in Business

Topic 2: Responsibility Centers and Reporting Segments

- Types of Responsibility Centers
- Transfer Pricing Models
- Reporting of Organization Segments

Part 1, Section C, Topic 2: Responsibility Centers and Reporting Segments   5

The Association of
Accountants and
Financial Professionals
in Business

LOS P1.C.2.a.

Types of Responsibility Centers

- Revenue center
- Cost center
- Profit center
- Investment center

The Association of
Accountants and
Financial Professionals
in Business

LOS P1.C.2.a.

Question: Responsibility Accounting

Responsibility accounting defines an operating center that is responsible for revenue and costs as:

a. an operating unit.

b. a profit center.

c. an investment center.

d. a revenue center.

Answer: b.

Responsibility centers are classified by their primary effect on the organization as a whole. Since profit margin is a function of both revenue and costs, a manager for a revenue center or a profit center is responsible for generating profits or revenues and for controlling costs. Managers of these departments usually do not have control over investments.

The Association of
Accountants and
Financial Professionals
in Business

LOS P1.C.2.c.

Traditional versus Contribution Reporting

Traditional Approach (Costs Organized by Function)			Contribution Approach (Costs Organized by Behavior)		
Sales		$31,200	Sales		$31,200
– Cost of Goods Sold		15,600	– Variable Production	$5,200	
Gross Margin		15,600	– Variable Selling and Administrative	2,600	7,800
– Selling	$8,060		Contribution Margin		23,400
– Administrative	4,940	13,000	– Fixed Production	10,400	
Net Operating Income		$2,600	– Fixed Selling and Administrative	10,400	20,800
			Net Operating Income		$2,600

The Association of
Accountants and
Financial Professionals
in Business

LOS P1.C.2.c.

Segment Reporting Key Terms

- **Reporting segments.** Business divided into meaningful groups (product line, geography)
- **Segment margin.** Segment's contribution margin less traceable fixed costs (costs that would not exist without the segment)
- **Traceable fixed costs.** Fixed costs included in a segment's margin that would not exist were it not for the segment
- **Common costs.** Fixed costs that cannot be traced to a segment and are shared by two or more segments; must be allocated for segment reporting

The Association of
Accountants and
Financial Professionals
in Business

LOS P1.C.2.f. and g.

Allocating Common Costs

Stand-alone cost allocation

* Determines relative proportion of cost driver for each party that shares a common cost
* Allocates costs by those percentages

  Example: Office #1 receives 30% of a consultant's time while Office #2 receives 70% of a consultant's time. These percentages would be used to allocate the consultant's fees.

Incremental cost allocation

* Allocates costs by ranking parties by primary user and incremental users

  Example: The consultant is based in the same city as Office #1 but charges $5,000 in travel expenses for travel to Office #2. The 70/30 allocation still would be used to allocate the consultant's project fees, but the $5,000 in travel would be charged to Office #2 only.

The Association of
Accountants and
Financial Professionals
in Business

LOS P1.C.2.h.

Transfer Pricing

* Used for internally exchanged goods and services.
* If transferred goods/services also are sold externally, transfer price can be the external price.
* External price is also called "arm's-length price."
* If transferred items are not sold externally, a transfer price model must be used.
* Model chosen affects selling and purchasing manager behavior.
* Transfers can be between different legal entities, which can attract scrutiny by tax authorities.

The Association of
Accountants and
Financial Professionals
in Business

LOS P1.C.2.i.

Transfer Pricing Models

- **Market price model.** A true arm's-length model; sets the price for a good or service at going market prices.
- **Negotiated price model.** Sets the transfer price through negotiation between the buyer and the seller.
- **Variable cost model.** Sets transfer prices at the unit's variable cost, or the actual cost to produce the good or service less all fixed costs.
- **Full cost (absorption) model.** Starts with the seller's variable cost for the item and then allocates fixed costs to the price.

The Association of
Accountants and
Financial Professionals
in Business

LOS P1.C.2.i.

Question: Advantages and Disadvantages of Transfer Pricing Models

Method	Advantages	Disadvantages
Market price	Easy to maintain and document; preferred method	Focus on external customers could affect purchasing segment
Negotiated	Could help company as a whole	Non–market-based prices are subject to greater tax scrutiny by tax authorities
Variable cost	Simple and easy to understand	Tax scrutiny; has no incentive to control variable costs
Full cost	Simple and easy to understand	Tax scrutiny; seller has no incentive to control costs

The Association of
Accountants and
Financial Professionals
in Business

LOS P1.C.2.i.

Question: Method for Establishing Transfer Price

In theory, the optimal method for establishing a transfer price is:

a. incremental cost.

b. flexible budget cost.

c. actual cost with or without a markup.

d. market price.

e. budgeted cost with or without a markup.

Answer: **d.**

The market price model is a true arm's-length model because it sets the price for a good or service at market prices. The market price model keeps business units autonomous, forces the selling unit to be competitive with external suppliers, and is preferred by tax authorities.

The Association of
Accountants and
Financial Professionals
in Business

LOS P1.C.2.h.

Question: Transfer Pricing for Decentralized Profit Center

PQ Inc. has decentralized profit centers. PQ's Arcade Division (AD) makes arcade consoles using the products of PQ's Video Card Division (VCD). The video card needed by AD sells on the open market for $10.98/unit and has these actual costs:

DM = $2.40, DL = $3.00, Variable Overhead = $1.50,
      Fixed Overhead = $2.25, Total Cost = $9.15

Assume that AD is able to purchase unlimited video cards externally for $8.70 per unit. VCD, having excess capacity, agrees to lower its transfer price to $8.70 per unit. This action would:

a. subvert the profit goals of VCD while optimizing the profit goals of AD.

b. optimize the overall profit goals of PQ.

c. cause mediocre behavior in VCD as lost opportunity costs increase.

d. optimize the profit goals of AD while subverting the profit goals of PQ.

Answer: **b.**

The Association of
Accountants and
Financial Professionals
in Business

LOS P1.C.2.k.

Transfer Pricing

Internal Pricing methods are to stimulate managers to co-operate to provide the Company the greatest benefit, rather than to act in their own interest. (Goal congruence)

Company X (A buys from B)	Division A	Division B
Market Price (MP)	$50	
Var. Costs (VC)	$20	
Excess Capacity	1,000 units	Need: 900 units

Question: Natural Bargaining Range re. TP?

VC: $20	In-between	MP: $50

Idle Capacity: Apply VC approach

Part 1, Section C, Topic 2: Responsibility Centers and Reporting Segments
Wiley CMAexcel Learning System, Part 1: Financial Reporting, Planning, Performance, and Control.
Copyright © 2017, Institute of Management Accountants. Published by John Wiley & Sons, Inc.

16

The Association of
Accountants and
Financial Professionals
in Business

LOS P1.C.2.k.

Question: Transfer Price Company A, Example 1

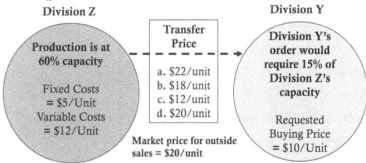

Division Z

Production is at 60% capacity

Fixed Costs = $5/Unit
Variable Costs = $12/Unit

Transfer Price

a. $22/unit
b. $18/unit
c. $12/unit
d. $20/unit

Market price for outside sales = $20/unit

Division Y

Division Y's order would require 15% of Division Z's capacity

Requested Buying Price = $10/Unit

Which transfer price would allow the divisions to reach goal congruence and allow both divisions to make a profit?

Answer: b.

Based on ICMA
question, used
with permission

Part 1, Section C, Topic 2: Responsibility Centers and Reporting Segments
Wiley CMAexcel Learning System, Part 1: Financial Reporting, Planning, Performance, and Control.
Copyright © 2017, Institute of Management Accountants. Published by John Wiley & Sons, Inc.

17

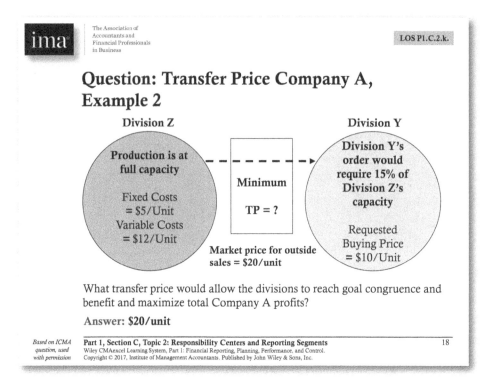

Based on ICMA question, used with permission

Part 1, Section C, Topic 2: Responsibility Centers and Reporting Segments   18
Wiley CMAexcel Learning System, Part 1: Financial Reporting, Planning, Performance, and Control.
Copyright © 2017, Institute of Management Accountants. Published by John Wiley & Sons, Inc.

The Association of
Accountants and
Financial Professionals
in Business

Topic 3: Performance Measures

- Product Profitability Analysis
- Business Unit Profitability Analysis
- Customer Profitability Analysis
- Return on Investment
- Residual Income
- Investment Base Issues
- Effect of International Operations
- Critical Success Factors
- Balanced Scorecard

Part 1, Section C, Topic 3: Performance Measures   19
Wiley CMAexcel Learning System, Part 1: Financial Reporting, Planning, Performance, and Control.
Copyright © 2017, Institute of Management Accountants. Published by John Wiley & Sons, Inc.

The Association of
Accountants and
Financial Professionals
in Business

LOS P1.C.3.b.

Product Profitability Analysis

	Tennis Balls	Racquet Balls	Total
Last year's sales	$780,000	$195,000	$975,000
Variable cost	585,000	175,500	760,500
Contribution margin	195,000	19,500	214,500
Advertising (traceable)	19,500	26,000	45,500
Contribution after all relevant costs	$175,500	($6,500)	169,000
Fixed cost (untraceable)			100,000
Net income with racquet balls			$69,000

The Association of
Accountants and
Financial Professionals
in Business

LOS P1.C.3.b.

Business Unit Profitability Analysis

Tennis Balls Unit	
Revenue	$780,000
Variable expenses	585,000
Contribution margin	195,000
Fixed expenses incurred in profit center	19,500
Direct/controllable profit	175,500
Corporate charges allocated to SBU	52,500
Income before taxes	123,000
Taxes	49,200
Net Income	$73,800

The Association of
Accountants and
Financial Professionals
in Business

LOS P1.C.3.b., e., and g.

Profitability Analysis Methods

Return on investment (ROI)

$$ROI = \frac{\text{*Income of a Business Unit}}{\text{Assets of a Business Unit}}$$

Residual Income (RI)

**RI = *Income of a Business Unit – (Assets of a Business Unit ×
Required Rate of Return)**

Note that "Income" means operating income unless otherwise noted.

The Association of
Accountants and
Financial Professionals
in Business

LOS P1.C.3.e., g., and i.

Factors Affecting ROI and RI

ROI can be affected by

- change in sales.
- change in operating expenses.
- change in assets.

RI can be affected by

- change in sales.
- change in operating expenses.
- change in assets.
- change in required rate of return.

$$ROI = \frac{\text{*Income of a Business Unit}}{\text{Assets of a Business Unit}}$$

**RI = *Income of a Business Unit
    – (Assets of a Business Unit × Required Rate of Return)**

Note that "Income" means operating income unless otherwise noted.

The Association of
Accountants and
Financial Professionals
in Business

LOS P1.C.3.e.

Question: Calculating ROI

The table lists selected financial information for the Western Division of the Hinzel Company for last year.

If Hinzel treats the Western Division as an investment center for performance measurement purposes, what is the ROI for last year?

a. 16.67%
b. 19.79%
c. 22.54%
d. 26.76%
e. 34.78%

Account	Amount (000s)
Working capital	$625
General and administrative expenses	75
Net sales	4,000
Plant and equipment	1,775
Cost of goods sold	3,525

Answer: a.
ROI = *Income of a Business Unit/Assets of a Business Unit
ROI = ($4,000 – $3,525 – $75)/($625 + $1,775)
ROI = $400/$2,400 = 0.16666 = 16.67%

*Note that "Income" means operating income unless otherwise noted.

Based on ICMA question, used with permission   Part 1, Section C, Topic 3: Performance Measures   24
Wiley CMAexcel Learning System, Part 1: Financial Reporting, Planning, Performance, and Control.
Copyright © 2017, Institute of Management Accountants. Published by John Wiley & Sons, Inc.

The Association of
Accountants and
Financial Professionals
in Business

LOS P1.C.3.g.

Question: Calculating Residual Income

The table lists selected financial information for the Western Division of the Hinzel Company for last year.

If Hinzel treats the Western Division as an investment center for performance measurement purposes and has a required rate of return of 15%, what is the residual income (RI) for last year?

a. $40
b. $42
c. $30
d. $38

Account	Amount (000s)
Working capital	$625
General and administrative expenses	75
Net sales	4,000
Plant and equipment	1,775
Cost of goods sold	3,525

Answer: a.
RI = *Income of a Business Unit – (Assets of Business Unit × Required Rate of Return)
RI = ($4,000 – $3,525 – $75) – [($625 + $1,775) × (0.15)]
RI = ($400) – [($2,400 × 0.15)] = $400 – $360 = $40

*Note that "Income" means operating income unless otherwise noted.

Based on ICMA question, used with permission   Part 1, Section C, Topic 3: Performance Measures   25
Wiley CMAexcel Learning System, Part 1: Financial Reporting, Planning, Performance, and Control.
Copyright © 2017, Institute of Management Accountants. Published by John Wiley & Sons, Inc.

The Association of
Accountants and
Financial Professionals
in Business

LOS P1.C.3.f., g., and i.

Decisions Based on ROI and RI

Decisions affecting assets:

- Asset replacement
- Investment in new assets or technology
- Disposal of large assets

Decisions that would affect profits:

- Research and development spending
- Spending on quality control
- Spending on maintenance
- Spending on human resource development
- Spending on advertising
- Transfer pricing disputes

The Association of
Accountants and
Financial Professionals
in Business

LOS P1.C.3.f. and h.

Maximize ROI or RI—Scenario 1

Scenario	Objective: Maximize ROI	Objective: Maximize RI (Required rate of return is 8%)
A business unit yields 18% ROI. It has the opportunity to invest in a project that yields 10% ROI. Accept or reject?	Reject, because it would dilute the business unit's current ROI. The project's 10% ROI would bring down the business unit's 18% ROI.	Accept, because it adds value on top of the existing assets invested. It is 2% above the required rate of return, so it would yield a positive residual income.

The Association of
Accountants and
Financial Professionals
in Business

LOS P1.C.3.f. and h.

Maximize ROI or RI—Scenario 2

Scenario	Objective: Maximize ROI	Objective: Maximize RI (Required rate of return is 8%)
The business unit in the Netherlands yields 8% ROI compared to an overall company 12% ROI. Should the company close the business unit in the Netherlands? Yes or no?	Yes. The Netherlands' 8% ROI would decrease the overall company's 12% ROI.	Yes. The Netherlands' business unit covers only the capital charge, so it does not add value.

The Association of
Accountants and
Financial Professionals
in Business

LOS P1.C.3.i.

Limitations of ROI and RI

ROI

- A business unit with high average ROI might reject lower-ROI projects that would be acceptable for the organization as a whole.

RI

- Highly dependent on the required rate of return.
- Is a flat dollar amount, so is less useful for comparing business units of different sizes.

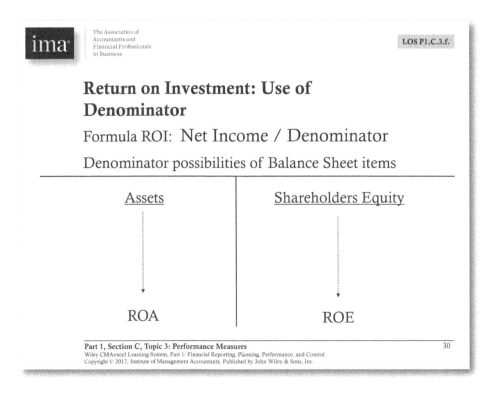

Part 1, Section C, Topic 3: Performance Measures
Wiley CMAexcel Learning System, Part 1: Financial Reporting, Planning, Performance, and Control.
Copyright © 2017, Institute of Management Accountants. Published by John Wiley & Sons, Inc.

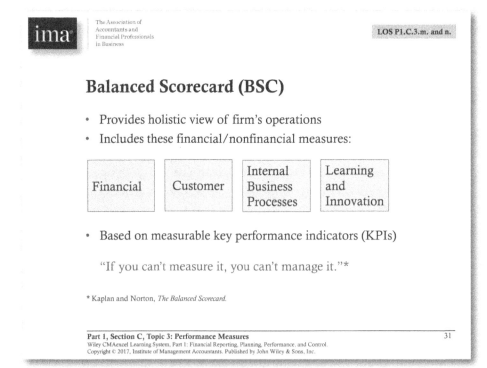

Part 1, Section C, Topic 3: Performance Measures
Wiley CMAexcel Learning System, Part 1: Financial Reporting, Planning, Performance, and Control.
Copyright © 2017, Institute of Management Accountants. Published by John Wiley & Sons, Inc.

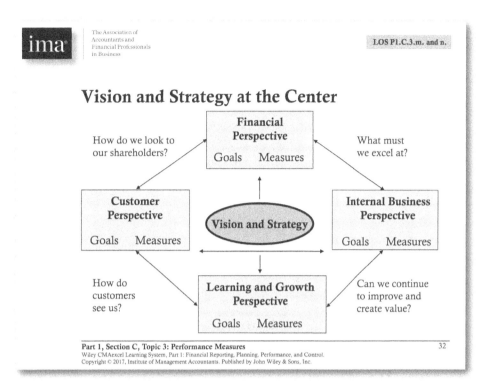

Part 1, Section C, Topic 3: Performance Measures   32
Wiley CMAexcel Learning System, Part 1: Financial Reporting, Planning, Performance, and Control.
Copyright © 2017, Institute of Management Accountants. Published by John Wiley & Sons, Inc.

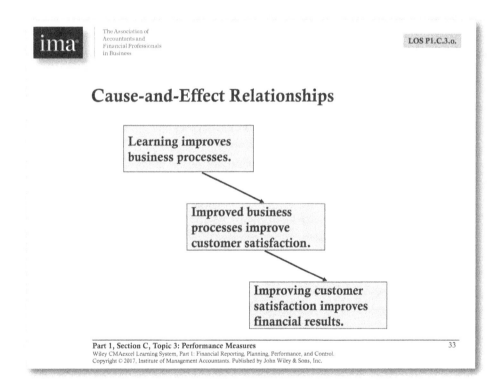

Part 1, Section C, Topic 3: Performance Measures   33
Wiley CMAexcel Learning System, Part 1: Financial Reporting, Planning, Performance, and Control.
Copyright © 2017, Institute of Management Accountants. Published by John Wiley & Sons, Inc.

The Association of
Accountants and
Financial Professionals
in Business

LOS P1.C.3.o.

Question: Matching Measure to Strategy

Alfa Inc. produces educational materials for children. The company prides itself on serving its customers better than its competitors do and has been able to grow its business by keeping a focus on customer service. Alfa recently has adopted a balanced scorecard performance measurement system.

Which of the following would be the primary measure used by Alfa in its balanced scorecard?

a. Gross margin
b. Timeliness of new products to market
c. Number of repeat sales by current customers
d. Cycle time

Answer: c.
Alfa's primary focus is on the customer perspective, which must include specific outcome measures and specific performance drivers. Number of repeat sales by current customers is a specific performance driver linked to the specific outcome measures of retention and satisfaction.

Based on ICMA question, used with permission

Part 1, Section C, Topic 3: Performance Measures   34
Wiley CMAexcel Learning System, Part 1: Financial Reporting, Planning, Performance, and Control.
Copyright © 2017, Institute of Management Accountants. Published by John Wiley & Sons, Inc.

The Association of
Accountants and
Financial Professionals
in Business

LOS P1.C.3.o. and p.

Question: Balanced Scorecard

What three principles link key performance indicators to the firm's strategy?

Answer:

Cause-and-effect relationship

Outcome measures and performance drivers

Links to financial measures

Part 1, Section C, Topic 3: Performance Measures   35
Wiley CMAexcel Learning System, Part 1: Financial Reporting, Planning, Performance, and Control.
Copyright © 2017, Institute of Management Accountants. Published by John Wiley & Sons, Inc.

The Association of
Accountants and
Financial Professionals
in Business

LOS P1.C.3.n. and q.

Financial Perspective

Category	Measures include...
Sales	Sales forecast accuracy, return on sales
Costs	Standards, budgets, variances
Liquidity	Asset, inventory and receivables turnover; cash flow
Solvency	Debt to equity ratio, interest, and fixed charge coverage
Profitability	ROI, RI
Market value	Share price

The Association of
Accountants and
Financial Professionals
in Business

LOS P1.C.3.n.

Customer Measures

The Association of
Accountants and
Financial Professionals
in Business

LOS P1.C.3.n.

Internal Business Processes Perspective

Innovation
- R&D outcomes
- Time to market
- Product development processes

Operations
- Process time, cycle time
- Productivity, throughput
- Safety
- Quality

Post-Sale Services
- Response time
- Customer service
- Warranty costs

The Association of
Accountants and
Financial Professionals
in Business

LOS P1.C.3.n.

Learning and Growth Perspective

Category	Measures include...
Employee skill sets (current and future state)	Training needed per employee, training offered, and analysis of qualified employees
Information systems capabilities	Availability of needed information and time to obtain
Empowerment, motivation, and organizational alignment	Suggestions per employee, cost savings per suggestion, employee turnover

The Association of
Accountants and
Financial Professionals
in Business

LOS P1.C.3.n.

Question: BSC Business Process Areas

The BSC considers all of the following to be business process areas that contribute most to companies' internal business process strategies EXCEPT which one?

a. **Employee skill sets**—increasing employees' investment in the company
b. **Innovation**—efficient use of research and development and product development
c. **Operations**—delivery of quality products and services to the customer
d. **Post-sale services**—providing additional value-added products and services to the customer

Answer: a.

Employee skill sets are part of the learning and growth measures category, not the internal business process measures category. The other items are all correct.

Part 1, Section C, Topic 3: Performance Measures   40
Wiley CMAexcel Learning System, Part 1: Financial Reporting, Planning, Performance, and Control.
Copyright © 2017, Institute of Management Accountants. Published by John Wiley & Sons, Inc.

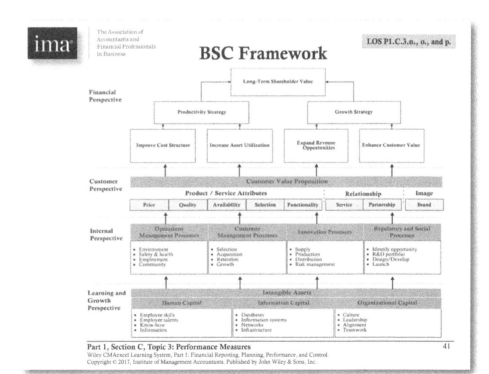

Part 1, Section C, Topic 3: Performance Measures   41
Wiley CMAexcel Learning System, Part 1: Financial Reporting, Planning, Performance, and Control.
Copyright © 2017, Institute of Management Accountants. Published by John Wiley & Sons, Inc.

The Association of
Accountants and
Financial Professionals
in Business

Section C Practice Questions

- We now review Practice Questions from the WCMALS self-study book, Section C.
- Questions are identified by topic.
- Not all topics are covered in this selection.
- More questions on each topic and full section test is included in the Online Test Bank.

The Association of
Accountants and
Financial Professionals
in Business

Section C Conclusion

- Section C content represents 25% of the multiple-choice questions on the Part 1 exam.
- This content also may be covered in essay question format.

To reinforce your learning:

- Study all the LOS for this section.
- Study all material in Section C of WCMALS self-study.
- Use the practice test questions in WCMALS self-study.
- Take the Section C practice test in the Online Test Bank for a wider range of questions on all topics in this section.

The Association of
Accountants and
Financial Professionals
in Business

Session 8 Wrap-Up

Content covered in Session 8

- Section C, Topic 2: Responsibility Centers and Reporting
- Section C, Topic 3: Performance Measures
- Section C Practice Questions

Content to be covered in Session 9

- Section D, Topic 1: Measurement Concepts
- Session 9 Exercise 1: Absorption versus Variable Costing
- Section D, Topic 2: Costing Systems
- Session 9 Exercise 2: Equivalent Units in Process Costing

Session 9

The Association of
Accountants and
Financial Professionals
in Business

Wiley
CMAexcel Learning System
Exam Review 2017

Part 1: Financial Reporting, Planning, Performance, and Control

Session 9

Learning Outcome Statements (LOS) identifiers appear on the
slides as applicable to highlight where we address each LOS
within the material.

The Association of
Accountants and
Financial Professionals
in Business

Session 8 Recap

- Section C, Topic 2: Responsibility Centers and Reporting Segments
- Section C, Topic 3: Performance Measures
- Section C Practice Questions

The Association of
Accountants and
Financial Professionals
in Business

Session 9 Overview

- Section D, Topic 1: Measurement Concepts
- Session 9 Exercise 1: Absorption versus Variable Costing
- Section D, Topic 2: Costing Systems
- Session 9 Exercise 2: Equivalent Units in Process Costing

Section D: Cost Management

- Topic 1: Measurement Concepts
- Topic 2: Costing Systems
- Topic 3: Overhead Costs
- Topic 4: Supply Chain Management
- Topic 5: Business Process Improvement

Topic 1: Measurement Concepts

- Fixed and Variable Costs
- Actual, Normal, and Standard Costs
- Absorption and Variable Costing
- Joint Product and By-Product Costing

The Association of
Accountants and
Financial Professionals
in Business

LOS P1.D.1.a.

Cost Behavior

- **Variable costs** vary directly and proportionately in total with changes in the activity level. The variable cost per unit remains the same over the relevant range. As activity increases so does the total variable costs. Examples: direct materials, direct labor

- **Fixed costs** remain the same in total over the relevant range. The fixed cost per unit varies with changes in the level of activity. As activity increases the fixed cost per unit decreases. Examples: rent, depreciation, property taxes.

- **Step costs** increase in steps as activity level increases. Examples: supervisory costs, maintenance.

The Association of
Accountants and
Financial Professionals
in Business

LOS P1.D.1.a.

Cost Behavior: Variable versus Fixed versus Step Costs

Variable Cost per Period

Fixed Cost per Period

Example of Step Cost

Maintenance $ per Year

000 of DLH/Month

The Association of
Accountants and
Financial Professionals
in Business

LOS P1.D.1.d. and e.

Actual, Normal, and Standard Costing

1. **Actual costing.** Material, labor, and manufacturing overhead are all charged at actual cost.

2. **Normal costing.** Materials and labor are charged at actual cost; manufacturing overhead is charged using a predetermined rate.

3. **Standard costing.** Expected or target costs are used for material, labor, and manufacturing overhead costs.

- The three are *not* mutually exclusive.

- One of the three methods is used to track manufacturing costs from *Raw Materials* to *Work-in-Process* to *Finished Goods* to *COGS*

The Association of
Accountants and
Financial Professionals
in Business

LOS P1.D.1.e.

Developing Standard Cost per Output Unit

- DM based on budgeted pounds and budgeted cost per pound

  100 pounds at **$2/pound** = *$200/unit*

- DL based on budgeted hours and budgeted cost per hour

  4 hours at **$12/hour** = *$48/unit*

- Predetermined overhead based on 150% of labor costs

  $48 × 1.5 = *$72/unit*

- Total standard cost = *$320/output unit*

The Association of
Accountants and
Financial Professionals
in Business

LOS P1.D.1.e.

Question: Roles in Establishing Standard Costs

Which one of the following is LEAST likely to be involved in establishing standard costs?

a. Budgetary accountants
b. Industrial engineers
c. Top management
d. Quality control personnel
e. Line management

Answer: c.
Setting cost standards is not the responsibility of top management and is best left to lower-level managers and planners due to both the level of detail required and the breadth of the task.

Based on ICMA question, used with permission   **Part 1, Section D, Topic 1: Measurement Concepts**   Wiley CMAexcel Learning System, Part 1: Financial Reporting, Planning, Performance, and Control. Copyright © 2017, Institute of Management Accountants. Published by John Wiley & Sons, Inc.   10

The Association of
Accountants and
Financial Professionals
in Business

LOS P1.D.1.b. and g.

Cost Behavior, Cost Objects, and Cost Drivers

- **Cost Behavior:** Variable or Fixed
- **Cost Objects:** Anything a cost needs to be determined for. *Examples:* a product, project, or department .
- **Cost Driver:** An activity with high correlation to the cost object. *Examples:* number of setups, machine hours, labor costs, labor hours, number of inspections.

Part 1, Section D, Topic 1: Measurement Concepts   Wiley CMAexcel Learning System, Part 1: Financial Reporting, Planning, Performance, and Control. Copyright © 2017, Institute of Management Accountants. Published by John Wiley & Sons, Inc.   11

The Association of
Accountants and
Financial Professionals
in Business

LOS P1.D.1.e. and j.

Steps to Develop a Predetermined Overhead Rate

- Create overhead budget in dollars.
- Select cost driver(s) for overhead costs.
- Estimate total quantity of cost driver(s).
- Calculate the rate:

$$\text{Predetermined Overhead Rate} = \frac{\text{Budgeted Overhead}}{\text{Cost Driver Activity}}$$

The Association of
Accountants and
Financial Professionals
in Business

LOS P1.D.1.e. and j.

Overhead Variances: Over- or Underapplied

- Overhead variances are the difference between overhead applied/allocated to WIP and actual overhead incurred.
- The actual overhead and the overhead applied/allocated often are charged to an overhead control account.
- Overhead variances, the net amount in the overhead control account, need to be closed out at the end of the period (at least annually) according to GAAP.

The Association of
Accountants and
Financial Professionals
in Business

LOS P1.D.1.e. and k.

Disposition of Over- or Underapplied Overhead

There are two methods for disposition. Determining which to use is based on the materiality or significance of the dollar amount.

1) **If immaterial**, journalize the amount to COGS only:

COGS	xxx	
Overhead control account		xxx

2) **If material**, prorate the amount to WIP, Finished Goods, and COGS:

WIP	xxx	
Finished goods	xxx	
COGS	xxx	
Overhead control account		xxx

The Association of
Accountants and
Financial Professionals
in Business

Question: Costing Examples

How would each of the following examples be journalized?

Example 1: Immaterial and underapplied overhead: $5,000 variance
Example 2: Material and overapplied overhead: $50,000 variance

Account balances: COGS of $300,000; WIP and FG of $100,000 each

Example 1

- Increase (debit) COGS by $5,000.

- Decrease (credit) overhead control account by $5,000 (brings account to 0).

Example 2

- Increase (debit) overhead control account by $50,000 (brings account to 0).

- Decrease (credit) COGS by $30,000 ($300/$500 = 60% of variance).

- Decrease (credit) WIP by $10,000 ($100/$500 = 20% of variance).

- Decrease (credit) FG by $10,000 ($100/$500 = 20% of variance).

Variable and Absorption Costing

Variable (Direct) Costing

- Inventoriable costs include material, labor, and variable overhead *only*.
- *Does not* include fixed overhead.
- *Is not* GAAP compliant.

Absorption (Full) Costing

- Inventoriable costs include material, labor, and both variable and fixed manufacturing overhead.
- *Does* include fixed overhead.
- *Is* GAAP compliant.

Variable versus Absorption Costing

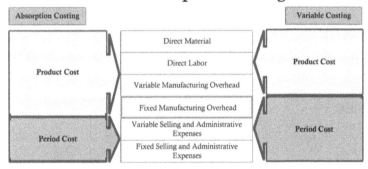

The difference between variable and absorption costing is in the treatment of fixed manufacturing overhead. Absorption costing treats fixed manufacturing overhead as a *product cost*. Variable costing treats it as a *period cost*.

The Association of
Accountants and
Financial Professionals
in Business

LOS P1.D.1.g. and h.

Difference between Variable Costing and Absorption Costing Income Is the Amount of Reconciliation Factor

- Fixed manufacturing overhead is the only difference between variable costing and absorption costing.
- Therefore, the change in fixed costs in inventory is the reconciling item between the two costing systems.

Change in inventory × Fixed overhead cost/unit = Reconciliation factor

The Association of
Accountants and
Financial Professionals
in Business

LOS P1.D.1.h. and i.

Using the Reconciliation Factor

Facts for the example:
- Units made and sold: 700 made and 500 sold at $200
- Variable manufacturing costs per unit: $30
- Variable selling (marketing) costs per unit: $20
- Fixed manufacturing costs per unit: $25 ($17,500 in total)
- Fixed selling (marketing) costs: $14,000

Calculations:

Revenue (500 @ $200)	$100,000
Variable cost (500 @ $50)	25,000
Fixed cost ($17,500 + $14,000)	31,500
Operating income$_{VC}$	**$ 43,500**
Reconciliation factor (200 @ $25)	5,000
Operating income$_{AC}$ =	**$ 48,500**

The Association of
Accountants and
Financial Professionals
in Business

Question: Costing Methods

Assuming that a management accountant wants to maximize reported net income, which of the following costing methods would show the greatest net income when the company increases its ending inventory?

a. Standard costing
b. Absorption costing
c. Normal costing
d. Variable costing

Answer: **b.**

When more units are produced than sold, absorption costing will generate a higher net income than variable costing because absorption costing will include the fixed overhead costs associated with the increased inventory. Lower costs for the items actually sold equate to a higher net income.

Based on ICMA question, used with permission   Part 1, Section D, Topic 1: Measurement Concepts
Wiley CMAexcel Learning System, Part 1: Financial Reporting, Planning, Performance, and Control.
Copyright © 2017, Institute of Management Accountants. Published by John Wiley & Sons, Inc.   20

The Association of
Accountants and
Financial Professionals
in Business

LOS P1.D.1.j.

Joint and By-Product Costing

- Joint products and by-products are made when one raw material is processed into two or more products

  ▸ **Joint products** are considered the main products.

  ▸ Relative sales value of joint products is higher than that of by-products

  ▸ **By-products** are not usually sellable or processed further

Part 1, Section D, Topic 1: Measurement Concepts
Wiley CMAexcel Learning System, Part 1: Financial Reporting, Planning, Performance, and Control.
Copyright © 2017, Institute of Management Accountants. Published by John Wiley & Sons, Inc.   21

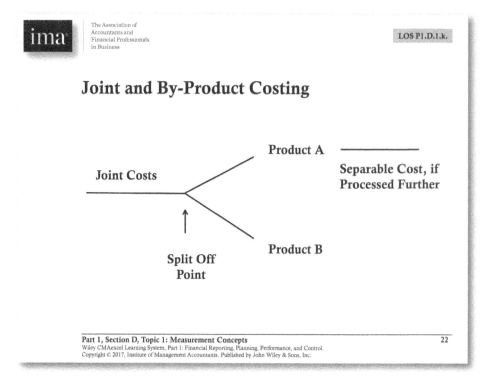

ima

The Association of
Accountants and
Financial Professionals
in Business

LOS P1.D.1.k.

Joint and By-Product Costing

ima

The Association of
Accountants and
Financial Professionals
in Business

Question: Joint Product Costing

In joint product costing, which one of the following costs is relevant when deciding the point at which a product should be sold in order to maximize profits?

a. Separable costs after the split-off point
b. Joint costs to the split-off point
c. Purchase costs of the materials required for the joint products
d. Sales salaries for the period when the units were produced

Answer: a.
Separable costs are additional processing costs that can be identified specifically with a product and occur after the split-off point.

Methods to Allocate Joint Costs

* Market-based methods:
  * ▶ Sales value at split-off
  * ▶ Net realizable value
  * ▶ Gross profit

* Physical unit method:
  * ▶ Based on each product's pro rata share of total quantity produced

Facts for Joint Cost Allocations

* **Joint costs are $8,000/day and result in:**
  * ▶ 2,000 lb./day of fine paper
  * ▶ 4,000 lb./day of semi-finished paper
* **Selling prices:**
  * ▶ Fine paper sells for $2.00/lb.
  * ▶ Semi-finished paper sells for $1.50/lb.
* **Separable processing costs:**
  * ▶ $2,000/day upgrades fine paper to a product that sells for $3.50/lb.

The Association of
Accountants and
Financial Professionals
in Business

LOS P1.D.1.l.

Allocating Costs Using Sales Value at Split-Off

- Sales value at split-off is the value that each of the products could be sold for at the split-off point
- To use this method, there must be a market for each of these products

The Association of
Accountants and
Financial Professionals
in Business

LOS P1.D.1.l.

Allocation of Joint Costs Using Sales Value at Split-Off Method

Product	Quantity	Price	Sales Value	% of SV	Joint Cost Allocated
Fine	2,000 lbs.	$2.00	$4,000	40%	$3,200
Semi-finished	4,000 lbs.	$1.50	$6,000	60%	$4,800
			$10,000	100%	$8,000

LOS P1.D.1.1.

Allocating Joint Costs Using Net Realizable Value (NRV)

- Used if all market prices are not available
- Uses final sales value less additional processing costs to allocate costs at the split-off point

LOS P1.D.1.1.

Allocation of Joint Costs Using Net Realizable Value Method

	Final			Less: Sep.	Net Realizable	% of	Joint Cost
Product	Quantity	Price	Sales Value	Cost	Value	NRV	Allocated
Fine	2,000	$3.50	$7,000	$2,000	$5,000	45.45%	$3,636
Semi-finished	4,000	$1.50	6,000		6,000	54.55%	4,364
	6,000		$13,000		$11,000	100.00%	$8,000

The Association of Accountants and Financial Professionals in Business

LOS P1.D.1.i.

Allocating Joint Costs Using Gross Profit Method

- Also known as *constant gross margin percentage* method
- Provides the same gross margin percentage for each product, after including separable processing costs after the split-off point
- Accounts for additional processing costs

The Association of Accountants and Financial Professionals in Business

LOS P1.D.1.i.

Allocation of Joint Costs Using Constant Gross Profit % Method

Product	Quantity	Price	Sales Value	×	Cost %	Total Cost	Separable Process Cost	Joint Cost	Gross Profit	Gross Margin
Fine	2,000 lbs.	$3.50	$7,000	×	.76923	$5,385	$2,000	$3,385	$1,615	23.1%
Semi-Finished	4,000 lbs.	$1.50	6,000	×	.76923	4,615		4,615	1,385	23.1%
			$13,000		$10,000/$13,000 = .76923	$10,000	$2,000	$8,000	$3,000	23.1%

LOS P1.D.1.1.

Allocating Joint Costs Using Physical Measure Method

Uses a common physical measure such as pounds, feet, cans, etc. to determine each product's share of the total joint costs.

32

LOS P1.D.1.1.

Allocating Joint Costs Using the Physical Measure Method

Product	Quantity	% of Qty.	Jt. Costs
Fine	2,000 lbs.	33.3%	$2,664
Semi-Finished	4,000 lbs.	66.7%	5,336
	6,000 lbs.	100.0%	$8,000

33

The Association of
Accountants and
Financial Professionals
in Business

Session 9 Exercise 1

Absorption versus Variable Costing

Session 9 Exercise 1: Absorption versus Variable Costing

Consider this information:

Units made	1,000
Units sold	750
Variable manufacturing costs per unit	$ 35
Variable selling costs per unit	$ 25
Fixed manufacturing costs per unit	$ 20
Fixed selling costs	$ 20,000
Beginning inventory (in units)	0
Ending inventory (in units)	250
Unit selling price	$150

Question 1: In the space provided, prepare a variable costing and absorption costing income statement.

Session 9 Exercise 1 Solution: Absorption versus Variable Costing

Question 1:

Variable Costing Operating Income Statement		
Revenues		$112,500
Variable cost of goods sold:		
Beginning inventory	$ –	
Variable manufacturing costs	35,000	
Cost of goods available for sale	35,000	
Less: Ending inventory	(8,750)	
Variable cost of goods sold	26,250	
Variable selling costs	18,750	
Total variable costs		45,000
Contribution margin		$ 67,500
Fixed costs		
Fixed manufacturing	$20,000	
Fixed selling costs	20,000	
Total fixed costs		$ 40,000
Operating income		$ 27,500

Absorption Costing Operating Income Statement		
Revenues		$ 112,500
Cost of goods sold:		
Beginning inventory	0	
Variable manufacturing costs	$ 35,000	
Fixed manufacturing costs	20,000	
Cost of goods available for sale	$ 55,000	
Less: ending inventory*	(13,750)	
Cost of goods sold		$ 41,250
Gross margin		$ 71,250
Operating costs:		
Variable selling costs	18,750	
Fixed selling costs	20,000	
Total operating costs		$ 38,750
Operating income		$ 32,500
Difference in Absorption Costing vs. Variable Costing		**$ 5,000**

*Includes both fixed and variable costs

Question 2: Describe two advantages of using variable costing rather than absorption costing.

Two of the several advantages of using variable costing rather than absorption costing are as follows.

- Financial statements using variable costing are understood more easily because they show that profits move in the same direction as sales. This effect is more logical than that shown with absorption costing, where profit is affected by changes in inventory.
- Variable costing facilitates the analysis of cost-volume-profit relationships by separating fixed and variable costs on the income statement.

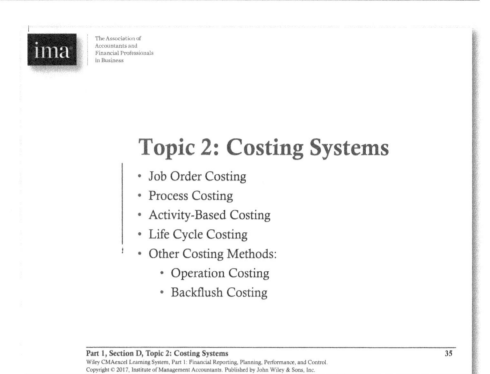

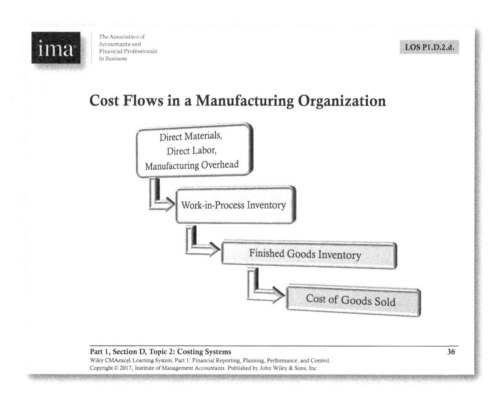

The Association of
Accountants and
Financial Professionals
in Business

LOS P1.D.2.a.

Job Order Costing

- Assigns costs to a specific job, most often based on customer order. Each order is a unique product or service. For example:
  - Wedding invitations or flyers ordered at a print shop
- Each order has its own job cost sheet
- Uses one work-in-process account. All unfinished jobs will total the amount in WIP.

The Association of
Accountants and
Financial Professionals
in Business

LOS P1.D.2.b.

Job Order Costing Process

1. Identify the job and setup a job cost sheet.
2. Trace the direct costs to the job.
3. Allocate indirect costs to the job.
4. Add all costs together to determine the total cost of the job.

The Association of
Accountants and
Financial Professionals
in Business

LOS P1.D.2.b.

Question: Job Order Costing

Lucy Sportswear manufactures a specialty line of T-shirts using a job order costing system. Lucy started and completed Job ICU2. During March the following costs were incurred:

- Direct materials: $13,700
- Direct labor: $4,800
- Administrative expenses: $1,400
- Selling expenses: $5,600

Factory overhead was applied at the rate of $25 per machine hour. Job ICU2 required 800 machine hours. If Job ICU2 resulted in 7,000 shirts, what was the cost of goods sold per unit?

a. $5.50
b. $5.70
c. $6.00
d. $6.30

Answer: a.

COGS = $13,700 + $4,800 + ($25/machine hour × 800 machine hours) = $38,500

COGS per unit = $38,500/7,000 units = $5.50/unit

Note: Selling & Administrative expenses are not product costs, they are period costs. They are not included in COGS.

The Association of
Accountants and
Financial Professionals
in Business

LOS P1.D.2.a.

Process Costing

- Accumulates product or service costs by process or department. It then assigns the costs to a large number of identical or "homogenous" products by dividing the total costs by the total number of units produced. For example:
  - Producing a batch of 10,000 bottles of juice
- Each batch has a standard cost sheet
- Can have one or more WIP accounts

Process Costing Concepts

Unique accounting and terms

- Partially completed units:
    - ▶ Work in process (WIP) at the end of a period
    - ▶ First units completed the following period
- Equivalent units (EUs) determined for WIP at the end of each period. For example:
    - ▪ 100% completed for material when materials are added at beginning of manufacturing process
    - ▪ 50% complete for conversion if labor and overhead are added throughout the process

Note: Labor and overhead costs are often combined and called "**conversion costs**."

Question: Job Order or Process Costing

Which one of the following alternatives correctly classifies the business application to the appropriate costing system?

a. Job costing system: Paint manufacturer
       Process costing system: Retail banking
b. Job costing system: Microcomputer manufacturer
       Process costing system: Construction company
c. Job costing system: Wallpaper manufacturer
       Process costing system: Oil refinery
d. Job costing system: Print shop
       Process costing system: Beverage manufacturer
e. Job costing system: Aircraft assembly
       Process costing system: Public accounting firm

Answer: **d.**

The Association of
Accountants and
Financial Professionals
in Business

LOS P1.D.2.c.

Spoilage, Rework, and Scrap

- Spoilage
  - ▸ Unacceptable material that is discarded or sold
  - ▸ Total Spoilage = Beginning Inventory + Units Started – Units Completed and Transferred Out – Ending Inventory
- Rework
  - ▸ Finished products needing additional remedial processing
- Scrap
  - ▸ Left over after production
  - ▸ Little or no economic value

The Association of
Accountants and
Financial Professionals
in Business

LOS P1.D.2.c.

Accounting for Spoilage, Rework, and Scrap

Type	Charged To:
Abnormal spoilage	Abnormal loss account
Normal spoilage and scrap-specific jobs	Specific job*
Normal spoilage and scrap-common jobs	Factory overhead

* Scrap sales are credited to the account to which the scrap was charged to offset scrap costs.

The Association of
Accountants and
Financial Professionals
in Business

LOS P1.D.2.f.

Process Costing Methods and Treatment of Equivalent Units

Process costing methods

- **First-in, first-out (FIFO).** Calculates unit cost using only costs incurred and work performed during the current period.
- **Weighted average.** Calculates unit cost using all costs including current period and prior periods that are part of current-period beginning WIP inventory.

The Association of
Accountants and
Financial Professionals
in Business

LOS P1.D.2.f.

Process Costing: Equivalent Units of Production

A process costing environment usually will have some partially completed units in its beginning and ending inventory.

Equivalent units represent the number of partially completed units in beginning or ending inventory.

LOS P1.D.2.f.

Basic Concept of Equivalent Units

Two half-completed products are **equivalent to**
one completed product.

10,000 units 50% complete are **equivalent to**
5,000 complete units.

LOS P1.D.2.f.

Process Costing Illustration

This is the first operation to manufacture the product.

- All materials are put into process at the beginning.
- The period starts with 100 units in process that are 40% complete: direct materials costs are $3,000 and conversion costs are $2,200.
- 700 units are started during the period.
- $29,998.80 of direct materials and $23,000 of conversion cost are added during the period.
- 600 units are transferred to the next operation.
- 200 units are in process at the end of the period and are 80% complete.

LOS P1.D.2.f.

Process Costing Generic Steps

1. Prepare a materials balance.
2. Calculate equivalent units of production.
3. Determine costs to be accounted for.
4. Determine the cost per equivalent unit.
5. Assign costs to ending WIP and to completed units sent to the next operation/department.

LOS P1.D.2.f.

Prepare the Materials Balance

Beginning WIP (40% complete)	100
Units Started	700
Units to Account for	**800***
Units Completed from Beginning WIP	100
Units Started and Completed	500
Units Completed	600
Ending WIP (80% complete)	200
Units Accounted for	**800***

Must equal

The Association of
Accountants and
Financial Professionals
in Business

LOS P1.D.2.f.

Production Report—Weighted-Average Method

		Calculation of EU	
		DM	CC
Units Completed from Beginning WIP	100		
Units Started and Completed	500		
Units Completed	600	600	600
Ending WIP	200	200	160
Units Accounted for	800	800	760

Costs to Be Accounted for:			
Beginning WIP	$5,200.00	$3,000.00	$2,200.00
Costs Added during the Period	52,998.80	29,998.80	23,000.00
Total Costs to be Accounted for	$58,198.80	$32,998.80	$25,200.00
		÷ 800	÷ 760
Unit Cost per Equivalent Unit:		= $41.24850	= $33.15789
Costs Transferred Out	$44,643.84	$24,749.10*	$19,894.74*
Ending WIP	13,554.96	8,249.70*	5,305.26*
Total Costs Accounted for	$58,198.80	$32,998.80	$25,200.00

* 600 × $41.24850 = $24,749.10   600 × $33.15789 = $19,894.74
* 200 × $41.24850 = $ 8,249.70   160 × $33.15789 = $ 5,305.26

The Association of
Accountants and
Financial Professionals
in Business

LOS P1.D.2.f.

Production Report—FIFO Method

		Calculation of EU	
		DM	CC
Units Completed from Beginning WIP	100	0	60
Units Started and Completed	500	500	500
Units Completed	600		
Ending WIP	200	200	160
Units Accounted for	800	700	720

Costs to Be Accounted for:			
Beginning WIP	$5,200.00	$3,000.00	$2,200.00
Costs Added during the Period	52,998.80	29,998.80	23,000.00
Total Costs to be Accounted for	$58,198.80	$32,998.80	$25,200.00
Costs Added during the Period	$52,998.80	$29,998.80	$23,000.00
		÷ 700	÷ 720
Cost per Equivalent Unit		$42.85543	$31.94444
Assignment of Costs:			
Beginning WIP Inventory	$5,200.00	$3,000.00	$2,200.00
Cost of Completing Units in WIP	1,916.67	0.00	1,916.67
Cost of Started and Completed Units	37,399.94	21,427.72	15,972.22
Cost of Units Transferred Out	$44,516.60	$24,427.72	$20,088.89
Ending WIP Inventory	13,682.20	8,571.09	5,111.11
Total Costs Accounted for	$58,198.80	$32,998.80	$25,200.00

The Association of
Accountants and
Financial Professionals
in Business

LOS P1.D.2.a., b., e., and i.

Activity-Based Costing (ABC)

- Based on the principle that all products produced or services performed by an organization do not require same amount of overhead.
- Recognizes that **activities** consume resources, and **products or services** use activities.
- Allocates overhead costs to products or services based on consumption of resources.
- Overhead costs are put into cost pools and the cost driver is determined based on a cause and effect relationship.
- Yields more accurate assignment of overhead costs.
- Is not a substitute for job costing or process costing used for manufacturing.
- Requires additional effort to set up and maintain.

The Association of
Accountants and
Financial Professionals
in Business

LOS P1.D.2.a. and b.

Key Steps in ABC

Step 1: Identify activities to be used as cost drivers and resource costs:

  ▸ Unit level, batch level, or customer level.
  ▸ Product sustaining or facility sustaining.

Step 2: Assign resource costs to cost pools.

Step 3: Determine the cost pool rate:

$$\text{Rate} = \frac{\text{Cost Pool}}{\text{Driver Units}}$$

Step 4: Assign overhead costs to cost objects.

LOS P1.D.2.a. and b.

Question: Costing Using ABC

New Cosmetics has a traditional cost accounting system that applies quality control costs uniformly to all products at a rate of 14.5% of DL cost. New's monthly DL cost = $27,500. To more equitably distribute quality control costs, New is considering ABC. New's monthly data:

Activity	Cost Driver	Cost Rates	Quantity
Incoming DM inspection	Type of material	$11.50/type	12 types
In-process inspection	Number of units	$0.14/unit	17,500 units
Product certification	Per order	$77/order	25 orders

The monthly quality control cost assigned to New Cosmetics using ABC is

a. $88.64 per order.
b. $525.50 lower than the cost using the traditional system.
c. $525.50 higher than the cost using the traditional system.
d. $3,987.50.

Answer: c.

Based on ICMA
question, used
with permission

Part 1, Section D, Topic 2: Costing Systems
Wiley CMAexcel Learning System, Part 1: Financial Reporting, Planning, Performance, and Control.
Copyright © 2017, Institute of Management Accountants. Published by John Wiley & Sons, Inc.

55

LOS P1.D.2.a. and b.

Explanation of Costing Using ABC

Quality control under traditional cost accounting system: 14.5% of DL cost, with monthly DL cost = $27,500
Traditional cost of quality control = $27,500 × 0.145 = $3,987.50

Activity	Cost Driver	Cost Rates	Quantity	Cost × Qty.
Incoming DM inspection	Type of material	$11.50/type	12 types	$138
In-process inspection	Number of units	$0.14/unit	17,500 units	$2,450
Product certification	Per order	$77/order	25 orders	$1,295

Quality control under ABC = $138 + $2,450 + $1,925
= $4,513
Difference = $4,513 − $3,987.50
= $525.50 (amount that ABC is higher than traditional)

The Association of
Accountants and
Financial Professionals
in Business

LOS P1.D.2.g., h., and i.

Question: ABC's Two Stages of Allocation

What are ABC's two stages of allocation?

Answer:

- **Stage 1:** Resource cost **assignment of overhead to activity cost pools** or centers using resource cost drivers
- **Stage 2:** Activity cost **assignment of activity costs to cost objects** using activity cost drivers

The Association of
Accountants and
Financial Professionals
in Business

LOS P1.D.2.h.

Comparing ABC and Traditional Costing

ABC	Traditional Costing
Firms with high product diversity or complexity; high likelihood of cost distortion	Firms with simple, standard products, no custom orders
Multiple cost drivers; best of activity based and volume based	Fewer cost drivers with best general fit: usually volume based
Overhead assigned to activities and then from activities to products or services	Overhead assigned to departments and then from departments to products or services
Focus on solving costing and processing issues that cross departmental lines	Focus on assigning responsibility to department managers for own cost savings

Life-Cycle Costing

- Considers all costs from product *conception* through *sales* through *warranty service.* These are all the costs along the value chain
- Is strategic basis for costing and pricing
- Includes:
  - Upstream costs for R&D and design
  - Manufacturing costs
  - Downstream costs for marketing, distribution, service costs, and warranty costs

Other Costing Methods

- **Operation Costing**:
  - Combines job costing and process costing
    - DM and DL assigned using job costing
    - Overhead assigned using process costing
  - Suitable for the following industries:
    - Clothing manufacturer, metalworking, and furniture
  - Clothing manufacturer example:
    - Has standard operations for cutting and sewing
    - The fabrics used vary by item, size, color, and price

Other Costing Methods (cont.)

- **Backflush Costing**:
    - Used for JIT (Just In Time) production systems
    - Assumes materials are put into production and products are finished immediately
        - Does not use WIP accounts
    - Is not in strict accordance with GAAP

Session 9 Exercise 2

Equivalent Units in Process Costing
Section D, Topic 2: Costing Systems

Session 9 Exercise 2: Equivalent Units in Process Costing

Section D, Topic 2: Costing Systems

Kristina Company, which manufactures quality paint sold at premium prices, uses a single production department. Production begins with the blending of various chemicals, which are added at the beginning of the process, and ends with the canning of the paint. Canning occurs when the mixture reaches the 90% stage of completion. The gallon cans are then transferred to the shipping department for crating and shipment. Labor and overhead are added continuously throughout the process. Factory overhead is applied on the basis of direct labor hours at the rate of $3.00 per hour.

Prior to May, when a change in process was implemented, work-in-process inventories were insignificant. The change in the process enables greater production but results in material amounts of work in process for the first time. The company has always used the weighted-average method to determine equivalent production and unit costs. Now production management is considering changing from the weighted-average method to the FIFO method.

The following data relate to actual production during the month of May.

Costs for May	
Work-in-process inventory, May 1 (4,000 gallons 25% complete)	
Direct materials—chemicals	$45,600
Direct labor ($10 per hour)	6,250
Factory overhead	1,875
May costs added	
Direct materials—chemicals	228,400
Direct materials—cans	7,000
Direct labor ($10 per hour)	$35,000
Factory Overhead	$10,500

Units for May	Gallons
Work-in-process inventory, May 1 (25% complete)	4,000
Sent to shipping department	20,000
Started in May	21,000
Work-in-process inventory, May 31 (80% complete)	5,000

Question 1: Prepare a schedule of equivalent units for each cost element for the month of May using the weighted-average method.

Question 2: Prepare a schedule of equivalent units for each cost element for the month of May using the FIFO method.

Question 3: Calculate the cost (to the nearest cent) per equivalent unit for each cost element for the month of May using the weighted-average method.

Question 4: Calculate the cost (to the nearest cent) per equivalent unit for each cost element for the month of May using the FIFO method.

Question 5: Discuss the advantages and disadvantages of using the weighted-average method versus the FIFO method, and explain under what circumstances each method should be used.

Session 9 Exercise 2 Solution: Equivalent Units in Process Costing

Question 1: Prepare a schedule of equivalent units for each cost element for the month of May using the weighted average method.

The equivalent units for each cost element, using the weighted-average method, are presented next.

	Direct Materials		
	Chemicals	Cans	Conversion*
Units completed and transferred to shipping	20,000	20,000	20,000
Work in process at 5/31			
Chemicals (100%)	5,000		
Cans (0%)		0	
Conversion costs (80%)			4,000
Equivalent units	25,000	20,000	24,000

*Conversion Cost = Direct Labor + Factory Overhead

Question 2: Prepare a schedule of equivalent units for each cost element for the month of May using the FIFO method.

The equivalent units for each cost element, using the FIFO method, are presented next.

	Direct Materials		
	Chemicals	Cans	Conversion
Transferred to shipping from 5/1 work in process (4,000 @ 25%)			
Chemicals	0		
Cans (100%)		4,000	
Conversion costs (75%)			3,000
Current production transferred to shipping (100%)	16,000	16,000	16,000
5/31 work in process (5,000 @ 80%)			
Chemicals (100%)	5,000		
Cans (0%)		0	
Conversion costs (80%)			4,000
Equivalent units	21,000	20,000	23,000

Question 3: Calculate the cost (to the nearest cent) per equivalent unit for each cost element for the month of May using the weighted-average method.

The cost per equivalent unit for each cost element, using the weighted-average method, is presented next.

	Direct Materials		
	Chemicals	Cans	Conversion
Work in process at 5/1	$45,600	$0	$8,125
May costs added	228,400	7,000	45,500
Total costs	$274,000	$7,000	$53,625
÷			
Weighted-average equivalent units	25,000	20,000	24,000
Cost per equivalent units	$10.96	$0.35	$2.23

Question 4: Calculate the cost (to the nearest cent) per equivalent unit for each cost element for the month of May using the FIFO method.

The cost per equivalent unit for each cost element, using the FIFO method, is presented next.

	Direct Materials		
	Chemicals	Cans	Conversion
May costs incurred	$228,400	$7,000	$45,500
÷			
First-in, first-out equivalent units	21,000	20,000	23,000
Cost per equivalent units	$10.88	$0.35	$1.98

Question 5: Discuss the advantages and disadvantages of using the weighted-average method versus the FIFO method, and explain under what circumstances each method should be used.

The weighted average method generally is easier to use because the calculations are simpler. This method tends to obscure current-period costs because the cost per equivalent unit includes both current costs and prior costs that were in the beginning inventory. This method is the most appropriate when conversion costs, inventory levels, and raw material prices are stable.

The FIFO method is based on the work done in the current period only. This method is most appropriate when conversion costs, inventory levels, or raw material prices fluctuate. In addition, this method should be used when accuracy in current equivalent unit costs is important or when a standard cost system is used.

The Association of
Accountants and
Financial Professionals
in Business

Session 9 Wrap-Up

Content covered in Session 9

- Section D, Topic 1: Measurement Concepts
- Session 9 Exercise 1: Absorption versus Variable Costing
- Section D, Topic 2: Costing Systems
- Session 9 Exercise 2: Equivalent Units in Process Costing

Content to be covered in Session 10

- Section D, Topic 3: Overhead Costs
- Section D, Topic 4: Supply Chain Management
- Section D, Topic 5: Business Process Improvement
- Section D Practice Questions

Part 1: Financial Reporting, Planning, Performance, and Control   63
Wiley CMAexcel Learning System, Part 1: Financial Reporting, Planning, Performance, and Control.
Copyright © 2017, Institute of Management Accountants. Published by John Wiley & Sons, Inc.

Session 10

The Association of
Accountants and
Financial Professionals
in Business

Wiley
CMAexcel Learning System
Exam Review 2017

Part 1: Financial Reporting, Planning, Performance, and Control

Session 10

Learning Outcome Statements (LOS) identifiers appear on the
slides as applicable to highlight where we address each LOS
within the material.

Session 9 Recap

- Section D, Topic 1: Measurement Concepts
- Session 9 Exercise 1: Absorption versus Variable Costing
- Section D, Topic 2: Costing Systems
- Session 9 Exercise 2: Equivalent Units in Process Costing

Session 10 Overview

- Section D, Topic 3: Overhead Costs
- Section D, Topic 4: Supply Chain Management
- Section D, Topic 5: Business Process Improvement
- Section D Practice Questions

The Association of
Accountants and
Financial Professionals
in Business

Topic 3: Overhead Costs

- Fixed and Variable Overhead Expenses
- Plant-Wide versus Departmental Overhead
- Activity-Based Costing Overhead Allocation
- Determination of Allocation Base
- Allocation of Service Department Costs

The Association of
Accountants and
Financial Professionals
in Business

LOS P1.D.3.a. and b.

Fixed and Variable Overhead Costs

- Fixed overhead costs
  - ▸ Are fixed over the relevant range most often for one year and based on operating capacity. The amounts change less frequently than variable overhead costs.

- Variable overhead costs
  - ▸ The total can be influenced on a day-to-day basis based on activity. Amounts are estimated over the same relevant range but could be updated during the time period.

The Association of
Accountants and
Financial Professionals
in Business

LOS P1.D.3.q.

Two Techniques to Separate Fixed and Variable Overhead Cost Components

1. **High-Low Method**

Month	Production Activity	Wages
July	2,000 units	$30,000
August	1,800 units	$28,000
September	1,900 units	$29,000
October	2,100 units	$31,000

Highest Activity—October	2,100 units	$31,000	
Lowest Activity—August	1,800 units	$28,000	
Difference	300 units	$ 3,000 / 300 units = $10	

Total cost	$28,000
Minus: VC $10 ×,800	$18,000
= Fixed Cost	$10,000

Part 1, Section D, Topic 3: Overhead Costs   6
Wiley CMAexcel Learning System, Part 1: Financial Reporting, Planning, Performance, and Control.
Copyright © 2017, Institute of Management Accountants. Published by John Wiley & Sons, Inc.

The Association of
Accountants and
Financial Professionals
in Business

LOS P1.D.3.q.

Two Techniques to Separate Fixed and Variable Overhead Cost Components (cont.)

2. **Regression Analysis Method**

Simple rules apply:

- Need a computer program such as Excel
- Need many observations in time series data. Do not want to have too few
- Need confidence that another variable is not influencing the variation in the data

Part 1, Section D, Topic 3: Overhead Costs   7
Wiley CMAexcel Learning System, Part 1: Financial Reporting, Planning, Performance, and Control.
Copyright © 2017, Institute of Management Accountants. Published by John Wiley & Sons, Inc.

The Association of
Accountants and
Financial Professionals
in Business

LOS P1.D.3.j.

Allocation of Fixed and Variable Manufacturing Costs

Allocated to products through predetermined overhead rates as discussed in the previous session:

1. Determine accounting period; normally annual basis
2. Determine allocation base or cost driver
3. Determine overhead costs associated with the cost driver
4. Calculate the overhead rate:

$$\frac{\text{Overhead Costs}}{\text{Allocation Base}} = \text{Overhead Rate}$$

The Association of
Accountants and
Financial Professionals
in Business

LOS P1.D.3.c.

Question: Departmental versus Plant-Wide Overhead Rates

Generally, individual departmental rates rather than a plant-wide rate for applying overhead would be used if

a. a company's manufacturing operations are all highly automated.
b. manufacturing overhead is the largest cost component of its product cost.
c. the manufactured products differ in the resources consumed from the individual departments in the plant.
d. a company wants to adopt a standard cost system.

Answer: c.

LOS P1.D.3.c.

Departmental versus Plant-Wide Overhead Rates

A key factor in determining how to develop and use overhead costs is to allocate overhead to individual products based on each product's usage of the overhead.

Allocation base should influence the overhead costs—meaning there should be a cause-and-effect relationship.

LOS P1.D.3.c. and I.

ABC Overhead Costing

- Generally more accurate than plant-wide and department rates.
- Allocation base uses cost drivers that have a cause-and-effect relationship with the overhead costs.
- Separate costs into cost pools with identifiable cost drivers. For example:
    - Cost pool: Equipment maintenance
    - Cost driver: Machine hours by machine type

LOS P1.D.3.c. and m.

Costing System Comparison: Zeta Company

Zeta Company is preparing its annual profit plan. As part of its analysis of the profitability of individual products, the controller estimates the amount of overhead that should be allocated to the individual product lines from the following information:

	Wall Mirrors	Specialty Windows
Units produced	25	25
Material moves per product line	5	15
Direct labor hours per unit	200	200
Budgeted materials handling costs = $50,000		

Based on ICMA question, used with permission   **Part 1, Section D, Topic 3: Overhead Costs**   12
Wiley CMAexcel Learning System, Part 1: Financial Reporting, Planning, Performance, and Control.
Copyright © 2017, Institute of Management Accountants. Published by John Wiley & Sons, Inc.

LOS P1.D.3.c.

Allocating Overhead Based on DL Hours

Under a costing system that allocates overhead on the basis of direct labor hours, calculate the materials handling costs for one wall mirror.

Wall Mirror   200 DLH per unit × 25 units = 5,000 DLH
Specialty Window   200 DLH per unit × 25 units = 5,000 DLH
   Total Units and DLH   **50   10,000**

$50,000 / 50 total finished units = $1,000 material handling cost/unit

Or

$50,000 / 10,000 = $5.00 × 200 DLH = $1,000 material handling cost/unit

Based on ICMA question, used with permission   **Part 1, Section D, Topic 3: Overhead Costs**   13
Wiley CMAexcel Learning System, Part 1: Financial Reporting, Planning, Performance, and Control.
Copyright © 2017, Institute of Management Accountants. Published by John Wiley & Sons, Inc.

The Association of
Accountants and
Financial Professionals
in Business

LOS P1.D.3.c. and g.

Allocating Overhead Based on Material Moves Using ABC

Under an ABC system that allocates overhead on the basis of material moves, calculate the materials handling costs for one wall mirror.

Wall Mirror	5 moves per unit × 25 units = 125 moves
Specialty Window	15 moves per unit × 25 units = 375 moves
Total Material Moves	**20** **500**

$50,000 / 500 moves = $100 of material handling costs per material move

Wall Mirror	**5 moves × $100 = $500 per unit**
Specialty Window	**15 moves × $100 = $1,500 per unit**

Based on ICMA question, used with permission

Part 1, Section D, Topic 3: Overhead Costs

Wiley CMAexcel Learning System, Part 1: Financial Reporting, Planning, Performance, and Control.
Copyright © 2017, Institute of Management Accountants. Published by John Wiley & Sons, Inc.

14

The Association of
Accountants and
Financial Professionals
in Business

LOS P1.D.3.d. and n.

Benefits and Limitations of the Methods to Determine Overhead Rates

Method:	Benefits	Limitations
Plant-Wide Rate	-Simple, easy to use -Works well if strong cause and effect relationship of the single cost driver	Allocation of costs is not as accurate if many, complex products
Departmental Rates	More accurate allocation of costs than the plant-wide rate	-Only works well if each department is homogenous. -Strong cause and effect relationship of the cost driver
ABC	-Helps identify inefficient operations -Most accurate allocation of costs	-Requires time and effort to set up and maintain -May require new accounting system

Based on ICMA question, used with permission

Part 1, Section D, Topic 3: Overhead Costs

Wiley CMAexcel Learning System, Part 1: Financial Reporting, Planning, Performance, and Control.
Copyright © 2017, Institute of Management Accountants. Published by John Wiley & Sons, Inc.

15

The Association of
Accountants and
Financial Professionals
in Business

LOS P1.D.3.i. and o.

Allocation of Service Department Costs

* Operating/Production departments
  ▶ Carry out the central purposes or operations of the organization
* Service departments
  ▶ Provide support or assistance to operating departments

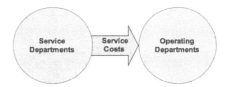

Service department costs are allocated to operating departments.

The Association of
Accountants and
Financial Professionals
in Business

LOS P1.D.3.e., f., and g.

Service Departments May Be Allocated In Total or Separately by Fixed and Variable

* In total is known as "single-rate cost allocation method."
* Separately by fixed and variable is known as "contribution margin cost allocation method."

The Association of
Accountants and
Financial Professionals
in Business

LOS P1.D.3.e. and f.

Using the Single-Rate Allocation Method

- The single-rate method creates a single allocation base for a service department's combined fixed and variable costs.
- When fixed costs are grouped with variable costs, the entire cost seems to be a variable cost.
- Gives the appearance of a higher rate compared to the outsource rate.
- However, fixed department costs would continue to be incurred, at least in the short term.
- Department would be adding new external costs while still incurring the fixed portion of internal costs.
- Managers should apply the contribution margin method before making a decision.

The Association of
Accountants and
Financial Professionals
in Business

LOS P1.D.3.e. and f.

Question: Single-Rate Cost Allocation Method

A company uses a single-rate method for allocation of its human resources (HR) department costs at a rate of $200/direct labor hour (DLH). Management is contacted by an HR outsourcer charging only $175/DLH.

Which of the following would be the MOST appropriate choice in the short term?

a. Go with the outsourcer and keep using the single-rate method for evaluations.
b. Apply the contribution margin method before making a decision.
c. Go with the outsourcer but apply the contribution margin method for evaluations.

Answer: **b.**

LOS P1.D.3.o. and p.

Allocating Service Department Costs

- Phase 1: Trace all planned costs directly to the individual service and production departments responsible for controlling them. This is implicit in responsibility accounting.

- Phase 2: Allocate service department costs to production departments or other service departments using one of the following:
  - Direct method
  - Step-down method
  - Reciprocal method

- Phase 3: Allocate production department costs to products.

LOS P1.D.3.o. and p.

Allocating Service Department Costs to Production Costs (Phase 2)

- Direct method (direct allocation method)
  - Allocates service department costs to production departments only
- Step-down method (proportional method)
  - Allocates service department costs to both production and other service departments
- Reciprocal method
  - Allocates service department costs to all service departments and to production departments

LOS P1.D.3.p.

Service Department Allocation: Direct Method

Service costs allocated directly to production using relevant cost drivers

	Service		Production		
	HR	Janitorial	Metal Dept.	Chrome Dept.	Total
Dept. costs before allocation	$200,000	$80,000	$400,000	$100,000	$780,000
Allocate HR	(200,000)	0	160,000	40,000	
Allocate Jan.	0	(80,000)	60,000	20,000	
New Totals	$0	$0	$620,000	$160,000	$780,000
Labor hours	10,000	5,000	20,000	5,000	
Space (sq. ft.)	15,000	500	60,000	20,000	

LOS P1.D.3.p.

Calculating Service Department Allocations: Direct Method

$$\text{Department Allocation} = \frac{\text{Production Dept. Units}}{\text{Total Units for All Prod. Depts.}} \times \text{Dept. Costs}$$

$$\text{HR Costs to Metal Dept.} = \frac{20,000}{20,000 + 5,000} \times \$200,000$$

$$= 0.8 \times \$200,000 = \$160,000$$

$$\text{HR Costs to Chrome Dept.} = 0.2 \times \$200,000 = \$40,000$$

$$\text{Janitorial Costs to Metal Dept.} = \frac{60,000}{60,000 + 20,000} \times \$80,000$$

$$= 0.75 \times \$80,000 = \$60,000$$

$$\text{Janitorial Costs to Chrome Dept.} = 0.25 \times \$80,000 = \$20,000$$

LOS P1.D.3.p.

Service Department Allocation: Step-Down Method

Service department costs allocated to other service departments and then to production

	Service		Production		
	HR	Janitorial	Metal Dept.	Chrome Dept.	Total
Dept. costs before allocation	$200,000	$80,000	$400,000	$100,000	$780,000
First step:	($200,000)	$33,333	$133,334	$33,333	
Subtotal	$0	$113,333	$533,334	$133,333	
Second step:		($113,333)	$85,000	$28,333	
New Totals	$0	$0	$618,334	$161,666	$780,000
Labor hours	10,000	5,000	20,000	5,000	30,000
Space (sq. ft.)	15,000	500	60,000	20,000	60,500

LOS P1.D.3.p.

Reciprocal Method Illustrated

Requires setting up and solving a system of simultaneous equations.

$$HR = \$200,000 + (15,000/95,000 \times J)$$

$$J = \$80,000 + (5,000/30,000 \times HR)$$

$$HR = \$200,000 + (0.15789 \times J)$$

$$J = \$80,000 + (0.16667 \times HR)$$

$$HR = \$200,000 + 0.15789 \, (\$80,000 + 0.16667 \times HR)$$
$$HR = \$200,000 + \$12,631.20 + (0.02632 \times HR)$$
$$1HR - (0.02632 \times HR) = \$212,631.20$$
$$0.97368HR = \$212,631.20$$
$$HR = \$212,631.20 / 0.97368 = \$218,378.93$$

Note: you need to consider the support the service departments provides to itself.

The Association of
Accountants and
Financial Professionals
in Business

LOS P1.D.3.p.

Question: Using Step-Down Method

M&P Tool has three service departments that support the production area. Estimated overhead by department for the upcoming year:

Service Departments	Estimated Overhead	# of Employees	Production Departments	# of Employees
Receiving	$25,000	2	Assembly	25
Repair	$35,000	2	Bolting	12
Tool	$10,000	1		

The Repair Department supports the most departments, followed by the Tool Department. Overhead cost is allocated to departments based on the number of employees. Using the step-down method of allocation, the allocation from the Repair Department to the Tool Department would be

a. $0.
b. $875.
c. $7,000.
d. $11,667.

Answer: **b.**
One employee in Tool Department/(2 + 1 + 25 + 12 total employees) = 1/40 × $35,000 = $875.
Note: Total employees amount of 40 does not include the Repair Department employees.

Based on ICMA question, used with permission   **Part 1, Section D, Topic 3: Overhead Costs**   26
Wiley CMAexcel Learning System, Part 1: Financial Reporting, Planning, Performance, and Control.
Copyright © 2017, Institute of Management Accountants. Published by John Wiley & Sons, Inc.

The Association of
Accountants and
Financial Professionals
in Business

Topic 4: Supply Chain Management

- Supply Chain Management
- Materials Resources Planning (MRP)
- Enterprise Resource Planning (ERP)
- Just-in-time Manufacturing (JIT)
- Lean Manufacturing
- Theory of Constraints and Throughput Costing
- Capacity concepts
- Other production management theories

Part 1, Section D, Topic 4: Supply Chain Management   27
Wiley CMAexcel Learning System, Part 1: Financial Reporting, Planning, Performance, and Control.
Copyright © 2017, Institute of Management Accountants. Published by John Wiley & Sons, Inc.

The Association of
Accountants and
Financial Professionals
in Business

LOS P1.D.4.a.

What Is Supply Chain Management?

- Involves the management of the flow of goods.
- Includes the planning and management of all activities involved in sourcing and procuring raw materials, converting those materials to a finished product, and delivering that finished product to customers.
- Objective is to integrate procurement, operations management, logistics, and information technology, while creating value through a chain of key processes and activities.

The Association of
Accountants and
Financial Professionals
in Business

LOS P1.D.4.d. and e.

Materials Requirements Planning versus Just-in-Time

Materials Requirement Planning (MRP)

- Demand forecast is push-through
- Uses bill of materials including components and subassembly tasks
- Specified quantities of ingredients forecast needed for outputs
- Master production schedule sets timing and all departments follow, regardless of demand

Just-in-Time (JIT)

- Demand-pull
- Comprehensive production and inventory control
- Materials arrive exactly when needed
- Reduce/eliminate waste, lowers inventory
- Requires close coordination

LOS P1.D.4.e.

Components of JIT and Use of Kanban

Characteristics of a JIT environment:

- Production organized into manufacturing cells
- Multiskilled workers
- Reduced setup times
- Reduced manufacturing lead times
- Reliable suppliers

Kanban in JIT implementation:

- Visual record or card signals demand between departments

Part 1, Section D, Topic 4: Supply Chain Management
Wiley CMAexcel Learning System, Part 1: Financial Reporting, Planning, Performance, and Control.
Copyright © 2017, Institute of Management Accountants. Published by John Wiley & Sons, Inc.

30

LOS P1.D.4.e.

Advantages and Limitations of JIT

Advantages	Limitations
• Obvious production priorities • Reduced setup/lead time • No overproduction • Faster feedback for quality control and less waste • Easier inventory control • Less paperwork • Strong supplier relationships • Minimize inventories	• No buffer inventory; production may wait • Reliance on suppliers; highly dependent on supply chain • Potential stockouts at suppliers • Potential overtime (unexpected orders)

Part 1, Section D, Topic 4: Supply Chain Management
Wiley CMAexcel Learning System, Part 1: Financial Reporting, Planning, Performance, and Control.
Copyright © 2017, Institute of Management Accountants. Published by John Wiley & Sons, Inc.

31

LOS P1.D.4.f.

Enterprise Resource Planning (ERP)

- An expansion of MRP
- Intended to improve operational efficiency and reduce waste by allowing department and functions across an organization to use resources and send workflow through a single computer system.
- Fundamental advantage: Saves time and expense by integrating a myriad of business processes.
- Disadvantages include: problems with customization, higher costs than less comprehensive solutions, extensive training, overcoming resistance to sharing sensitive information between departments, diversion of focus on critical activities associated with the re-engineering of business processes to fit the ERP system.

Based on ICMA question, used with permission   **Part 1, Section D, Topic 4: Supply Chain Management**   32
Wiley CMAexcel Learning System, Part 1: Financial Reporting, Planning, Performance, and Control.
Copyright © 2017, Institute of Management Accountants. Published by John Wiley & Sons, Inc.

LOS P1.D.4.b. and c.

Lean Manufacturing

- Lean manufacturing, also called lean enterprise, lean production, or simply "lean," is a production practice that considers the use of resources for any goal other than creation of customer value to be wasteful, and a target for elimination.
- Goal is to *maximize customer value*, while *minimizing waste*.
- "Waste" is not just scrap or rework; it is anything the customer does not want to pay for, or that does not create value for the customer.
- The concept of "lean" can apply to business practices and other processes in addition to manufacturing.
- Primary benefits are reduced waste and improved production flow. Both lead to reduced costs.
- *Just-in-time (JIT) manufacturing* is an outcome of *lean manufacturing*.

Based on ICMA question, used with permission   **Part 1, Section D, Topic 4: Supply Chain Management**   33
Wiley CMAexcel Learning System, Part 1: Financial Reporting, Planning, Performance, and Control.
Copyright © 2017, Institute of Management Accountants. Published by John Wiley & Sons, Inc.

The Association of
Accountants and
Financial Professionals
in Business

LOS P1.D.4.g.

Outsourcing

Decision to purchase product/service from outside supplier

- Make versus buy analysis
- Contract manufacturing

Allows firm to concentrate on core business

The Association of
Accountants and
Financial Professionals
in Business

LOS P1.D.4.g.

Advantages and Limitations of Outsourcing

Advantages	Limitations
• Focus on strategic revenue-generating activities • Outside expertise improves efficiency and effectiveness • Access to current technology at low cost and no risk of obsolescence • Allows the organization to shift some of its fixed costs to variable costs • May improve quality and timeliness of products/services	• May cost more • Loss of in-house expertise • Can reduce process control • May reduce quality control • May lead to less flexibility (depending on external supplier) • May result in less personalized service • Can result in knowledge give-away • Creates privacy/confidentiality issues • Potential for employee morale/loyalty issues

The Association of
Accountants and
Financial Professionals
in Business

LOS P1.D.4.g.

Question: Reasons to Outsource

Which of the following is a reason to outsource?

a. Reduced privacy issues from improved supplier relationships
b. Access to new technology without obsolescence risk
c. Less dependence on a traditional supply chain
d. Improved employee morale and loyalty

Answer: **b.**
**Outsourcing can provide access to current technologies at
reasonable cost without the risk of obsolescence if purchased
by the firm.**

36

The Association of
Accountants and
Financial Professionals
in Business

LOS P1.D.4.h.

Theory of Constraints (TOC) Terminology

TOC is a management philosophy based in a manufacturing
environment. Terminology:

- System
- Constraint
- Cycle time
- Constraint management
- Inventory (I)
- Operating expenses (OE)
- Throughput (T)
- Drum-buffer-rope (DBR) system

37

The Association of
Accountants and
Financial Professionals
in Business

LOS P1.D.4.j., k., and n.

Three Measurements Used in TOC

1. Throughput Contribution = Sales Revenue – Direct Material Costs

2. Inventory = Cost of Direct Materials in DM, WIP, and FG
    Inventories + R&D Cost + Costs of Equipment and Buildings

3. Operating Expenses = All Costs of Operations, except Direct
    Materials

Throughput Contribution or Costing is considered to be a super-
variable costing method.

The Association of
Accountants and
Financial Professionals
in Business

LOS P1.D.4.k.

Throughput Contribution Example

Throughput Contribution = Sales Revenue – Direct Material Costs

$200 = sales revenue for a product

$45 = cost of parts purchased from external vendors

$20 = sales commissions paid (10% of each sale)

$22 = transportation costs

Throughput Contribution = $200 – $45 = $155

The Association of
Accountants and
Financial Professionals
in Business

LOS P1.D.4.h.

Managing Constraints

- **Exploiting** the constraint changes how the organization uses the constraint without spending more money

- **Elevating** the constraint requires spending money to increase the constrained resource's capacity (purchase or outsource)

See Statement on Management Accounting, *Theory of Constraints (TOC) Management System Fundamentals.*

The Association of
Accountants and
Financial Professionals
in Business

LOS P1.D.4.i.

Steps in the Theory of Constraints

1. Identify the system constraint (weakest link).
2. Decide how to *exploit* the constraint. Use every part of constraining component without committing to expensive changes/upgrades.
3. Subordinate everything else. Adjust the rest of system to give constraint maximum throughput.
4. *Elevate* the constraint. Take whatever action is needed to eliminate it. Using this step means Steps 2 and 3 were insufficient.
5. Go back to Step 1, but beware of inertia.

The Association of
Accountants and
Financial Professionals
in Business

TOC Management Fundamentals

TOC focuses on three things:

T = Throughput   **I = Inventory**   **OE = Operating Expenses**

- Net profit increases when T goes up or OE go down.
- T can go up by increasing sales revenues or reducing variable costs of production.
- Measures that increase net profit increase ROI—as long as I remains the same.
- If I can be decreased, ROI goes up even without an increase in net profit.
- Cash flow increases when either T goes up or the time to generate T is reduced (assuming the time saved is applied toward generating more T).

The Association of
Accountants and
Financial Professionals
in Business

Theory of Constraint Reports

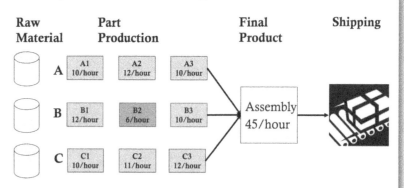

The slowest operation is B2 (6/hour); output from this constraint (the weakest link) determines output of the entire system.

The Association of
Accountants and
Financial Professionals
in Business

LOS P1.D.4.h.

Question: Theory of Constraints (TOC)

The theory of constraints

a. focuses on eliminating constraints and improving/speeding up cycle or delivery time.
b. uses long-term time horizon.
c. assumes direct labor costs are fixed.
d. implies all of the above.

Answers: a and c.

The Association of
Accountants and
Financial Professionals
in Business

LOS P1.D.4.l. and m.

Allocation of Overhead Based on Capacity

Allocation of overhead is tied to capacity level:

- **Theoretical capacity.** Capacity achieved under ideal conditions.
- **Practical capacity.** Highest level of capacity achievable under normal operating conditions.
  - Takes into account equipment maintenance, breakdowns, employee vacations, and so on.
  - Is realistic and achievable

The Association of
Accountants and
Financial Professionals
in Business

LOS P1.D.4.a.

Other Production Management Techniques

- Automation and robotics
- Computer-aided design (CAD)
- Computer-aided manufacturing (CAM)
- Computer-integrated manufacturing (CIM)
- Concurrent engineering (simultaneous engineering)
- Flexible manufacturing system (FMS)
- Capacity management and analysis (capacity planning)

The Association of
Accountants and
Financial Professionals
in Business

Topic 5: Business Process Improvement

- Value chain analysis
- Value-added concepts
- Process analysis
- Benchmarking
- Activity-based management
- Continuous improvement concepts
- Best practice analysis
- Cost of quality analysis
- Business process improvement in accounting operations

The Association of Accountants and Financial Professionals in Business

LOS P1.D.5.a.

Value Chain Analysis (VCA)

Strategic tool to assess the importance of each customer's value perceptions by defining current costs and performance measures and how to reduce costs and increase customer value through:

- Value
- Value-added activities
- Value chain
- Cost driver (structural, executional)
- Supply chain

Part 1, Section D, Topic 5: Business Process Improvement 48

Wiley CMAexcel Learning System, Part 1: Financial Reporting, Planning, Performance, and Control.

The Association of Accountants and Financial Professionals in Business

LOS P1.D.5.b.

Typical Value Chain for Manufacturing

NOTE:
Production includes the acquisition of Raw Materials. *Marketing* includes the selling function. *Customer Service* is provided after the sale is made. *Customer Service* feeds back into *Research and Development* making the value chain a continuous cycle.

Part 1, Section D, Topic 5: Business Process Improvement 49

Wiley CMAexcel Learning System, Part 1: Financial Reporting, Planning, Performance, and Control.

LOS P1.D.5.c.

Value Chain Approach to Assess Competitive Advantage

1. **Internal cost analysis should:**

   Determine sources of profitability and relative cost of internal processes or activities; evaluate opportunities for achieving relative cost advantage.

2. **Internal differentiation analysis should:**

   Examine sources for creating superior differentiation, with primary focus on customers' value perceptions.

3. **Vertical linkage analysis is:**

   Broader application of Steps 1 and 2; includes all upstream and downstream value-creating processes.

See Statement on Management Accounting, *Value Chain Analysis for Assessing Competitive Advantage*.

LOS P1.D.5.d.

Customer–Supplier Value Chain

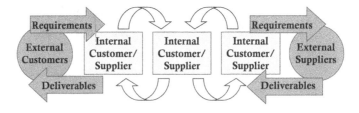

The Association of
Accountants and
Financial Professionals
in Business

LOS P1.D.5.e.

Process Analysis

- Process: Activity or group of interrelated activities that takes an input (materials, resources), adds value to it, and provides an output to internal or external customers.
- Characteristics of a good process:
  - ▸ Effectiveness
  - ▸ Efficiency
  - ▸ Adaptability

The Association of
Accountants and
Financial Professionals
in Business

LOS P1.D.5.e.

Process Reengineering and BPR

- **Process reengineering:** Evaluates process flow, reduces opportunities for error, eliminates all non-value-added activities, lowers cost
- **Business process reengineering (BPR)**
  - ▸ Fundamental
  - ▸ Radical
  - ▸ Dramatic
  - ▸ Process

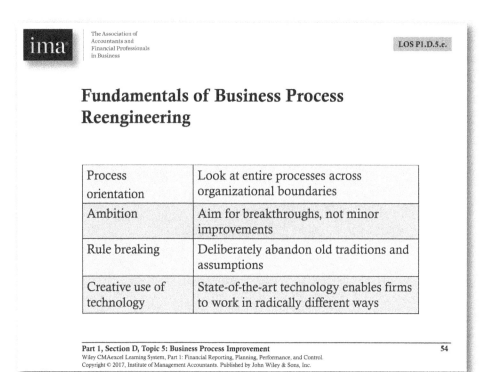

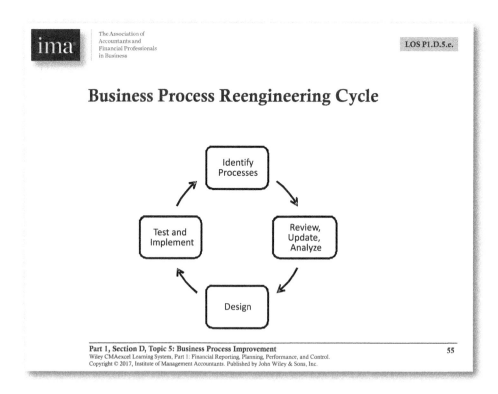

The Association of
Accountants and
Financial Professionals
in Business

LOS P1.D.5.e.

Process Analysis Linkages

- **Productivity**. Improving what already exists
- **Productivity increase**. Continuous quality improvement
- **Continuous improvement**. Ongoing organizational learning, process improvements, and reengineering

The Association of
Accountants and
Financial Professionals
in Business

LOS P1.D.5.g.

Benchmarking Process

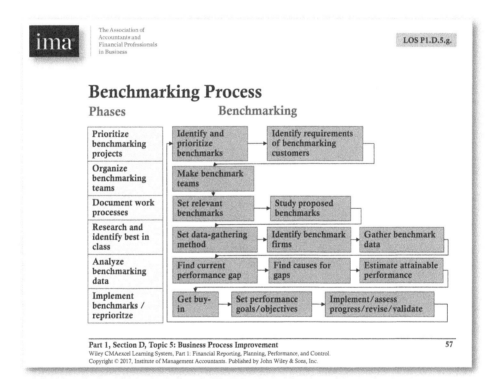

The Association of
Accountants and
Financial Professionals
in Business

LOS P1.D.5.h.

Question: Benchmarking

What issues can strategic benchmarking help an organization address?

Answer:

- **Building core competencies to sustain competitive advantage**
- **Developing new business line**
- **Targeting specific shift in strategy**
- **Making an acquisition**
- **Creating organization with quick response to uncertainties**

The Association of
Accountants and
Financial Professionals
in Business

LOS P1.D.5.i.

Activity-Based Costing versus Activity-Based Management

	Activity-Based Costing (ABC)	Activity-Based Management (ABM)
Definition	Assigns resources to activities, and activities to cost objects (via causal relationships determined by ABM)	Management of activities to improve customer value and profit; gets data from ABC and provides data to ABC
Answers the question	What do things cost?	What causes costs to occur?
Analysis	Static (controlling existing costs)	Forward looking and change oriented

The Association of
Accountants and
Financial Professionals
in Business

LOS P1.D.5.i.

General Applications for ABM

If operations are ...	Then ABM can be useful to ...
Growing	Redeploy non-value-added work. Improve processes and activities.
Flat	Identify non-value-added costs. Set priorities and make improvement. Isolate/eliminate cost drivers. Determine product/service costs.
Declining	Cut costs/downsize/lay off.
Capacity constrained	Determine product/service costs. Make product/service decisions. Determine activity capacity. Identify bottlenecks.

The Association of
Accountants and
Financial Professionals
in Business

LOS P1.D.5.i.

Question: Using ABM to Enhance Quality

How can ABM be used to enhance quality efforts and facilitate quality implementation?

Answer:

ABM's integrated system supports quality management by:

- **Establishing accountability.**
- **Facilitating result measurement.**
- **Enabling priority setting.**

ABM facilitates quality implementation by

- **Identifying activity costs.**
- **Increasing visibility of associated quality costs.**
- **Providing quality cost measures to use in cost-of-quality reports.**

LOS P1.D.5.k.

Continuous Improvement

Continuous improvement (CI or kaizen) values innovation, but continuous incremental improvements are valued more because they are consistent and cumulative.

- Staircase of improvement
- Standards based on:
  - Activity analysis
  - Historical data
  - Benchmarking
  - Market expectations
  - Strategic decisions

Part 1, Section D, Topic 5: Business Process Improvement   62

LOS P1.D.5.f.

Best Practice Analysis

Best practice. Successful process or technique that can be applied to another situation to improve performance

Best practice analysis. Compares current performance to best practice and identifies steps toward best practice

- Define the gap (compare internal data).
- Determine reasons for the gap.
- Examine factors that contribute to best practices.
- Develop recommendations and approach to implement best practices.

Part 1, Section D, Topic 5: Business Process Improvement   63

The Association of
Accountants and
Financial Professionals
in Business

LOS P1.D.5.f.

Question: Improving Performance with Best Practices

A technique for improving performance of activities and processes that searches for best practices is

a. benchmarking.
b. kaizen costing.
c. trend reporting.
d. value-added reporting.

Answer: **a.**

Wiley CMAexcel Learning System, Part 1: Financial Reporting, Planning, Performance, and Control.
Copyright © 2017, Institute of Management Accountants. Published by John Wiley & Sons, Inc.

The Association of
Accountants and
Financial Professionals
in Business

LOS P1.D.5.l.

Cost of Quality (COQ) Components

Improving quality requires analysis of costs associated with quality.

1. Prevention costs: training, analysis of supplier capabilities

2. Appraisal costs: inspections, testing of raw materials

3. Internal failure costs: rework, spoilage

4. External failure costs: cost of shipping defective product, such as customer complaints, returns, warranty claims

A focus on prevention and appraisal costs will minimize/eliminate external failure costs.

Wiley CMAexcel Learning System, Part 1: Financial Reporting, Planning, Performance, and Control.
Copyright © 2017, Institute of Management Accountants. Published by John Wiley & Sons, Inc.

BPI in Accounting Operations

- Services, particularly routine activities, provided by "back office" departments or "cost centers" are prime for continuous improvement and cost reduction.
- Specific to accounting operations:
  - ▸ Conduct process walk-throughs to evaluate opportunities for improvement
  - ▸ Identify ways to reduce the accounting cycle (realize a "fast close")
  - ▸ Implement shared services for routine, lower level, accounting tasks

Section D Conclusion

- Section D content represents 20% of the multiple-choice questions on the Part 1 exam.
- This content also may be tested in essay question format.

To reinforce your learning:

- Study all the LOS for this section.
- Study all material in Section D of the WCMALS self-study book.
- Use the practice test questions in the WCMALS self-study book.
- Take the Section D practice test in the Online Test Bank for a wider range of questions on all topics in this section.

The Association of
Accountants and
Financial Professionals
in Business

Section D Practice Questions

- We now review the Practice Questions from the WCMALS self-study book, Section D.
- Questions are identified by topic.
- Not all topics are covered in this selection.
- More questions on each topic and full section test are included in the Online Test Bank.

The Association of
Accountants and
Financial Professionals
in Business

Session 10 Wrap-Up

Content covered in Session 10
- Section D, Topic 3: Overhead Costs
- Section D, Topic 4: Supply Chain Management
- Section D, Topic 5: Business Process Improvement
- Section D Practice Questions

Content to be covered in Session 11
- Section E, Topic 1: Governance, Risk, and Compliance

Session 11

The Association of
Accountants and
Financial Professionals
in Business

Wiley
CMAexcel Learning System
Exam Review 2017

Part 1: Financial Reporting, Planning, Performance, and Control

Session 11

Learning Outcome Statements (LOS) identifiers appear on the
slides as applicable to highlight where we address each LOS
within the material.

The Association of
Accountants and
Financial Professionals
in Business

Session 10 Recap

- Section D, Topic 3: Overhead Costs
- Section D, Topic 4: Supply Chain Management
- Section D, Topic 5: Business Process Improvement
- Section D Practice Questions

The Association of
Accountants and
Financial Professionals
in Business

Session 11 Overview

- Section E, Topic 1: Governance, Risk, and
  Compliance

The Association of
Accountants and
Financial Professionals
in Business

Section E: Internal Controls

- Topic 1: Governance, Risk, and Compliance

The Association of
Accountants and
Financial Professionals
in Business

LOS P1.E.1.i.

Warmup Question: Custody of Cash

Which one of the following actions would most effectively
address the issue of internal control risk related to the custody of
cash receipts?

a. Establishing a lockbox deposit system at a regional bank.

b. Assigning a single employee to be responsible for the receipt
   and posting of cash receipts to customer accounts.

c. Preparing a control total of cash receipts immediately upon
   opening incoming payments.

d. Installing a surveillance system to monitor the processing of
   cash receipts and custody of cash.

The Association of
Accountants and
Financial Professionals
in Business

Topic 1: Governance, Risk, and Compliance

- The Internal Control Framework and Principles of Internal Control
- Enterprise Risk Management

The Association of
Accountants and
Financial Professionals
in Business

LOS P1.E.1.i.

Topic 1: Governance, Risk, and Compliance (continued)

- Control Environment Components
- Risk
- Corporate Governance and Responsibility
- Foreign Corrupt Practices Act (FCPA)

The Association of
Accountants and
Financial Professionals
in Business

LOS P1.E.1.a. and q.

Framework for Establishing Internal Controls

- *2013 Internal Control—Integrated Framework*
  - ‣ Widely-accepted and recognized model for designing and assessing internal control; Public Company Accounting Oversight Board (PCAOB) and the American Institute of Certified Public Accountants (AICPA) recognize this framework as the primary model within which an organization's internal controls can be tested, assessed, and opined upon.
  - ‣ Initially developed in 1992 (and updated in 2013) by the Committee of Sponsoring Organizations of the Treadway Commission (COSO)
  - ‣ Tested on Part 1, Section E of the CMA Examination

The Association of
Accountants and
Financial Professionals
in Business

LOS P1.E.1.a. and q.

Framework for Establishing Internal Controls (continued)

- 2004 Enterprise Risk Management (ERM) Integrated Framework
  - ‣ An expansion of the original 1992 COSO Internal Control Framework
  - ‣ ERM Framework still current in light of 2013 COSO Internal Control—Integrated Framework update
  - ‣ Two Frameworks are complementary
  - ‣ ERM tested in Part 2, Section D on CMA Examination

The Association of
Accountants and
Financial Professionals
in Business

LOS P1.E.1.u.

2013 COSO Framework Components

- The *2013 COSO Internal Control—Integrated Framework* consists of **five core integrated internal control components**:
  - ▸ Control environment
  - ▸ Risk assessment
  - ▸ Control activities
  - ▸ Information and communication
  - ▸ Monitoring activities

The Association of
Accountants and
Financial Professionals
in Business

LOS P1.E.1.u.

2013 COSO Framework Components (continued)

- These control components represent what is required in order to achieve **key organizational objectives**—*operations, reporting (both internal and external), and compliance*—and are applicable to all aspects of an **organization's structure**—*entity level, division, operating unit, and function.*

The Association of
Accountants and
Financial Professionals
in Business

LOS P1.E.1.i.

Question: Reconciliations

A company has designed its accounting system to have an automated reconciliation between its payroll and general ledger systems. Which type of control has the company implemented?

a. Output control

b. Input control

c. Processing control

d. Transaction control

The Association of
Accountants and
Financial Professionals
in Business

LOS P1.E.1.u.

2013 COSO *Internal Control—Integrated Framework* ("Cube")—Explained

The Association of
Accountants and
Financial Professionals
in Business

LOS P1.E.1.u.

17 Core Principles of COSO Internal Control

- The COSO *2013 Internal Control—Integrated Framework* establishes 17 principles that represent fundamental concepts of each internal control component.
- An organization is presumed to achieve effective control by applying all principles.
- Control environment contains five core principles.
- Risk assessment contains four core principles.
- Control activities contains three core principles.
- Information and communication contains three core principles.
- Monitoring activities contains two core principles.

The Association of
Accountants and
Financial Professionals
in Business

LOS P1.E.1.a. and u.

17 Core Principles Control Environment

Control environment (5 Principles)
- Commitment to integrity and ethical values
- Directors' independence from management
- Structures, lines, and responsibilities
- Attract, develop, and retain competent staff
- Individual accountability for internal controls

17 Core Principles Risk Assessment

Risk assessment (4 Principles)

- Identify and assess risks.
- Determine how to manage risks.
- Assess fraud risks.
- Identifies and assesses changes.

17 Core Principles Control Activities

Control activities (3 Principles)

- Select and develop control activities.
- Develop control activities over.
- Deploy control activities.

The Association of
Accountants and
Financial Professionals
in Business

LOS P1.E.1.a. and u.

17 Core Principles Information and Communication

Information and communication (3 Principles)

- Obtain, generate, and use quality information.
- Internally communicate control information.
- Externally communicate selective control information.

The Association of
Accountants and
Financial Professionals
in Business

LOS P1.E.1.a. and u.

17 Core Principles Monitoring Activities

Monitoring activities (2 Principles)

- Ongoing internal control evaluations.
- Evaluate and communicate internal control deficiencies.

LOS P1.E.1.a.

Question: Management Responsibilities

Which of the following are responsibilities of management?
I.   Aid in the choice of accounting methods and policies.
II. Document internal control procedures.
III. Sign quarterly and annual financial reports.
IV. Choose the auditor and approve auditor compensation.
V.   Review the auditor's suggestions for improved internal controls.
a.   I, II, III, and V only
b.   I, III, IV, and V only
c.   I, II, III, IV, and V
d.   I and IV only

LOS P1.E.1.u.

Question: Monitoring Control

Which one of the following is an example of monitoring controls?

I.   Internal audits

II. Audit committee reviews

III. Management reviews

a.   I only

b.   III only

c.   II only

d.   I, II, and III

The Association of
Accountants and
Financial Professionals
in Business

LOS P1.E.1.u.

Effective Control Principles

- Two-fold risk in designing internal controls
  - May be too "lax"
  - May be too complex and detailed
- Four principles of accounting system design apply to the creation of effective internal controls:

  ✓Control principle
  ✓Compatibility principle
  ✓Flexibility principle
  ✓Cost-benefit principle

The Association of
Accountants and
Financial Professionals
in Business

LOS P1.E.1.l.

Types of Internal Controls

- Preventive
- Detective
- Corrective
- Directive
- Compensating

The Association of
Accountants and
Financial Professionals
in Business

LOS P1.E.1.l.

Question: Safeguarding Control

Locked doors, security systems, ID badges, passwords,
and similar controls are designed to:

a. Safeguard the firm's assets.

b. Lower production costs.

c. Protect the firm's reputation.

d. Ensure that internal controls are followed.

The Association of
Accountants and
Financial Professionals
in Business

LOS P1.E.1.o.

Preventive versus Detective Controls

Preventive

- Attempt to deter or prevent errors or irregularities from occurring
- Examples
  - ✓ Separation of duties
  - ✓ Supervisory review
  - ✓ Completeness checks
  - ✓ Computer passwords
  - ✓ Prenumbered documents

Detective

- Attempt to detect errors or irregularities after the have occurred
- "Back up" and complement to preventive controls
- Examples
  - ✓ Bank reconciliations
  - ✓ Physical inventory counts
  - ✓ Review of exception reports

LOS P1.E.1.o.

Question: Type of Controls

When designing internal controls, a company would develop prenumbered forms as a type of

a. detective control.
b. preventive control.
c. directive control.
d. corrective control.

Answer: **b.**
Because all such forms must be accounted for, prenumbered forms are a way of preventing lost and false transactions.

LOS P1.E.1.o.

Question: Compensating Controls

An example of a compensating or mitigating control would be

a. dual control, such as two signers on every check.
b. an error report that an employee can use to follow up on and resolve the discrepancy.
c. a bank reconciliation process performed by a party who is independent of accounting and cash handling.
d. a policy to use local vendors as often as possible.

Answer: **c.**
This is exactly a mitigating control, which can compensate for a number of flaws in the controls over cash transactions.

The Association of
Accountants and
Financial Professionals
in Business

LOS P1.E.1.g.

Inherent Limitations of Internal Controls

- A well-designed internal control system is not infallible
- Internal controls are designed to provide reasonable (not absolute) assurance that an organization's key internal control objectives are met
- Internal control limitations may result from certain human factors or other exceptions such as:

The Association of
Accountants and
Financial Professionals
in Business

LOS P1.E.1.g.

Inherent Limitations of Internal Controls— Human Factors and Other Exceptions

- Management override
- Fraud/collusion
- Conflicts of interest
- Human error/carelessness
- Misunderstandings
- Cost–benefit limitations

LOS P1.E.1.a.

Enterprise Risk Management (ERM)

The goals of risk management include:

- Aligning risk appetite and strategy
- Improving risk responses
- Reducing operational surprises and losses
- Identifying and managing multiple and cross-enterprise risks
- Seizing opportunities
- Improving capital deployment

LOS P1.E.1.a., c., h., i., j., k., and u.

Control Environment Components

- Tone at the top
- Policies and Standards
- Segregation of Duties
  - Authorizing events
  - Recording events
  - Safeguarding resources related to events (custody)
  - Reconciling, overseeing and auditing
- Documenting Control Policies and Procedures

The Association of
Accountants and
Financial Professionals
in Business

LOS P1.E.1.h. and v.

Question: Unauthorized Access

A company has just completed construction of a new computer facility. To limit unauthorized access to this facility, which one of the following is the most effective procedure that the company can implement?

a. Data encryption

b. Access control software

c. Input controls

d. Biometric identification system

The Association of
Accountants and
Financial Professionals
in Business

LOS P1.E.1.v.

Question: Network Access

The internal auditors of a company are assessing controls over network access. The best source of evidence to determine that terminated employees do not continue to have access to the company's network is to

a. Discuss password removal procedures with the database administrator.

b. Review access control software to determine whether the most current version is implemented.

c. Review computer logs for access attempts.

d. Reconcile current payroll lists with database access lists.

The Association of
Accountants and
Financial Professionals
in Business

LOS P1.E.1.c., h., and p.

Documentation of Control Policies and Procedures

- Essential for assessing controls
  - ▶ Reports on controls mandated by SOX
- Relate to specific responsibilities, authority, and reporting relationships
  - ▶ Helpful for job training

The Association of
Accountants and
Financial Professionals
in Business

LOS P1.E.1.h.

Personnel Policies and Procedures

"People" (Human Resource) Controls:
- Recruiting, Selecting, Hiring, and Supervision
- Orientation, Training, Development, and Performance Reviews
- Bonding, Rotation, and Vacations

The Association of
Accountants and
Financial Professionals
in Business

LOS P1.E.1.u.

Internal Control Monitoring

Why is control monitoring important?

Benefits of well-designed control monitoring:

- Timely identification of Internal control problems
- Receive more timely and accurate information for decision makers
- Timely, reliable, and accurate financial and nonfinancial reports and statements
- Timely certifications of internal control
- Maximize organizational efficiencies and reduce costs

The Association of
Accountants and
Financial Professionals
in Business

LOS P1.E.1.a. and q.

Risk

Audit risk consists of two parts:

1. The financial statements are materially misstated.
2. The auditor expresses an inappropriate audit opinion.

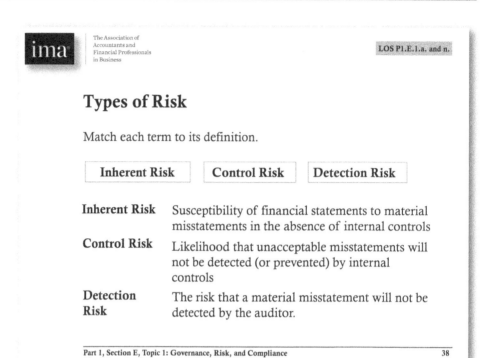

Types of Risk

Match each term to its definition.

Inherent Risk	Control Risk	Detection Risk

Inherent Risk	Susceptibility of financial statements to material misstatements in the absence of internal controls
Control Risk	Likelihood that unacceptable misstatements will not be detected (or prevented) by internal controls
Detection Risk	The risk that a material misstatement will not be detected by the auditor.

Question: Inherent Risk

Inherent risk is

a. The risk that internal controls will not be followed.

b. That an internal audit will not uncover incidents where controls have not been followed.

c. That the business will naturally experience, regardless of internal controls.

d. That measures the effectiveness of a firm's internal controls.

The Association of
Accountants and
Financial Professionals
in Business

LOS P1.E.1.a., g., u., and w.

Audit Risk (AR)

$$AR = IR \times CR \times DR$$

Inherent Risk (IR) × Control Risk (CR) × Detection Risk (DR)

The Association of
Accountants and
Financial Professionals
in Business

LOS P1.E.1.a. and u.

Governance, Risk, and Compliance

Inherent Risk		Material Error?
Control Risk		Caught by Controls?
Detection Risk		Caught by Audit?
Audit Risk		Wrong Opinion!

The Association of
Accountants and
Financial Professionals
in Business

LOS P1.E.1.p., q., s., and w.

External Auditor Responsibilities

- The external auditor has dual governance-related responsibilities:
  - ➤ Financial statement audit attestation
    - ▪ Issues opinion as to whether company's financial statements are free from material error
      - ➤ Unmodified opinion
      - ➤ Unmodified opinion with emphasis-of-matter or other-matter paragraph
      - ➤ Modified opinion, which may include a qualified opinion, an adverse opinion, or a disclaimer of opinion
  - ➤ Attestation on management's assessment of effectiveness of internal controls in connection with SOX Section 404
    - ▪ Provides evaluation as to whether company's internal control structure and procedures allow for accurate and fair reporting of the company's transactions and that recorded transactions will permit preparation of financial statements in accordance with generally accepted accounting (GAAP).
    - ▪ Must also address and describe any material weaknesses in internal controls identified.

The Association of
Accountants and
Financial Professionals
in Business

LOS P1.E.1.p., s., and w.

Public Company Accounting Oversight Board (PCAOB) Standards and SOX 404

PCAOB Auditing Standard No. 5 requires auditors to:

- Follow a risk-based approach to develop auditing procedures and performing an audit under provisions of SOX Section 404.
- Scale the audit to the size of the organization under audit.
- Follow a principles-based approach to determine reliance on work of others.
- Follow a top-down risk-assessment (TDRA) approach to auditing financial statements and internal controls.

The Association of
Accountants and
Financial Professionals
in Business

LOS P1.E.1.p. and r.

Internal Control Assessment Using the TDRA Approach

The *Top-Down Risk Assessment Approach (TDRA)* to performing an internal control assessment in connection with SOX Section 404 includes the following six steps:

1. Identify and evaluate entity-level controls.

2. Identify significant accounts or disclosures.

3. Identify material misstatement risks within the accounts or disclosures identified in step #2.

4. Determine which entity-level controls sufficiently address the risks identified in step #3.

5. Determine which transaction-level controls compensate for possible entity-level control failures.

6. Determine the nature, extent, and timing of evidence-gathering tests needed to complete the assessment of internal controls.

The Association of
Accountants and
Financial Professionals
in Business

LOS P1.E.1.d., e., and f.

Corporate Governance and Responsibility

- Corporate governance
    - System by which a corporation is directed and controlled
    - Specifies roles and responsibilities of key participants both internal (board of directors) and external (shareholders, external auditors)
    - Specifies rules and procedures for decisions about corporate affairs
- Corporate governance structure
    - Must comply with federal and state laws
        - Submission of corporate charter/articles of incorporation—defines the purpose and basic structure of a corporation
    - Shareholders elect board of directors; board of directors appoint senior management
    - Bylaws, which establish operating procedures for the corporation
- Structure influences the scope and effectiveness of the control environment

The Association of
Accountants and
Financial Professionals
in Business

LOS P1.E.1.a. and u.

Question: Control Activities

The Internal Control Integrated Framework from 1992 comprises five mutually-reinforcing components including control activities. Control activities include all of the following except:

a. Adequate separation of duties.

b. Risk management.

c. Independent verifications.

d. Adequate documentation and records.

The Association of
Accountants and
Financial Professionals
in Business

LOS P1.E.1.a., m., and u.

Question: Completeness Control

Which of the following is an example of a completeness control?

a. Pre-numbered forms that allow for reconciliation of form numbers against shipping reports.

b. Facilities utilization reports.

c. Thorough training on proper accounting classes to which transactions should be posted.

d. Employees time sheets that must be completed before employees can receive their paychecks.

The Association of
Accountants and
Financial Professionals
in Business

LOS P1.E.1.c. and u.

Key Components of Internal Control Structure

- Organizational structure influences the design and effectiveness of controls.

- Key components of an organization's internal control structure fall into three categories:

  ✓ Control environment
  ✓ Information (accounting) system
  ✓ Control procedures

The Association of
Accountants and
Financial Professionals
in Business

LOS P1.E.1.c. and d.

Key Stakeholders in Internal Controls and the Control Environment

- Board of Directors and Audit Committee
  ‣ Provide oversight and define corporate culture
- Senior Management
  ‣ Provides leadership, ensures internal control efforts communicated and supported with sufficient resources
  ‣ Must demonstrate how controls meet needs of business
- Staff and Line Managers
  ‣ Contribute to design and implementation of internal control programs
  ‣ Review and monitor controls
- External Auditors
  ‣ Attest to fair presentation of financial results
  ‣ Attest to management's assessment of internal control
- Internal Auditors
  ‣ Assess internal control environments
  ‣ Validate internal control efforts and compare current practices to industry standards
  ‣ Recommend improvements

Sarbanes-Oxley Act of 2002 (SOX) and Management's Responsibilities (Sections 302 and 404)

- Regulation passed by U.S. Congress in 2002 to protect investors from the possibility of fraudulent accounting activities by corporations.
- SOX introduced major changes to, and increased regulation over, corporate governance, corporate financial reporting and disclosure, and auditing practice, and established more stringent guidelines for internal control implementation, assessment, and effectiveness.
- While the Act contains numerous sections and titles, CMA candidates are required to be familiar with four key sections:

  ➤ *Section 201: Services Outside the Scope of Practice of Auditors*
  ➤ *Section 203: Audit Partner Rotation*
  ➤ *Section 302: Corporate Responsibility for Financial Reports*
  ➤ *Section 404: Management Assessment of Internal Controls*

Question: SOX

All of the following statements in regard to management's report on internal controls over financial reporting in accordance with the Sarbanes-Oxley Act are true except that the report must

a. Include a statement of management's responsibility for establishing effective internal controls over financial reporting.

b. Include a statement that the design of the internal controls is the responsibility of the company's audit committee.

c. Assess the effectiveness of the company's internal controls over financial reporting, as of the end of the period.

d. Be attested to by an independent auditor.

The Association of
Accountants and
Financial Professionals
in Business

LOS P1.E.1.t.

Foreign Corrupt Practices Act (FCPA)

- Prohibits payments by U.S. companies to foreign government officials to secure favorable action
- Prohibited even if such payments are normal business practice in that country
- Officers of the firm face personal penalties including fines and imprisonment

The Association of
Accountants and
Financial Professionals
in Business

LOS P1.E.1.l. and t.

FCPA Internal Control Provisions

- In addition to prohibitions associated with bribery payments, the FCPA also addresses accounting transparency requirements under the SEC's 1934 Act
- In connection with these requirements, publicly traded companies must maintain a system of internal control to ensure transactions adhere to the following general control objectives:

✓ Authorization

✓ Recording

✓ Safeguarding

✓ Reconciliation

LOS P1.E.1.t.

Question: FCPA

Which of the following are required under the Foreign Corrupt Practices Act (FCPA)?

I.   A firm must design internal control procedures.

II. A firm must have an internal audit department.

III. Transactions must be executed with management's authorization.

IV. Access to assets must be authorized.

a. I, II, III, and IV

b. I, III, and IV only

c. I and III only

d. I and II only

Session 11 Wrap-Up

Content covered in Session 11

• Section E, Topic 1: Governance, Risk, and Compliance

Content to be covered in Session 12

• Section E, Topic 2: Internal Auditing

• Section E, Topic 3: Systems Controls and Security Measures

• Section E, Practice Questions

Session 12

The Association of
Accountants and
Financial Professionals
in Business

Wiley
CMAexcel Learning System
Exam Review 2017

Part 1: Financial Reporting, Planning,
Performance, and Control

Session 12

Learning Outcome Statements (LOS) identifiers appear on the
slides as applicable to highlight where we address each LOS
within the material.

The Association of
Accountants and
Financial Professionals
in Business

Session 11 Recap

- Section E, Topic 1: Governance, Risk, and Compliance

The Association of
Accountants and
Financial Professionals
in Business

Session 12 Overview

- Section E, Topic 2: Internal Auditing
- Section E, Topic 3: System Controls and Security Measures
- Section E, Practice Questions

The Association of
Accountants and
Financial Professionals
in Business

Topic 2: Internal Auditing— Summary of Learning Outcome Statements

a.   Internal audit definition, function, and scope

b.   Internal control objectives, components, and risks

c.   Internal audit plans

d.   Internal control breakdowns and risks

e.   Internal audit types and objectives

f.   Roles and responsibilities of the Chief Audit Executive (CAE)

g.   Reporting relationship of the Chief Audit Executive (CAE)

The Association of
Accountants and
Financial Professionals
in Business

Question: Internal Control

Internal control is a process effected by the:

a.   Public Company Accounting Oversight Board.

b.   Securities and Exchange Commission.

c.   Company's board, management, and other personnel.

d.   Committee on Sponsoring Organizations.

Internal Audit Definition, Function, and Scope

- Definition of internal auditing
- Internal auditing function
- Internal auditing scope
- Internal auditing standards and services
  - ➤ Attribute standards
  - ➤ Performance standards
  - ➤ Implementation standards
  - ➤ Assurance services
  - ➤ Consulting services

Internal Auditing Standards and Services

- Attribute standards
- Performance standards
- Implementation standards
- Assurance services
- Consulting services

The Association of
Accountants and
Financial Professionals
in Business

LOS P1.E.2.b.

Question: Assurance Audits

What is the effect of combining a compliance audit, an operational audit, and a financial audit into one big assurance audit?

a. Additive effect.

b. Dilution effect.

c. Multiplicative effect.

d. Synergistic effect.

The Association of
Accountants and
Financial Professionals
in Business

LOS P1.E.2.b.

Internal Control Objectives, Components, and Tests

- Control Types
  - ➢ Management Controls
  - ➢ Accounting Controls
  - ➢ Administrative Controls
- Control Objectives
- Control Components
- Control Tests
  - ➢ Sampling
  - ➢ Compliance
  - ➢ Substantive

LOS P1.E.2.b.

Internal Audit Plans

- Perform an internal audit risk assessment exercise
- Take an inventory of auditable activities
- Assign risk levels (L, M, or H) to each activity
- Set audit priorities based on risk levels
- Develop the audit plan for later scheduling of audits

LOS P1.E.2.c.

Risk-Based Approach to Planning and Executing an Internal Audit

- Internal audits should adopt a top-down, risk-based approach to planning and executing an audit.
  - ▸ Assess risk.
  - ▸ Prioritize high risk areas.
  - ▸ Addressing and improving internal controls and financial reporting systems.

The Association of
Accountants and
Financial Professionals
in Business

LOS P1.E.2.b.

Internal Control Breakdowns and Risks

- Limitations of internal controls
  - ➤ Internal control is not a cure-all for all problems
  - ➤ Reflection of actions and inactions
- Control breakdowns
  - ➤ Employees (fatigue, disgruntled, carelessness)
  - ➤ Control failures and inadequate controls
  - ➤ Management override
  - ➤ Management intervention
- Collusion
- Risks from control breakdowns
  - ➤ Stealing of assets and data
  - ➤ Accessing unauthorized websites

The Association of
Accountants and
Financial Professionals
in Business

LOS P1.E.2.d.

Risks to Internal Audit Function

- Risks to the internal audit function
  - ➤ Audit failures
  - ➤ Audit's false assurances
  - ➤ Audit's loss of reputation
- Reasons for the audit failures
  - ➤ Management gaps
  - ➤ Communication gaps
  - ➤ Competency gaps

The Association of
Accountants and
Financial Professionals
In Business

LOS P1.E.2.a.

Question: Audit Scope Gap

Internal audit's scope gap can be minimized or reduced in
which of the following phases of an audit process?

a. Audit program

b. Audit fieldwork

c. Audit preliminary survey

d. Audit reporting

The Association of
Accountants and
Financial Professionals
in Business

LOS P1.E.2.d.

Audit Failures, False Assurance, and Reputational Loss

- Audit failures manifest themselves when the auditor fails to
  detect a material misstatement or fraud. Audit failures
  embarrass internal audit management, functional
  management, executive management, and the board of
  directors.

- False assurance is a level of confidence or assurance based
  on perceptions or assumptions rather than facts.

- Unprofessional audit work combined with incompetent
  auditors can lead to reputation risk for internal auditors.

The Association of
Accountants and
Financial Professionals
in Business

LOS P1.E.2.d.

Reasons for False Assurance and Loss of Reputation

- Reasons for the audit's false assurances
  - ➤ Communication gaps
  - ➤ Expectation gaps
  - ➤ Competency gaps
- Reasons for the audit's loss of reputation
  - ➤ Competency gaps
  - ➤ Brand gaps
  - ➤ Compliance gaps

The Association of
Accountants and
Financial Professionals
in Business

LOS P1.E.2.d.

Lines of Defense

- Mitigating internal audit risks
  - ➤ Lines of defense mechanisms (single vs. multiple)
  - ➤ Defense-in-depth
  - ➤ Defense-in-breadth
  - ➤ Defense-in-technology
  - ➤ Defense-in-time

The Association of
Accountants and
Financial Professionals
in Business

LOS P1.E.2.e.

Question: Internal Audit Engagement

When an internal auditor with education and experience in law works with the human resource department of a company about employee lawsuits, the auditor is conducting a(n):

a. Compliance audit.

b. Operational audit.

c. Financial audit.

d. Consulting audit.

The Association of
Accountants and
Financial Professionals
in Business

LOS P1.E.2.e.

Internal Audit Types and Objectives

- Audit scope and objectives
  - ➤ Compliance audits
  - ➤ Operational audits
  - ➤ Financial audits
  - ➤ Consulting audits
- Audit evidence
  - ➤ Physical
  - ➤ Digital
  - ➤ Combination

The Association of
Accountants and
Financial Professionals
in Business

LOS P1.E.2.b.

Question: Managing and Mitigating Risks

Managing and mitigating organization-wide risks finally rests with which of the following management concepts?

a. Chain of authority

b. Chain of accountability

c. Chain of responsibility

d. Chain of delegation

The Association of
Accountants and
Financial Professionals
in Business

LOS P1.E.2.a.

Audit Scope and Objectives

- A compliance audit's scope includes governance audits, ethics audits, and due diligence reviews during mergers, acquisitions, and divestitures. The audit objectives include determining the ability of an organization to reasonably ensure conformity and adherence to its policies, plans, and legal requirements.

- An operational audit's scope consists of the recurring activities of an organization directed toward producing a product or rendering a service. The audit objectives are to ensure the effective, efficient, and economical utilization of an organization's resources.

- A financial audit's scope includes a review of specific line item, account balance, or class/group of transactions affecting financial statements. The audit objective is to ensure that the financial statements are correctly stated.

- The consulting audit's scope includes advisory and related client service activities where the nature and scope of work are agreed with the client in advance. The audit objectives are to add value and improve the organization.

The Association of
Accountants and
Financial Professionals
in Business

LOS P1.E.2.a.

Question: Internal Auditor Systems Work

Internal auditors can design, develop, implement,
and maintain which of the following?

a. Control systems

b. Computer systems

c. Audit systems

d. Audit trail systems

The Association of
Accountants and
Financial Professionals
in Business

LOS P1.E.2.f.

Roles and Responsibilities of the CAE

- Internal audit charter
  - ➤ Purpose, authority, and responsibility
  - ➤ Roles and reporting relationships
  - ➤ Authority to access resources
- Roles and responsibilities of the Chief Audit
  Executive (CAE)
  - ➤ Hiring the audit staff
  - ➤ Developing the audit plans
  - ➤ Planning the audit engagement
  - ➤ Issuing the audit reports
  - ➤ Monitoring the audit engagement results
  - ➤ Developing the succession plans
  - ➤ Coordinating with other auditors

Question: Chief Audit Executive (CAE)

LOS P1.E.2.f.

Which of the following is not a functional reporting item between the chief audit executive and his or her superior?

a. Approving the audit charter

b. Approving the audit manual

c. Approving the audit risk assessment program

d. Approving the audit plan

Reporting Relationship of the CAE

LOS P1.E.2.g.

- Internal audit status
  - Independence
  - Objectivity
- Reporting relationship of the CAE
  - Dual-reporting
  - Functional reporting
  - Administrative reporting

The Association of
Accountants and
Financial Professionals
in Business

LOS P1.E.2.b.

Question: Internal Auditor Value

Internal auditors can add a greater value to their organizations by doing more:

a. Compliance audits.

b. Operational audits.

c. Financial audits.

d. Consulting audits.

The Association of
Accountants and
Financial Professionals
in Business

Topic 3: Systems Controls and Security Measures

- General information systems controls
- Network, hardware, and facility controls
- Business continuity planning and related controls
- Accounting controls
- Flowcharting to assess controls

The Association of
Accountants and
Financial Professionals
in Business

Question Warmup: Types of Controls

Consider the following types of controls.

I.   Preventive

II. Corrective

III. Feedback

IV. Feedforward

V.   Detective

Which one of the following groups of controls are generally considered the most cost-effective controls?

a. I, II, and III.

b. I, II, and V.

c. I, III, and V.

d. III, IV, and V.

The Association of
Accountants and
Financial Professionals
in Business

Typical Information System

Financial accounting information

- Revenues
- Taxes
- Debts
- Profits/Losses

Data used in business operations

- Inventory
- Client Lists
- Schedules
- Vendors
- Prices/Costs

LOS P1.E.3.b.

General Information Systems Controls

These controls are related to the overall information technology (IT) function and include:

- Organizational, personnel, and operations controls
- Systems development controls
- Network, hardware, and facility controls
- Backup and disaster recovery controls (business continuance plans)
- Accounting controls

LOS P1.E.3.b.

Risks Associated with Information Systems

- Reduced visibility of the audit trail
- Malfunction of hardware or software
- Reduced human intervention to identify mistakes
- Systematic errors
- Alteration, deletion, or theft of information due to unauthorized access

- Loss of data
- Reduced segregation of duties
- Reduced traditional authorization
- Greater need for skilled and experienced IT personnel
- Viruses and Trojan horses
- Acts of sabotage
- Phishing communications

The Association of
Accountants and
Financial Professionals
in Business

LOS P1.E.3.a. and b.

Risk Commentary

- Lost or stolen data
- Information loss or fraud
- Hackers
- Lack of separation of duties
- Unauthorized file alteration

The Association of
Accountants and
Financial Professionals
in Business

LOS P1.E.3.h. and i.

Question: Inherent Risk

An inherent risk specifically related to conducting business over the internet includes:

a. Website denial of service attack.

b. Exposure to viruses.

c. Unauthorized access by hackers, exposure to viruses, and website denial of service attacks.

d. Unauthorized access by hackers.

The Association of
Accountants and
Financial Professionals
in Business

LOS P1.E.3.c.

Question: Weakness in EDP System Controls

Which one of the following represents a weakness in the internal control system of an electronic data processing system?

a. The systems analyst designs new systems and supervises testing of the system.

b. The accounts receivable clerk prepares and enters data into the computer system and reviews the output for errors.

c. The data control group reviews and tests procedures and handles the reprocessing of errors detected by the computer.

d. The computer operator executes programs according to operating instructions and maintains custody of programs and data files.

The Association of
Accountants and
Financial Professionals
in Business

LOS P1.E.3.a., c., d., and e.

Personnel Policies to Protect Information

- Segregation of duties and functions
- Mandatory vacations for employees in sensitive positions
- Control over computer accounts
    ▸ User profiles, passwords, access restrictions
    ▸ Tracking of user and file activity
- Knowledge of employees' habits

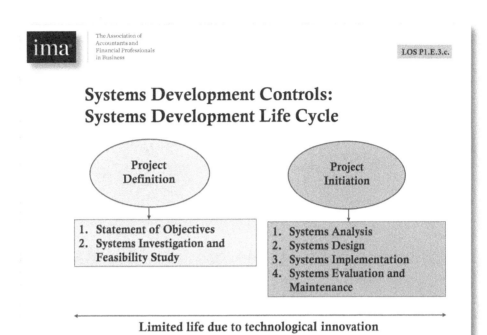

The Association of
Accountants and
Financial Professionals
in Business

LOS P1.E.3.c.

Systems Development Controls: Systems Development Life Cycle

Project Definition

1. **Statement of Objectives**
2. **Systems Investigation and Feasibility Study**

Project Initiation

1. **Systems Analysis**
2. **Systems Design**
3. **Systems Implementation**
4. **Systems Evaluation and Maintenance**

Limited life due to technological innovation

The Association of
Accountants and
Financial Professionals
in Business

LOS P1.E.3.c.

Project Initiation Details

1. Systems Analysis
2. Systems Design
3. Systems Implementation
4. Systems Evaluation and Maintenance

The Association of
Accountants and
Financial Professionals
in Business

LOS P1.E.3.c.

Question: Systems Implementation

All of the following are included in the systems implementation process except:

a. training.

b. systems design.

c. conversion.

d. testing.

The Association of
Accountants and
Financial Professionals
in Business

LOS P1.E.3.d.

Facility and Hardware Controls

The data center should be:

- Located in an area that does not provide easy public access.
- Protected through security passes, touchpad locks, and so on.
- Protected from the elements, natural disasters, and power disturbances and outages.
- Designed to handle periods of peak processing volume.

The Association of
Accountants and
Financial Professionals
in Business

LOS P1.E.3.i. and j.

Network Controls

- Enable authorized employees to access and use firm's data and programs

- Keep unauthorized users from accessing firm's data and programs

Network controls include:

- Data encryption and transmission
- Routing verification procedures
- Message acknowledgment procedures
- Virus protection
- Firewalls
- Intrusion detection systems

The Association of
Accountants and
Financial Professionals
in Business

LOS P1.E.3.i.

Question: Data Encryption

Data encryption:

a. Converts data from easily read local language into a secret code and helps prevent unauthorized usage of sensitive information.

b. Converts graphics into binary code that can be more easily transmitted over the Internet.

c. Is less necessary over the Internet than on a local area network (LAN) or wide area network (WAN) because e-mail and FTP cannot be intercepted.

d. Is not necessary unless a business is working on government defense contracts.

LOS P1.E.3.j.

Question: Restrict Access by Outsiders

Company ABC has installed a software/hardware system that restricts access by outsiders to the firm's network. This is called:

a. a firewall.

b. data encryption.

c. a disaster recovery procedure.

d. an intrusion detection system.

LOS P1.E.3.m.

Business Continuity Planning

- Business continuity planning (BCP) is a strategy that looks to:
  - ➤ identify an organization's exposure to internal and external threats
  - ➤ bring together critical resources and assets in order to protect those resources, and
  - ➤ ensure continuing operations and recovery, in the event of an adverse event or disaster.

- As part of the BCP process, a business continuance plan is developed, which provides for the implementation of key control policies and procedures:
  - Data backup policies and procedures
  - Disaster recovery policies and procedures (business continuance plans)

LOS P1.E.3.m. and n.

Business Continuance Plan and Disaster Recovery Procedures

- Define roles of team members
- Detailed backup plan
  - ▸ Use of hot, warm, or cold site
- Regular testing

Part 1, Section E, Topic 3: Systems Controls and Security Measures
Wiley CMAexcel Learning System, Part 1: Financial Reporting, Planning, Performance, and Control.
Copyright © 2017, Institute of Management Accountants. Published by John Wiley & Sons, Inc.

Data Backup Policies and Procedures

- Grandfather-father-son method for backup media (tapes)
- Checkpoint procedures
- Backup of system configurations
- Offsite storage of backup files and documentation

Part 1, Section E, Topic 3: Systems Controls and Security Measures
Wiley CMAexcel Learning System, Part 1: Financial Reporting, Planning, Performance, and Control.
Copyright © 2017, Institute of Management Accountants. Published by John Wiley & Sons, Inc.

The Association of
Accountants and
Financial Professionals
in Business

LOS P1.E.3.i.

Question: Database Use

Which of the following provides protection from unauthorized use of databases?

a. Storing the data center in a secured area.

b. Data encryption.

c. Input entry screens with validity checks.

d. File transfer protocol.

The Association of
Accountants and
Financial Professionals
in Business

LOS P1.E.3.i.

Question: File Retention

Which one of the following would most compromise the use of the grandfather-father-son principle of file retention as protection against loss or damage of master files?

a. Inadequate ventilation

b. Failure to encrypt data

c. Storing of all files in one location

d. Use of magnetic tape

LOS P1.E.3.f.

Question: Accounting Controls

An accounting system should contain controls that readily confirm or question the reliability of recorded data.

What are the five standard accounting controls?

Answer:

1. **Batch totals**
2. **Control accounts**
3. **Voiding or canceling**
4. **Feedback controls**
5. **Feed-forward and preventive controls**

LOS P1.E.3.f.

Question: Accounting Controls

Accounting controls are concerned with the safeguarding of assets and the reliability of financial records. Consequently, these controls are designed to provide reasonable assurance that all of the following take place except:

a. Comparing recorded assets with existing assets at periodic intervals and taking appropriate action with respect to differences.

b. Recording transactions as necessary to permit preparation of financial statements in conformity with generally accepted accounting principles and maintaining accountability for assets.

c. Executing transactions in accordance with management's general or specific authorization.

d. Compliance with methods and procedures ensuring operational efficiency and adherence to managerial policies.

The Association of
Accountants and
Financial Professionals
in Business

LOS P1.E.3.f.

Question: Disaster Recovery

Disaster recovery policies and procedures are designed to enable a company to carry on business in the event of an unpredicted disaster where the business would not be able to function normally. A company's disaster recovery plan should include all of the following except:

a. Specify backup sites for alternate computer processing.

b. Define the roles of all members of the disaster recovery team.

c. Document all processing and output controls.

d. Appoint a primary leader for the process.

The Association of
Accountants and
Financial Professionals
in Business

LOS P1.E.3.f.

Application and Transaction Controls Flowchart

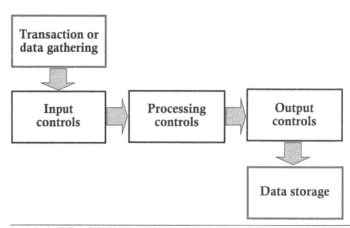

The Association of
Accountants and
Financial Professionals
in Business

LOS P1.E.3.f.

Question: Feed-Forward Controls

Which of the following is not an example of feed-forward controls?

a. Performance plans.

b. Performance metrics.

c. Performance scorecards.

d. Performance dashboards.

The Association of
Accountants and
Financial Professionals
in Business

LOS P1.E.3.f. and g.

Application and Transaction Controls

- **Input Controls**
    - Batch controls
    - Approval mechanism
    - Dual observation
    - Supervisory procedure
    - Preprinted recording forms or preformatted screens
    - Redundant data checks
    - Unfound records tests (validity tests)
    - Check digits
    - Interactive edit checks, field checks

- **Processing Controls**
    - Run-to-run totals

- **Output Controls**
    - Controls for validating processing results
    - Controls regulating distribution of output

The Association of
Accountants and
Financial Professionals
in Business

Documenting and Assessing Controls

For each set of internal controls, auditor and
management need to answer such questions
as:

- What is the actual process? Does it
  function as planned? Are there
  unnecessary procedures?

- Where are the decision points, and who
  can make decisions?

- Where are there interactions with other
  systems?

- Are there gaps between systems that
  allow possibility of error or fraud?

- General information
  systems controls
- Application and
  transaction controls
- Network, hardware,
  and facility controls
- Backup and disaster
  recovery controls

The Association of
Accountants and
Financial Professionals
in Business

LOS P1.E.3.f.

Question: Check Number

Sam needs to send a check to a contract
worker. The check
number is on the check, and the computer program adds a
second number while printing the check to aid in tracking the
transaction. This is an example of:

a. An input control.

b. A processing control.

c. A program access control.

d. An output control.

The Association of
Accountants and
Financial Professionals
in Business

LOS P1.E.3.f.

Question: Data Accuracy

Which controls provide reasonable assurance that data is complete, accurate, and authorized?

a. Output controls.

b. Input controls.

c. Physical controls.

d. Processing controls.

The Association of
Accountants and
Financial Professionals
in Business

LOS P1.E.3.k.

Commonly Used Flowchart Symbols

Symbol	Description	Symbol	Description
Diamond	A diamond usually denotes a point of decision.		This symbol represents online data storage.
Rectangle	A rectangle usually denotes a process.	Inverted triangle	An inverted triangle may represent offline storage, such as a file cabinet.
Circle	A circle denotes a connector with a different element on the flow chart.	Cylinder	The cylinder represents a database (also used for "magnetic disk" storage.
Pentagon	This pentagonal shape usually denotes connection to an off-page element.		This symbol usually represents manual operation (an offline process).
Document	This figure usually represents a document.		This symbol usually represents manual input to a computer system.
			This symbol indicates a keying operation.

LOS P1.E.3.k.

Question: Flowchart of Activities

Flowcharts of activities are used to:

a. help detect intrusion past the firewall into the network.

b. visually inspect, observe, and document a process in order to assess effectiveness of control procedures.

c. help ensure that data transmitted over the Internet is not intercepted by unauthorized personnel.

d. ensure that data can be recovered if it is lost.

LOS P1.E.3.k.

Use of Flowcharts to Document Internal Control

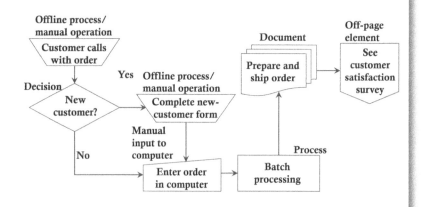

The Association of
Accountants and
Financial Professionals
in Business

LOS P1.E.3.k.

Flowchart of Transactions Process

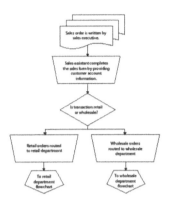

The Association of
Accountants and
Financial Professionals
in Business

LOS P1.E.3.c.

Question: Revenue Cycle Assurance

The accounting controls surrounding the revenue cycle should provide assurances of all of the following except the

a. Accurate recording, shipping, and billing of all valid sales transactions.

b. Approval of all credit sales transactions after they are processed.

c. Proper authorization of all sales return and allowance transactions.

d. Accurate recording of customer accounts and finished goods inventories.

The Association of
Accountants and
Financial Professionals
in Business

Section E Practice Questions

- We now review the Practice Questions from the WCMALS self-study book, Section E.
- Questions are identified by topic.
- More questions on each topic and full section test are included in the Online Test Bank.

The Association of
Accountants and
Financial Professionals
in Business

Section E Conclusion

- Section E content represents 15% of the multiple-choice questions on the Part 1 exam.
- This content also may be tested in essay question format.

To reinforce your learning:

- Study all the LOS for this section.
- Study all material in Section E in the WCMALS self-study.
- Use the practice test questions in the WCMALS self-study.
- Take the Section E practice test in the Online Test Bank for a wider range of questions on all topics in this section.

The Association of
Accountants and
Financial Professionals
in Business

Session 12 Wrap-Up

Content covered in Session 12

- Section E, Topic 1: Internal Auditing
- Section E, Topic 2: Systems Controls and Security Measures
- Section E Practice Questions